FEAR OF LIFE

Other Books by ALEXANDER LOWEN, M.D.

The Language of the Body

Love and Orgasm

The Betrayal of the Body

Pleasure

Depression and the Body

Bioenergetics

The Way to Vibrant Health

FEAR OF LIFE

ALEXANDER LOWEN, M.D.

COLLIER BOOKS

A Division of Macmillan Publishing Co., Inc.

NEW YORK

COLLIER MACMILLAN PUBLISHERS

LONDON

Macmillan Publishing Co., Inc.
866 Third Avenue, New York, N.Y. 10022
Collier Macmillan Canada, Inc.

Library of Congress Cataloging in Publication Data

Lowen, Alexander.
    Fear of life.

    1. Neuroses.   2. Fear.   3. Life.   I. Title.
RC530.L68   1981   616.85′2   81-9991
ISBN 0-02-077330-7 (pbk.)   AACR2

First Collier Books Edition 1981

10   9   8   7   6   5   4   3

Fear of Life is also published in a hardcover edition
by Macmillan Publishing Co., Inc.

Printed in the United States of America

Dedicated with love to

ROWFRETA L. WALKER

I hitched my wagon to your star.

Contents

What a thing is man! Among all wonders
The wonder of the world is man himself.

———————

Yea, wondrous is man's Sagacity:
Through this he climbeth on high
Through this also he falleth.
In the confidence of his power he stumbleth;
In the stubbornness of his will he goeth down.

—SOPHOCLES, *Antigone*

FEAR OF LIFE

Introduction

Neurosis is not usually defined as a fear of life, but that is what it is. The neurotic person is afraid to open his heart to love, afraid to reach out or strike out, afraid to be fully himself. We can explain these fears psychologically. Opening one's heart to love makes one vulnerable to being hurt; reaching out, to being rejected; striking out, to being destroyed. But there is another dimension to this problem. More life or feeling than one is accustomed to is frightening to the person because it threatens to overwhelm his ego, flood his boundaries, and undermine his identity. Being more alive and having more feeling is scary. I worked with a young man whose body was very unalive. It was tight and contracted, his eyes were dull, his skin color sallow, his breathing shallow. By breathing deeply and doing some of the therapeutic exercises, his body became more alive. His eyes brightened, his color improved, he felt tingling sensations in parts of his body, and his legs began to vibrate. But then, he said to me, "Man, this is too much life. I can't stand it."

I believe that to some degree we are all in the same situation as this young man. We want to be more alive and feel more, but we are afraid of it. Our fear of life is seen in the way we keep busy so as not to feel, keep running so as not to face ourselves, or get high on liquor or drugs so as not to sense our being. Because we are afraid of life, we seek to control or master it. We believe that it is bad or dangerous to be carried away by our emotions. We admire the person who is cool, who acts without feeling. Our hero is James Bond, Secret Agent 007. The emphasis in our culture is upon doing and achieving. The modern individual is committed to being successful, not to being a person. He belongs rightly to the "action generation," whose motto is do more but feel less. This attitude characterizes much of modern sexuality: more action but less passion.

Regardless of how well we perform, we are failures as people. I believe that most of us sense the failure in ourselves. We are dimly aware of the pain, anguish, and despair that lie just below the surface. But we are determined to overcome our weaknesses, override our fears, and surmount our anxieties. This is why books on self-improvement or How to Do It are so popular. Unfortunately, these efforts are bound to fail. Being a person is not something one can do. It is not a performance. It may require that we stop our frantic business, that we take time out to breathe and to feel. In the process we may feel our pain, but if we have the courage to accept it, we will also have pleasure. If we can face our inner emptiness, we will find fulfillment. If we can go through our despair, we will discover joy. In this therapeutic undertaking, we may need help.

Is it the fate of modern man to be neurotic, to be afraid of life? My answer is yes, if we define modern man as a member of a culture whose dominant values are power and progress. Since these values characterize Western culture in the twentieth century, it follows that every person who grows up in this culture is neurotic.

The neurotic individual is in conflict with himself. Part of his being is trying to overcome another part. His ego is trying to master his body; his rational mind, to control his feelings; his will, to overcome his fears and anxieties. Though this conflict is in large part unconscious, its effect is to deplete the person's energy and to destroy his peace of mind. Neurosis is internal conflict. The neurotic character takes many forms, but all of them involve a struggle in the individual between what he is and what he believes he should be. Every neurotic individual is caught in this struggle.

How does such a state of internal conflict arise? Why is it the fate of modern man to suffer from these conflicts? In the individual case the neurosis arises within the context of a family situation. But the family situation reflects the cultural one, since the family is subject to all the forces in the society of which it is a part. To understand the existential condition of modern man and to know his fate, we must investigate the sources of conflict in his culture.

We are familiar with some conflicts in our culture. For example, we talk peace, but we prepare for war. We advocate conservation, but we ruthlessly exploit the earth's natural resources for economic gain. We are committed to the goals of power and progress, yet we want pleasure, peace of mind, and stability. We don't realize that power and pleasure are opposing values and that the former often precludes the latter. Power inevitably leads to a struggle for its possession, which often pits father against son and brother against brother. It is a divisive force in a community. Progress denotes a constant activity to change the old into the new under the belief that the new is always superior to the old. While this may be true in some technical areas, it is a dangerous belief. By extension, it implies that the son is superior to the father or that tradition is merely the dead weight of the past. There are cultures in which other values dominate, where respect for the past and for tradition is more important than the desire for change. In these cultures conflict is minimized and neurosis is rare.

Parents as representatives of the culture have the responsibility to inspire their children with the values of the culture. They make demands upon a child in terms of attitudes and behavior that are designed to fit the child into the social and cultural matrix. On one hand the child resists these demands because they amount to a domestication of his animal nature. He must be "broken in" to make him part of the system. On the other hand the child wishes to comply with these demands to keep the love and approval of his parents. The outcome depends upon the nature of the demands and the way they are enforced. With love and understanding it is possible to teach a child the customs and practices of a culture without breaking his spirit. Unfortunately, in most cases the process of adapting the child to the culture does break his spirit, which makes him neurotic and afraid of life.

The central issue in the process of cultural adaptation is the control of sexuality. There is no culture that does not impose some restraint upon sexual behavior. This restraint seems necessary to prevent discord from developing within a community. Human beings are jealous creatures and prone to violence. Even in the most primitive societies the bond of marriage is sacred. But conflicts that arise from such restrictions are external to the personality. In Western culture the practice has been to make the person feel guilty about sexual feelings and sexual practices like masturbation that in no way threaten the peace of the community. When guilt or shame are attached to feelings, the conflict is internalized and creates a neurotic character.

Incest is taboo in all human societies, but the sexual feelings of a child for the parent of the opposite sex are reprehensible only in modern societies. Such feelings are believed to pose a danger to the exclusive right of a parent to the sexual affections of the partner. The child is seen as a rival by the parent of the same sex. Although no incest occurs, the child is made to feel guilty for this most natural feeling and desire.

When Freud investigated the causes of the emotional problems of his patients through analysis, he found that in all cases they involved infantile or childhood sexuality, in particular, sexual feelings for the parent of the opposite sex. He also found that associated with these incestuous feelings were death wishes toward the parent of the same sex. Noting the parallel with the legend of Oedipus, he described the child's situation as oedipal. He believed that if a boy did not suppress his sexual feelings for his mother, he would suffer the fate of Oedipus; namely, he would kill his father and marry his mother. To prevent that fate the child is threatened with castration if he does not repress both his sexual desire and his hostile feelings.

Analysis also revealed that not only were these feelings suppressed but the oedipal situation itself was repressed; that is, the adult had no memory of the triangle in which he was involved between three and six years of age. My own clinical experience confirms this observation. Few patients can recall any sexual desire for the parent. Freud believed, further, that this repression was necessary if the person was to establish a normal sexual life in adulthood. He thought that the repression made it possible to transfer the early sexual desire from the parent to a peer; otherwise, the person would remain fixated on the parent. Thus, for Freud, repression was the way the oedipal situation was resolved, allowing the child to advance through a latency period to normal adulthood. If the repression was incomplete, the person became a neurotic.

According to Freud, the neurotic character represents an inability to adapt to the cultural situation. He recognized that civilization denies the individual full instinctual gratification, but he believed that this denial was necessary for cultural progress. In effect he accepted the idea that it was the fate of modern man to be unhappy. That fate was not a concern of psychoanalysis, which was limited to helping a person function adequately within the cultural system. The neurosis was seen as a symptom (phobia, obsession, compulsion, melancholia, etc.), which interfered with that functioning.

Wilhelm Reich had a different view. Although he had studied with Freud and was a member of the Vienna Psychoanalytic Society, he realized that the absence of a disabling symptom was no criterion of emotional health. In working with neurotic patients he found that the symptom developed out of a neurotic character structure and could be fully eliminated only if the person's character structure was changed. For Reich it was not a question of functioning adequately in the culture but of an individual's ability to give himself fully to sex and to work. That ability allowed the person to experience full satisfaction in his life. To the degree that this ability was lacking, the person was neurotic.

In his therapeutic work Reich focused upon sexuality as the key to the understanding of character. Every neurotic person had some disturbance in his orgastic response. He could not give in fully to the involuntary pleasurable convulsions of the orgasm. He was afraid of the overwhelming feeling of total orgasm. The neurotic was orgastically impotent to some degree. If, as a result of therapy, the person gained this ability, he became emotionally healthy. Whatever neurotic disturbances he suffered from disappeared. Further, his freedom from neurosis continued as long as he retained his orgastic potency.

Reich saw the connection between orgastic impotence and the oedipal problem. He claimed that neurosis had its roots in the patriarchal authoritarian family in which sexuality was suppressed. He would not accept that man was inexorably bound to an unhappy fate. He believed that a social system that denied to people the full satisfaction of their instinctual needs was sick and had to be changed. In his early years as a psychoanalyst Reich was also a social activist. However, in his later years he came to the conclusion that neurotic people cannot change a neurotic society.

I have been greatly influenced by Reich's thinking. He was my teacher from 1940 to 1953. He was my analyst from 1942 to 1945. I became a psychotherapist because I believed that his approach to human problems both theoretically (character analysis) and technically (vegetotherapy) represented an important advance in the treatment of the neurotic character. Character analysis was Reich's great contribution to psychoanalytic theory. For Reich the neurotic character was the terrain in which the neurotic symptom developed. He believed therefore, that the analysis should focus upon the character rather than the symptom to effect a major improvement. Vegetotherapy marked the breakthrough of the therapeutic process into the somatic realm. Reich saw that the neurosis was manifested in a disturbed vegetative functioning as well as in psychic conflicts. Breathing, motility, and the involuntary pleasurable movements of orgasm were markedly restricted in the neurotic individual by chronic muscular tensions. He described these tensions as a process of armoring, which reflected the character on the somatic level. He stated that the bodily attitude of a person is functionally identical with his psychic attitude. Reich's work is the basis for my development of bioenergetic analysis, which extends Reich's ideas in several important ways.

One, bioenergetic analysis provides a systematic understanding of character structure on both the psychic and somatic levels. That understanding enables one to read the person's character and emotional problems from the expression of his body. It makes it possible, also, to imagine the history of the person, since his life experiences are structured in his body.[1] The information gained from this reading of the language of the body is integrated into the analytic process.

Two, through its concept of grounding, bioenergetic analysis offers a deeper understanding of the energy processes in the body

1. The reader is referred to Alexander Lowen, *The Language of the Body* (New York: Collier Books, 1971) for a fuller presentation of this concept.

as they affect personality. Grounding refers to the energetic connection between a person's feet and the earth or ground. It reflects the amount of energy or feeling the person allows into the lower part of his body. It denotes the relationship of the person to the ground he stands on. Is he well grounded or is he up in the air? Are his feet well planted? What is his standing? One's feelings of security and independence are intimately related to the function of his legs and feet. These feelings strongly influence his sexuality.

Three, bioenergetic analysis employs many active bodily techniques and exercises to help a person strengthen his standing, increase his energy, enlarge and deepen his self-perception, and further his self-expression. In bioenergetic analysis the body work is coordinated with the analytic process, making this therapeutic modality a combined body-mind approach to emotional problems.

For more than thirty years I have been a practicing therapist, working to help patients gain some measure of joy and happiness in their lives. That endeavor has necessitated a continuing effort to understand the neurotic character of modern man from both the cultural and the individual positions. My focus has been and is upon the individual as he struggles to find some meaning and satisfaction in his life; in other words, as he struggles against his fate. However, the background of that struggle is the cultural situation. Without a knowledge of the cultural process we cannot comprehend the depth of the problem.

The cultural process that gave rise to modern society and modern man was the development of the ego. This development is associated with the acquisition of knowledge and the gaining of power over nature. Man is part of nature like any other animal, fully subject to her laws; but he is also above nature, acting upon and controlling her. He does the same with his own nature; part of his personality, the ego, turns against the animal part, the body. The antithesis between ego and body produces a dynamic tension that furthers the growth of culture, but it also contains a destructive potential. This can be seen best through analogy with a bow and arrow. The more one draws the bow, the further the arrow will fly. But if one overdraws the bow, it will break. When the ego and the body pull apart to the point where there is no contact between them, the result is a psychotic break. I believe we have reached this danger point in our culture. Psychotic breakdowns are quite common, but even more widespread is the fear of breakdown, on both the personal and the social levels.

Given his culture and the character it produces, what is the fate of modern man? If the story of Oedipus can serve as a prophecy, it is a prophecy of achieving the success and power one seeks only to find one's world coming apart or breaking down. If success is measured by material possessions, as it is in the industrialized countries, and power by the ability to *do* and *go* (machines and energy), most people in the Western world have both success and power. The collapse of their world is the impoverishment of their inner or emotional lives. Having committed themselves to success and power, they have little else to live for. And like Oedipus they have become wanderers on the earth, uprooted beings who can find no peace anywhere. Each individual feels alienated, to some degree, from his fellowman, and each carries within him a deep sense of guilt that he does not understand. This is the existential condition of modern man.

The challenge to modern man is to reconcile the antithetical aspects in his personality. On the body level he is an animal, on the ego level a would-be god. The fate of the animal is death, which the ego in its godlike aspirations is trying to avoid. But in trying to avoid this fate man creates an even worse one, namely, to live in fear of life.

Human life is full of contradictions. It is the mark of wisdom to recognize and accept these contradictions. It may seem like a contradiction to say that accepting one's fate leads to a change in that fate, but it is true. When one stops struggling against fate, one loses his neurosis (internal conflict) and gains peace of mind.

The result is a different attitude (no fear of life), expressed in a different character and associated with a different fate. Such a person will have the courage to live and to die, and he will know the fulfillment of life. This is how the story of Oedipus ends, the figure whose name identifies the key problem in the personality of modern man.

1/ The Neurotic Character

The Oedipal Problem

It is said that people learn from experience, and in general this is true. Experience is the best and, perhaps, the only real teacher. But when something falls within the area of a person's neurosis, the rule does not seem to apply. The person doesn't learn from experience but repeats the same self-destructive behavior again and again. For example, there is the person who always finds himself in the position of helping others. He responds eagerly when someone appeals to him for aid. Afterward he feels used and resentful because he doesn't believe that the person he helped appreciated his effort. He turns against the person he befriended and resolves to be less available and more critical of the need for his help next time. Yet when he senses someone in difficulty, he offers his services often even before they are requested, thinking that this time the result will be different. But it happens again as before. He doesn't learn because his helping has a compulsory quality. He is driven to help by forces beyond his control.

Take the case of the woman who in her relationships with men assumes a mothering role. The effect of this position is to infantilize the man and so to deprive her of sexual fulfillment. She may end the relationship feeling used and cheated and blaming the man's immaturity and weakness for its failure. Next time, she says, she will choose someone who can stand on his own two feet and not need to be mothered. But the next time turns out like the others. A strange fate seems to impel her into the very situation she is trying to avoid. She is driven to mother her men by unknown forces in her personality,

Such behavior can be regarded as neurotic because of the unconscious conflict that underlies it. In the case of the man, part of his personality wants to help, another part doesn't. If he helps he feels resentful, if he doesn't he feels guilty. This is a typical neurotic trap from which there is no way out except by retracing the steps that led into it. There is a similar unconscious conflict behind the behavior of the woman. That conflict is between her desire for a healthy and satisfying sexual relationship with a man and her fear of such a relationship. Mothering a man is her way of attempting to overcome her sexual anxiety, for it allows her to deny her fear of surrendering to a man. By acting as a mother, she feels needed and superior.

Here is still another example. A certain woman had great difficulty establishing a relationship with a man. When she met someone she was attracted to, she became hypercritical. She saw all his weaknesses and faults and rejected him. Since no one is perfect, her reactions made forming any relationship impossible. Although she says that she wants a relationship very much, she seems incapable of changing this pattern of behavior even after it is pointed out to her. It is not difficult to see that her hypercritical attitude is a defense against the feared danger of being rejected herself. She protects herself by rejecting the man first. But knowing this doesn't help much either. Her neurotic response is beyond her control.

To help her we must know what forces in her personality dictated this behavior. It only happened when she met someone to whom she was attracted. With others the problem did not arise, she could be friendly and relaxed. Since the difficulty developed only when she had some feeling for the person, we can assume that it was related to the feeling of desire or longing. She could not stand this feeling, it was too painful, and so she withdrew from the situation. Here, too, we must find out what happened to this person as a child to create this problem. Through analysis we will discover that she experienced a rejection by a parent, the pain of which was so overwhelming that she locked it up to survive. She closed her heart so as not to feel her heartache, and now she dares not open it. To love is to open the heart, and she is afraid to do so because of the pain in it. In her case the neurotic conflict is between the desire for love and the fear of it.

What makes such conflict neurotic is the person's repression of its negative element. Thus, the helping man denies his resentment at being asked for help, the mothering woman denies her fear of sex, and the hypercritical person denies her inability to love. Unable to face his pain and the anger to which it gives rise, the neurotic individual strives to overcome his fears, anxieties, hostilities, and anger. One part of himself seeks to rise above another, which splits the unity of his being and destroys his integrity. The neurotic person struggles to win over himself. In this, of course, he must fail. Failure seems to mean submission to an unacceptable fate, but actually it amounts to self-acceptance, which makes change possible. To the degree that most people in Western culture are struggling to be different, they are neurotic. And since this is a fight one can't win, all who engage in this struggle will fail. Strangely, through the acceptance of failure, we become free from our neurosis.

A typical example is the man who repeatedly loses money in bad investments by following the advice of others. He is a sucker for the promise of quick and easy money. Although he had been burned enough to know that the promise is illusory, he cannot resist its lure. He functions under the drive of a compulsion that is more powerful than his rational judgment. It may be a compulsion to lose, for there are people who seem fated to be losers. But such a fate can be changed if the nature of the compulsion and its origin are carefully explored through analysis.

The classic example is the woman who, after divorcing her first husband because he was an alcoholic and determining that her second marriage will be different, discovers that her new husband is also a heavy drinker. Although she didn't know this before the marriage, she had been blind to many indications of this tendency. Through analysis it can be shown that she is attracted to men who drink but repelled when the drinking gets out of control. Like the man in the preceding example, she is not aware of her deep feelings and motivations. This lack is typical of a neurotic character.

The term *neurotic character* refers to a pattern of behavior based upon internal conflict and represents a fear of life, of sex, and of being. It reflects the person's early life experience because it was formed as a result of those experiences. The most crucial experience for the development of the neurotic character is the oedipal one. This key experience occurs between the ages of three and six, when the oedipal situation develops, namely, the sexual interest of the child in the parent of the opposite sex and the resulting rivalry with the parent of the same sex. Both parents play an active role in this triangular situation in which the child feels trapped. The child develops a neurotic character as the only possible solution to a situation that in his mind is fraught with danger to life and sanity. Whether the danger is as real as the child believes, one cannot say. No child in this situation can afford to test the validity of his belief. He must compromise by bridling his passion and suppressing his sexuality. I shall illustrate this process with the following cases.

Margaret consulted me because she was depressed and felt that her life was empty. She was an attractive woman in her middle thirties and a nurse by profession. She had never married, though she had had many relationships with men. None had worked out satisfactorily for her. Years earlier her depression had been so severe that she was suicidal. Her suicidal tendencies had diminished through psychoanalytic treatment, but her depressive tendencies continued. However, she had never ceased to work. She was a hard worker and was highly regarded in her profession.

The outstanding expression of Margaret's body was its lifelessness. If she didn't talk or move, she might be taken for a wax figure. Her eyes were dull, her voice flat. However, from time to time while looking at me her eyes would light up and her face would become alive. It never lasted more than a few minutes, but it was an astounding transformation. When it happened, I was aware that she regarded me with feeling. Usually she appeared preoccupied and was aware of me only to communicate her thoughts. As we worked together I realized that her lifelessness went quite deep. When she opened her eyes wide, they had an almost hollow look. Her breathing was very shallow, her movements never animated.

The therapeutic task was to help Margaret discover why the light faded from her eyes. Why was she unable to maintain the glow of life? What was she unconsciously afraid of? Margaret's lack of life was the result of self-negation and a self-destructive attitude. In most neurotic persons this attitude is unconscious. Margaret was aware, however, that she was self-destructive. She said, "I am always trying to kill my body by not eating properly, not sleeping enough, by being worried about my image, and by being frantic about my work. I am never 'there' for myself, I am never able to enjoy myself, I don't take care of myself."

When I asked Margaret how and why that attitude developed, she replied, "I was literally destroyed by my mother, so frequently that I identified with her." Margaret had told me earlier that her mother used to beat her regularly. She described her mother as a hypochondriac who lay on a couch all day reading and complaining. However, the mother was really ill. She was a diabetic, but Margaret said that she was also self-destructive in that she took no responsibility for her own life. She died of heart trouble in her fifties. "But," Margaret said, "my father was equally self-destructive, working twenty hours a day and never taking time for pleasure. He was Christ, the martyr. He died of a heart attack in his forties."

She added, "My father was a burden to me. I felt I had to save him. He was in my mind all the time. He made me very sad and unhappy. I could never reach him. I remember looking at him when he was suffering from heart trouble, and he had such a pathetic look. It was actually worse than pathetic. It was the look of suffering. He was a sufferer. I need to help people."

We cannot understand Margaret or her problem without a picture of the family situation in which she grew up. In that picture the most important elements are the personalities of the parents. They affect the child more by who they are than by what they do. Children are very sensitive and pick up their parents' moods, feelings, and unconscious attitudes by osmosis, as it were. This was especially true for Margaret since she was an only child. Her parents' influence was unmitigated by the presence of other children. Consider the following.

"My mother said my father was a rough lover. I realize that I choose men who are somewhat like him in their suffering and in their rough intensity of sexual need. I don't see the suffering in these men until I get socked with it later. Then I find that I am taking care of them, helping them, and there is nothing in it for me. This is one way I am self-destructive. But I don't know if I could like anybody who is not suffering. My heart wouldn't open to that person. The last man I was involved with attempted suicide. I had a long line of men I had to help. It seems that if I can't do the neurotic thing, there is nothing else."

What exactly was Margaret's relationship to her father? She says that her mother told her that she was very close to her father until the age of four or five. She has no memory of that closeness nor any knowledge of why it ended. All she remembers is that her father was beyond reach. She felt close to him in her heart but there was no contact between them. "It was like in a dream. I am still in that dream. I relate to men on this basis. I build enormous fantasies of what life would be like with them, only to discover after a few meetings that they couldn't possibly fulfill my dreams."

From the above it is clear that in her contacts with men Margaret is looking for the kind of relationship that she had with her father before the age of five. It was a search for a lost paradise. She was trying to find her Shangri-la. She asked me, "Why am I always getting cuddled by men at bars? I must give off something." Her manner and her expression indicated that she, too, was a sufferer. Just as she is drawn to those who suffer, so they are drawn to her. Each hopes the other can relieve his suffering, but each only brings suffering to the other. Neither has any joy to offer.

From the above it is obvious that Margaret suffered a severe loss at about the age of five, when the loving relationship she had with her father ended. The depressive tendency is conditioned by such a loss.[1] Undoubtedly, there had been an earlier loss of love in her relationship with her mother, but the early loss had been mitigated by the warmth of her contact with her father. When that ended, Margaret was lost. She survived by a great effort of will, manifested today in the set of a grim and determined jaw. But memories of the time when she glowed in the warmth of her father's love are still reflected in the momentary brightening of her eyes and face.

What happened to cause the destruction of the loving relationship she had with her father? Why did it have such a devastating

1. See my book *Depression and the Body* (New York: Coward, McCann & Geoghegan, Inc., 1972) for a full discussion of the causes and treatment of depression. This book is also available as a Penguin paperback.

effect upon her personality? Margaret had no memories of that time. They were completely repressed. However, she has had many years of psychoanalysis and is familiar with the oedipal problem. During our discussion of this subject, she remarked, "I don't remember any sexual feelings for my father, but during my analysis I had a dream of sleeping with him. Having been in analysis for some time, I felt that I could have this dream without thinking I was crazy. However, in the dream I felt I couldn't let go. I couldn't really enjoy it."

Margaret still doesn't enjoy sex. She still can't let go and have an orgasm. She uses sex for contact and closeness. She cannot give in to her sexual feelings because she is afraid they would overwhelm her and drive her crazy. I shall explore this aspect of the fear of sex in a later chapter. My intention here is to show the relation between the neurotic character and the oedipal problem.

What really went on in her family? What was the relation between the parents? Margaret said, "I used to have the fantasy as a child that my parents were very close to each other and that I was the outsider. I felt isolated. Then, as I grew older, I saw that my mother was alone and my father, too. I realized that she talked about him as if he was a stranger." She did recollect a scene in which her father tried to throw her mother out of the window, but she doesn't know why. We can guess. Like so many other marriages, her parents' relationship had started on the high note of romance but ended on the bitter one of frustration. This is the terrain in which the oedipal problem develops. The frustrated parent generally turns to the child of the opposite sex for sympathy and affection.

The feelings between Margaret and her father were very deep. Despite the barrier between them, he was close to her heart and she to his. Margaret said that she was told that when she won some awards at school and church he cried. Why was any expression of these feelings restrained? There is only one answer. They had become sexual on both sides. The danger of incest seemed real. The father had to withdraw from any contact with the girl, and she had to be made to suppress her sexuality since it threatened him.

The child's sexual desire for the parent is an expression of her natural aliveness. The child is innocent until the parents project their sexual guilt upon her. Margaret was the bad one because her sexuality was alive and free. It had to be beaten out of her, which her mother did literally—with a horsewhip with which her father used to train horses. She was forced to deny her body and invest her energy in schoolwork. The father didn't protect her because he felt too guilty to interfere. She was effectively broken as one breaks the wild, free spirit of a horse so it can be ridden by a man. Since Eve, the female has been regarded as the temptress. This bias reflects the double standard of morality characteristic of patriarchal culture. In the past, Western society has found it necessary to suppress the woman's sexuality more than that of the man.

We can understand now why Margaret developed her neurotic character. She was not allowed to relate to her father on a sexual level, and that taboo became ingrained into her personality and extended to all men. She can be the child who wants to be cuddled or she can be the understanding and sympathetic helper who will try to ease a man's suffering. Since neither of these approaches fulfills her need for a sexual relationship (which is more than just having sex), she becomes depressed. I don't believe that she can overcome her depressive tendency until she regains her sexuality. Having lost her sexuality, she lost her life. To be sexual is to be alive, and to be alive is to be sexual. In subsequent chapters I will show what is involved in working through this problem.

Margaret's case is not unique. It may differ from the average in the severity of the beatings she received, in the degree of repressed sexuality in the family, and in the special form her neurotic character assumed. Yet it is typical of what goes on in modern families, namely, the incestuous feelings between parents and children, the rivalries, jealousies, and threats to the child.

It is also typical of the way the oedipal problem shapes the neurotic character of the individual. Here is a different case, which shows many similarities with Margaret's, although it involves a man.

Robert was a highly successful architect who consulted me because he was depressed. His depression was caused by the breakup of his marriage. When I asked why the marriage failed, he said that his wife complained that there was no communication between them, that he withdrew from contact, and that he was sexually passive. He admitted the truth of her complaints. He recognized that he had great difficulty expressing feelings. He had undergone psychoanalytic treatment earlier for a number of years. The treatment had helped him somewhat, but his emotional responsiveness was still very weak.

Robert was a handsome man in his late forties. He had a well-built and well-proportioned body and regular facial features. When I looked at him, he smiled too quickly. I sensed that eye contact embarrassed him. On closer examination I saw that his eyes were watchful and without feeling. The most notable aspect of his body, however, was its tightness and rigidity. Without his clothes he looked like a Greek statue. Dressed, he could be taken for a moving mannequin. He was so controlled that his body did not look alive.

What happened in Robert's childhood to account for his emotional deadness? Like Margaret, he was an only child. His mother, however, doted on him when he was young. Although his parents were not rich, he was dressed in very expensive clothes, which were always kept clean. He said that pictures showed him to be an adorable little boy. His biggest wrongdoing was to get dirty. He was immediately washed and his clothes changed. He was never beaten. Punishment for any transgression took the form of shame and the withdrawal of love.

Robert related that as a boy he had the fantasy that he was not the child of his parents. He said that they really wanted a girl. He imagined that someday his true parents would discover him.

This feeling of not belonging arises whenever there is a lack of emotional contact between parents and a child. In Robert's case his parents also felt that he didn't belong to them. They said he was different from them. Robert explained his feeling by the fact that his mother and father were so close that he felt on the outside. "I felt that I would pound on the door and say, 'Let me in.' At other times I felt I would run away and find my true family." It may be recalled that Margaret had a similar feeling of being an outsider and not belonging to her family. She discovered later that the apparent closeness of her parents was more of a façade than a reality. What was the situation in Robert's family?

Robert described his mother as an amazon driving wild horses with whips. Though she was not pretty, wore glasses, and was socially uncomfortable, she had made a splendid marriage. His father, he said, was handsome, charming, and very much sought after. He was a winner, a man bound to succeed. Robert recognized that his mother was ambitious. He said, "She tried to project an image of refinement. Her parents had been farmers. She wanted to show that she was the best wife for my father, that their union was the perfect marriage."

She also tried to project the image of being the perfect mother. To fulfill that image Robert had to be the perfect child, which he tried to be. But perfect children are not real, that is, not alive. Real children get dirty, make messes. To keep his mother's love Robert had to become an image, a statue or a mannequin. And for the same reason the father wasn't real either. Who can be a real man to a perfect wife? Robert has no memory of his parents ever fighting. Even as a child Robert sensed that the family situation had an air of unreality. To whatever degree he felt alive, he couldn't be their child. He could belong only by being unreal himself.

It would be a mistake to think that there were no passions in this family. Robert never talked about the sexual life of his parents, but they must have had one. He never mentioned any sexual feelings he may have had as a child, but he must have had some. He had repressed all memories of his early years. That repression went hand in hand with the deadness of his body. The information he related to me was mostly secondhand. However, we do have some evidence of the existence of an oedipal situation. Robert said that as a boy he had fantasies of winning his mother and trouncing his father. In his fantasy his mother preferred him to his father. Another significant piece of evidence is the fact that Robert did trounce his father. He said, "I have outshone him to a point where I am ashamed of it." Actually his father never proved to be a winner. It was Robert who became the big winner in the world and who fulfilled his mother's ambitions.

However, there was a price attached to this victory. That price was the loss of his orgastic potency, namely, the ability for a total body surrender in sex. Robert's sexuality was limited to his genital organ; the rest of his body did not participate in the excitement or the discharge. His inability to give himself fully to his sexual feeling was due to the rigidity and tension in his body, which was also responsible for his emotional deadness. Whether the emotional deadness resulted from a fear of sex or whether his orgastic impotence was caused by his emotional deadness need not be argued. The problem had to be worked out simultaneously on both levels, the sexual and the emotional. On a deeper level, both represented a fear of life.

Robert, however, was unaware of any fear of sex or of life. Fear, being an emotion like any other, is equally suppressed in a state of emotional deadness. This makes the problem very difficult, since all one can go on is the absence of feeling. For example, Robert had no recollection of any sexual feelings for his mother. He couldn't imagine such feelings, for he found his mother sexually unattractive. He did not recall ever seeing her naked, nor ever having had any curiosity about her body. He does remember that one night he decided to listen at their bedroom door, but he was quickly discovered and sent to his room. He did not associate this incident with sexual curiosity. Evidently his curiosity was crushed very early. When he was three he had occasion to see a little girl being bathed, but he was berated for looking.

Because Robert doesn't remember, it cannot be assumed that he had no sexual feelings as a child. Since such feelings are normal, it must be assumed that they were strongly suppressed and the memory of them repressed. This assumption is supported by the severity of the muscular tension and bodily rigidity that are the means of suppression. In discussing this matter Robert remarked that cutting off feeling was a common maneuver he used whenever someone hurt him. He cut off all feeling for the person and "cut" the person as if he didn't exist. He said that it was a tactic used against him by his mother and that he used it against her in return. As I see it, mother and son were engaged in a power struggle in which seduction and rejection were the means of control. His mother doted on him, dressing him as Little Lord Fauntleroy, to use his words, but she also "cut him off" whenever he didn't do what she wanted. He did what she demanded, but he also rejected her sexually.

There is another aspect to Robert's problem. His bodily rigidity must be interpreted as a sign that he was scared stiff. I worked with him long enough to know that it was true. But, he didn't feel it. Of course, being emotionally dead he didn't feel much. Nevertheless, it was necessary to find out of whom he was afraid and why.

Robert says that he was raised as Little Lord Fauntleroy. I saw him as a prince. His mother took the role of the queen. The situation would require that his father be the king, but he didn't carry off that role. Instead of being on top, he pushed his son into that position. The boy was to achieve what he couldn't. The prince was to take his place and become king. But, much as the father may have desired to see his son outshine him, it was only natural that he would also feel resentful and angry at being displaced and downgraded. When two males compete for the same female, the fight can be deadly. But a son is no match for a father and is terrified to make a real challenge. He must back off, admit defeat, and give up his sexual desire for his mother. He accepts psychological castration and, thereby, removes himself as a competitor and threat to his father.

The oedipal situation is now resolved. The boy can grow up and conquer the world, but on a sexual level he still remains a boy. Robert was aware that on one level of his personality he still felt immature, not fully a man. Emotionally, he remained a prince.

In a subsequent chapter I will discuss the treatment of the oedipal problem. First, we need to understand the problem both as a cultural phenomenon and as the result of family dynamics. In the next section we will look at the Oedipus legend in some detail to see how closely these cases parallel the myth.

The Oedipus Legend

Oedipus was a prince, the son of Laius, king of Thebes. When he was born, his father consulted the oracle at Delphi about his son's future. Told that when the boy grew up, he would kill his father and marry his mother, Laius, to avoid this calamity, had the boy staked out in a field to die of exposure. Oedipus was saved by a shepherd who took pity on him and brought him to Corinth, where he was adopted by Polybus, king of Corinth, who raised him as his own son. Because his foot was inflamed from being tied to the stake, he was given the name of Oedipus, which means "swollen foot."

When Oedipus grew to manhood, he, too, consulted the oracle at Delphi to learn his destiny. And he was told that he would kill his father and marry his mother. Since he believed Polybus to be his father, Oedipus decided to avoid the fate predicted by the oracle by leaving Corinth to seek his fortune elsewhere. On the road to Boeotia he was accosted by a traveler who ordered him out of his way. A quarrel ensued, and Oedipus struck the man with his staff, killing him. Not knowing who his victim was, Oedipus proceeded to Thebes. When he arrived, he learned that the city was being terrorized by the Sphinx, a strange monster with the face of a woman, the body of a lion, and the wings of a bird. The Sphinx posed a riddle to any traveler she caught. Those who failed to answer correctly were devoured.

Creon, who was ruling the city since the death of his brother

Laius, had promised the crown and the hand of the widowed queen Jocasta to anyone who would free the city from the ravages of the monster. Oedipus undertook the challenge and confronted the Sphinx. To the question "Which animal walks on four legs in the morning, two at midday, and three in the evening?" Oedipus answered, "Man." In his infancy he crawls on all fours, in his maturity he walks on two legs, and in the evening of his life he walks with a cane. When the Sphinx heard this answer, she threw herself into the sea and was drowned. Oedipus returned to Thebes, married the queen, and ruled the city for more than twenty years. From their union came two sons, Eteocles and Polyneices, and two daughters, Antigone and Ismene. Oedipus' reign in Thebes was prosperous, and he was honored as a just and devoted sovereign.

In Greek mythology there is often some tragedy in the life of the hero. For example, both Hercules, the great destroyer of monsters, and Theseus, who slew the Minotaur, perished tragically. Among others, Erichthonius, who as king of Athens introduced the worship of Athene and the use of silver, was killed by a thunderbolt from Zeus. The hero's achievement, which is supported by one god, offends another. His superhuman exploit makes him appear godlike. The gods are notoriously jealous. The hero must pay a price for his hubris, since he is a mortal after all.

Oedipus is regarded as a hero for his conquest of the Sphinx. The Erinyes, as the fates were called, were lying in wait. A terrible plague ravaged the city of Thebes. There was drought and famine. When the oracle at Delphi was consulted, he said that the scourges would not cease until the murderer of Laius was discovered and driven from the city. Oedipus vowed to find the culprit. To his surprise, his investigations revealed that he was the guilty one. He had killed his father on the highway to Thebes and, unwittingly, had married his mother.

Overwhelmed by shame, Jocasta hanged herself. Oedipus put out his own eyes. Then, accompanied by Antigone, his faithful daughter, he left Thebes and became a wanderer. After many years he found a final refuge in the town of Colonus near Athens.

There, reconciled to his fate and purified of his crimes, he disappeared mysteriously from the earth. The implication is that he was taken to the abode of the gods, as befits a Greek hero. Having provided a last haven for Oedipus, Colonus became a sacred place.

The legend relates the end of this unhappy family. Oedipus' two sons had agreed to share the rulership of the kingdom alternately. But when the time came for Eteocles to turn the power over to his brother, he refused. Polyneices gathered together an army of Aegeans and laid siege to Thebes. In the course of the battle the two brothers slew each other. Creon, who then became ruler of the city, decreed that Polyneices should be treated as a traitor and his body left unburied. Antigone defied the decree out of love for her brother and buried him with honors. For this disobedience she was condemned to be buried alive. Her sister Ismene shared her fate.

Looking back to the cases of Margaret and Robert, we can see that their lives did not parallel the history of Oedipus. Neither was guilty of the crimes of incest and parental murder, despite the fact that both were involved in oedipal situations in their childhood. How they avoided the fate of Oedipus is explained by Sigmund Freud, the first person to recognize the importance of the oedipal situation and the significance of the Oedipus story for modern man. In the next section we will examine the psychoanalytic view of the development of the Oedipus complex.

The Oedipus Complex

Freud was drawn to the story of Oedipus because he believed that the two crimes of Oedipus, the killing of his father and the marriage to his mother, coincide with "the two primal wishes of children, the insufficient repression or the reawakening of which forms the nucleus of perhaps every psychoneurosis."[2] This

2. Sigmund Freud, *Totem and Taboo* (New York: W. W. Norton & Co., 1956), p. 132.

nucleus became known as the Oedipus complex. Earlier, Freud had written, "It may be that we are all destined to direct our first sexual impulses towards our mothers and our first impulses of hatred and violence towards our fathers, our dreams convince us that we were."[3] If this were so, then the fate of Oedipus would be the common fate of all mankind. Freud recognized this possibility, for he said, "His fate moves us because it might have been our own, because the oracle laid upon us the very curse that rested on him."[4]

In psychoanalytic thinking all children are considered to go through an oedipal period, from about the ages of three to seven. In this period they have to deal with feelings of sexual attraction to the parent of the opposite sex, and jealousy, fear, and hostility toward the parent of the same sex. The complex also includes varying amounts of guilt associated with these feelings. Otto Fenichel says, "In both sexes, the Oedipus complex can be called the climax of infantile sexuality, the erogenous development from oral eroticism via anal eroticism toward genitality."[5]

It is important for our study to understand what is meant by infantile sexuality and how it differs from the adult form. The term "infantile sexuality" actually refers to all sexual manifestations from birth to about six years of age. The erotic pleasure a baby derives from nursing or thumbsucking is considered to be sexual in nature. Between the ages of three and five, childhood sexuality becomes focused on the genitals. In the fifth year, according to Freud, at the height of development of childhood sexuality, that focus comes close to that reached in maturity. The difference between childhood and adult sexuality is that the former lacks the elements of penetration and ejaculation, the reproductive

3. Sigmund Freud, "The Interpretation of Dreams," in *Basic Writings of Sigmund Freud* (New York: Random House, Modern Library Ed., 1938), p. 308.

4. Ibid., p. 308.

5. Otto Fenichel, *The Psychoanalytic Theory of Neurosis* (New York: W. W. Norton & Co., 1945), p. 91.

aspects of sexuality. Childhood sexuality is, therefore, a surface phenomenon. Freud described it as phallic rather than genital. This distinction is valid if we recognize that phallic refers to a rise in excitation rather than a discharge. Adult sexuality is characterized by its emphasis upon the latter. However, the feelings associated with childhood sexuality can hardly be distinguished from those relating to the adult form.

Although the Oedipus complex is regarded as a normal development for all children in our culture, this does not mean that it is biologically determined. We must distinguish between two different phenomena. One is the preliminary blooming of sexuality, which occurs at this time and which is manifested in masturbatory activities and a heightened sexual curiosity. It is also reflected in the child's sexual interest in the parent of the opposite sex. Evidence for this early blooming is provided by patients' dreams and memories. It can be confirmed by any observant parent, since children make no effort to hide their sexual feelings. And medical research has shown that there is an increased production of sexual hormones during this period. This preliminary awakening of sexuality is generally followed by a quiescent period, the latency period, which lasts until puberty, when both hormonal and sexual activity begin to assume their adult form. Another biological phenomenon parallels this double flowering of sexuality, and that is the development of teeth. We have two sets of teeth; the first, or baby teeth, reach their fullness at about the ages of six to seven, when they fall out and are replaced by the permanent teeth. It is also around this time, six years of age, that most children begin their formal education.

The other phenomenon is the creation of a triangle in which the mother is a sexual object for both father and son, or the father a sexual object for mother and daughter. When this happens, as it invariably does in our culture, we have to deal with the parent's jealousy and hostility to the child. It may be quite natural for a boy to feel some jealousy over his father's sexual relation with his mother. This jealousy in no way threatens the father. It is quite another story when the father becomes jealous of his son because he senses that his wife favors or prefers the boy. This situation is fraught with real danger for the child. In the same way the mother's jealousy of her daughter poses a serious threat to the girl. This aspect of the Oedipus complex is culturally determined. "In this sense," according to Fenichel, "the Oedipus complex is undoubtedly a product of family influence."[6] Its specific form will depend, therefore, upon the dynamics of the family situation.

Another element, namely, sexual guilt, also enters into this complex. Although all parties are involved in the triangle, the child is made to feel guilty about his sexual feelings and behavior. He acted innocently, following his instinctual impulses, but in the parents' eyes any sexual expression by the child is "bad," "dirty," or "sinful." Parents project their sexual guilt upon the child. Thus, the Oedipus complex of the child generally reflects the unresolved oedipal conflicts of his parents. The child's feeling of guilt about his sexuality derives less from what his parents say or do but, as Fenichel points out, even more from "the general attitude of the parents toward sex, which is constantly manifested by them, with or without their knowledge."[7]

But this statement only locates the problem in the preceding generation. To understand how this guilt arose in the first place, we must study the origin of those cultural forces that created the oedipal situation. In a subsequent chapter we will undertake this study by analyzing the mythology and history of ancient Greece. We can anticipate its result by saying that fear and hostility between parents and children and sexual guilt are both results of the change from the matriarchal to the patriarchal principle of relationships. That change occurred at the beginning of civilization, when mankind gained power over nature. The acquisition of power led to a struggle for power that goes on to this day in all "civilized" societies.

Finally, the complex also includes a murderous rage on the

6. Ibid., p. 97.
7. Ibid., p. 95.

part of the child toward the parent of the same sex. The child wants to kill the parent, but is more afraid that he will be killed by the parent. Because of the great fear, the rage is suppressed and comes out only in death wishes against the parent or as fear that the parent will die or be killed in an accident. In the end, the child is made to feel guilty about his hostility toward the parent.

The Freudian position has been that the child's rage and hostility against the parent is directly related to and associated with his incest wishes. Thus, Erik Erikson writes, "The 'oedipus' wishes (so simply and so trustingly expressed in the boy's assurance that he will marry his mother and make her proud of him and in the girl's that she will marry her father and take much better care of him) lead to secret fantasies of vague murder and rape. The consequence is a deep sense of guilt—a strange sense, for it forever seems to imply that the individual has committed a crime which, after all, was not committed but would have been biologically quite impossible. This secret guilt, however, helps to drive the whole weight of initiative toward desirable ideals and immediate practical goals."[8] This view supports the idea that the Oedipus complex is not only biologically determined but essential to the continued progress of culture. Doesn't it seem strange that such lovely feelings on the part of a child for a parent could lead to "secret fantasies of vague murder and rape"? It makes more sense to me to assume that it is only after the child is made to feel guilty about his incest wishes that the secret fantasies of murder and rape arise.

This was also the view of my teacher, Wilhelm Reich. In his study, *Der Triebhafte Charakter (The Impulsive Character)*, published in 1925 while he was still a member of the psychoanalytic movement, he writes, "The Oedipal phase is among the most meaningful in human experience. Without exception its

8. Erik Erikson, *Childhood and Society* (New York: W. W. Norton & Co., 1950), p. 86.

conflicts stand at the core of every neurosis and mobilize powerful guilt feelings. . . . These guilt feelings develop with particular intensity into attitudes of hate, which are part and parcel of the Oedipus complex."[9] Note that the hate is derived from the guilt, not the other way around. Reich also had a different view of the value of the guilt feelings. Erikson saw them as furthering cultural progress. For Reich, they stemmed from a sex-repressive upbringing, the function of which "is that of laying the foundation for authoritarian culture and economic slavery."[10]

Having delineated the Oedipus complex, we are interested next to learn its fate in the personality. How are the conflicts contained within it resolved? If it was merely a question of the sexual feelings of a child for his parent, these, being infantile in nature, would be superseded in the course of natural growth. No child hangs onto its baby teeth forever. They are pushed out by the permanent teeth as the latter emerge. The same should be true for infantile sexual feelings. With the onset of mature sexuality in puberty, the young person would direct his sexual feelings toward objects outside the family. Unfortunately, in our culture this natural development does not occur without disturbance. The infantile sexual feelings are too entangled with feelings of guilt, fear, and hatred for such a simple resolution to occur. The whole complex is repressed.

The repression of the Oedipus complex takes place under the threat of castration. In this, both Freud and Reich are in accord. The boy gives up his striving to be sexually close to his mother and his hostility to his father out of fear of castration. Freud says specifically that "the boy's Oedipus complex succumbs to the dread of castration."[11] The child is afraid that his penis will be

9. Wilhelm Reich, *The Impulsive Character*, trans. Barbara G. Koopman (New York: New American Library, 1974), p. 17.

10. Wilhelm Reich, *The Function of the Orgasm* (New York: The Orgone Institute Press, 1942), p. 20.

11. Sigmund Freud, "The Passing of the Oedipus-Complex," 1924 in *Collected Papers*, Vol. II (London: Hogarth Press, 1953), p. 276.

cut off or taken away. When children are threatened with punishment for masturbation, this threat to the genitals is often explicitly stated. But even where neither parent makes such an overt threat, the fear of castration is not absent. The boy is aware that he is competing with his father, and he can sense the latter's hostility. Since the penis is the offending organ, it is only natural to assume that it will be injured or cut off. Human castration was practiced in past times. People had their hands cut off for stealing. It is not difficult to see why boys would develop this image of the threatened punishment. Many people have typical anxiety dreams about this possibility. A patient of mine related one from his youth. He dreamed that his penis elongated and passed out the window, down the front of the building, across the street, and up the front of the building opposite to enter a window. On this street there was a tram railway. Just as his penis was about to enter the window, he heard the clang of an approaching streetcar. In all haste he was trying to get his penis back into his room before the car ran over it, when he awoke.

I could advance another hypothesis to account for the fact that all my patients have a fear of castration. Any hostility directed at a child for his sexuality by a parent will produce in the child a pulling up and contraction of his pelvic floor. Hostility will have this effect, even though it takes the form of a hateful look. And as long as the child is frightened of the parent, the tension in the pelvic floor will remain. Since tension and fear are equivalent, the contraction of the pelvic floor is associated with a fear of injury to the genitals. The person will not be conscious of the fear if he is not conscious of the tension. In that case, the fear of castration may be expressed in dreams or slips of the tongue. However, using body techniques that help the person become aware of the tension often brings the fear to consciousness.

My female patients also suffer from a fear of castration, experienced as a fear of injury to the genital area. However, in most cases this fear is not conscious, and it may require considerable analytic and body work before the person allows herself to feel the fear. Generally it is easier for the patient to experience the hostility of the parent as a threat to life. Such threats, because of the fear they evoke, function as threats of castration. In addition, girls are shamed and humiliated for any overt expression of sexual feeling, especially toward the father. Since the fear of humiliation produces a suppression of sexual feeling, it acts like a threat of castration.

The most effective weapon a parent has to control a child is the withdrawal of love or its threat. A young child between the ages of three and six is too dependent on parental love and approval to resist this pressure. Robert's mother, as we saw earlier, controlled him by "cutting him out." Margaret's mother beat her into submission, but it was the loss of her father's love that devastated her. Whatever the means parents use, the result is that the child is forced to give up his instinctual longing, to suppress his sexual desire for one parent and his hostility toward the other. In their place he will develop feelings of guilt about his sexuality and fear of authority figures. This surrender constitutes an acceptance of parental power and authority and a submission to the parents' values and demands. The child becomes "good," which means that he gives up his sexual orientation in favor of one directed toward achievement. Parental authority is introjected in the form of a superego, ensuring that the child will follow his parents' wishes in the acculturation process. In effect, the child now identifies with the threatening parent. Freud says, "The whole process, on the one hand, preserves the genital organ, wards off the danger of losing it; on the other hand, it paralyzes it, takes its function away from it."[12]

The effective suppression of the feelings associated with the Oedipus complex leads to the development of the superego. This, as we have seen, is a psychic function that represents the internalized parental prohibitions. But while this psychic process has been adequately described in the psychoanalytic literature,

12. Ibid., p. 273.

little has been written about the fact that the suppression of feeling occurs in the body. The mechanism for this suppression is the development of chronic muscular tensions, which block the movements that would express the feeling. For example, if a person wants to suppress an impulse to cry because he feels ashamed about crying, he would tense the muscles of his throat to prevent the sob from being expressed. We could say that he choked off the impulse or that he swallowed his tears. In this case the person is aware of the feeling of crying or sadness. However, if not crying becomes part of the person's way of being, that is, part of his character (only babies cry), then the tensions in the muscles of his throat develop a chronic quality and are removed from consciousness. Such a person may pride himself that he doesn't cry when hurt, but the fact is that he cannot cry even should he wish to because the inhibition has become structured in his body and is now beyond conscious control. An inability to cry is commonly encountered among men who complain about a lack of feeling. The person may be depressed and recognize that he is unhappy, but he cannot feel his sadness.

A similar mechanism operates in the suppression of sexual and other feelings. By sucking in the belly, pulling up the pelvic floor, and holding the pelvis immobile, one can reduce the flow of blood into the genital organs and block the natural sexual movements of the pelvis. At first, this is done consciously by tensing the appropriate muscles. But in time the tension becomes chronic and removed from consciousness. In some cases the tension is so severe that the person is not aware of any sexual feelings. I have a patient in therapy who is unable to feel any sexual desire, much as she would like to. In other cases the effect of the tension is to reduce the amount of sexual feeling the person can experience. In these persons one can find superego prohibitions against feeling and expressing sexual desire. The psychic and somatic determinants of behavior are functionally identical. But without acting upon the somatic component, one cannot effectively change character.

Broadly speaking, feeling is the perception of movement. If a person holds his arm absolutely immobile for five minutes, he will lose the feeling of his arm. He won't feel that he has an arm. The reader can experience this loss of sensation or feeling by letting his arm hang at his side without movement for five minutes or so. Similarly, if you put a hat on; notice how for a few minutes you are conscious of the hat, but then, if it doesn't move, that consciousness disappears and you forget about it. But not all movement leads to feeling. Perception is necessary; if one moves while asleep, there is no feeling. But without movement, there is nothing to perceive. Since the suppression of feeling is accomplished by chronic muscular tensions that immobilize the body, it is impossible for a person to sense a suppressed feeling. He may know logically that feelings are suppressed, but he cannot feel or perceive them. By the same token, character that is structured in the body as chronic tension is generally beyond the person's conscious perception.

An observer can see the tensions and, if he is trained, can interpret them to understand the person and his history. The common remark that "we do not see ourselves as others see us" is true because our eyes are turned outward. We "see" ourselves subjectively, that is, through feeling, whereas others see us objectively, through vision. Thus, an observer can see by the way we hold ourselves (stiff upper lip, set jaw, and tight throat) that we cannot allow ourselves to give in to crying. All we feel is that we have no desire to cry. The same thing is true of sexuality. The way we carry ourselves expresses our relation to our sexuality. If the pelvis is cocked back but loose and swinging, it denotes a strong identification with one's sexuality. If it is tucked forward (tail between legs) and held rigidly, it expresses the opposite attitude. We are our bodies, and they reveal who we are.

Both Freud and Fenichel held the belief that neurosis resulted from an inadequate repression of the Oedipus complex. Its persistence was supposed to fixate the individual at an infantile level of sexual development. We are familiar with the man who lives at home with his mother and who is neither married nor has a regular sex life. His life does seem to have an infantile quality. Most people are aware of the incestuous relationship between mother and son except the two persons involved. The man would strongly deny that he had any sexual feelings for or interest in his mother. I would believe him. He has suppressed all sexual desire for her and has effectively repressed the memory of any feeling he once had. His guilt would not permit him to remain in the situation if he had any conscious sexual feeling for his mother. He is "hung up" on her, not because of an inadequate repression but because the repression was too severe. He has no sexual feeling left with which to go out into the world as a man. Such severe suppression of sexual feeling can be explained only by assuming that there was an equally intense incestuous attachment during the oedipal period.

Repression of the Oedipus complex allows the child to advance into the latency period. Theoretically, this enables him to invest his energies in the outer world, but, as we have just seen, if the repression is severe, this avenue is very limited. The Freudian position poses a real dilemma, as Fenichel notes: "Superficially, no sexual attachment is completely attractive because the partner is never the mother; in a deeper layer, every sexual attachment has to be inhibited because every person represents the mother."[13] Given the repression of the Oedipus complex, there is no way the individual can find fulfillment; the most he can hope for is to find a place in society, do his work, get married, and raise a family. Neurosis for Freud represented an inability to function normally in society. He recognized that civilization exacted a price, imposed restraints upon the individual, and created discontents. If in an individual case the price was too high, the restraints too severe, the discontents too great, psychoanalysis was available to help the person gain the ego strength to adapt more successfully.

13. Fenichel, *The Psychoanalytic Theory of Neurosis*, p. 170.

Freud thought that only by repressing the Oedipus complex could one avoid the fate of Oedipus. But, as we saw, that doesn't work. The oedipal conflicts are not resolved by repression. They are only buried in the unconscious, where they operate as a fate to control one's behavior. Reich says, "When Freud said that the Oedipus complex vanishes as a result of castration anxiety, we have to add the following: True it vanishes, but it arises anew in the form of character reactions, which, on the one hand, perpetuate its main features in a distorted form, and are, on the other hand, reaction formations against its basic elements."[14]

I agree with Reich. The Oedipus complex vanishes as a conscious phenomenon through repression, but it then becomes active in the unconscious. Consequently, a person will marry someone who, superficially, is the opposite of his or her parent but then be compelled by the complex to treat the spouse as the parent. Another result is the superficial demonstration of the proper filial love and respect to the parent of the same sex while maintaining under the surface a great hostility. In effect, as I shall explain later, each boy marries his mother and each girl marries her father. And, while we do not kill the parent literally as Oedipus did, we do so psychologically by the hatred in our hearts. It is my argument that repressing the Oedipus complex assures that on a psychological level one will share the fate of Oedipus.

14. Wilhelm Reich, *Character Analysis*, 3d ed. (New York: The Orgone Institute Press, 1949), p. 156.

2 / Fate and Character

The Operation of Fate

I have long been familiar with the Oedipus story, but recently I returned to it with renewed interest because of the role that fate plays in the myth. Consider the fact that both Laius, the father, and Oedipus, the son, consulted the oracle on separate occasions and were foretold the same fate, and that both took steps to avoid that fate. Laius staked his infant son in the field to die; Oedipus left Corinth to avoid killing his father. Yet despite these efforts to avoid their fate, the prediction of the oracle came true. The question that came to my mind was: Did it happen just *because* they tried to avoid their fate? This question struck me with some force, since I had been aware for some time that one spect of the neurotic character is the neurotic's inability to accept himself. I realized that the neurotic individual struggles to avoid a feared fate, but by that very effort he ensures the fate he is attempting to escape.

Suppose, for example, that Laius had accepted his fate as prophesied by the oracle. Would the story be different? (Such an acceptance could be part of a religious attitude. If it is the will of the gods, so be it.) If Laius had raised Oedipus as his son, at least one incident in the story could not have occurred. Laius would not have been a stranger to his son and so could not have been killed in a chance encounter on the highway. Had Oedipus accepted his fate and remained in Corinth in obedience to the will of the gods, he could not have married his mother. The "ifs" can change a story, but it is because events happened just as they did that we have a meaningful story of human experience.

Freud had a similar feeling about the Oedipus story as dramatized by Sophocles in his play *Oedipus Rex*. He says, "The Oedipus Rex is a tragedy of fate. Its tragic effect depends on the conflict between the all-powerful will of the gods and the vain efforts of human beings threatened with disaster. Resignation to the divine will, and the perception of one's own impotence, is the lesson which the deeply moved spectator is supposed to learn from the play."[1] Yet Freud himself was not prepared to accept the inevitability of fate. He believed that "although the oracle placed the same curse on us," we could avoid the fate of Oedipus by repressing the feelings and memories associated with our infantile incest wishes. But, as I shall show, repression binds the individual to the traumatic situation and programs him to repeat it in later life.

The idea that the attempt to escape fate only serves to make that fate more certain is illustrated by John O'Hara in the introduction to his story "Appointment in Samarra." A servant, sent by

1. Sigmund Freud, "The Interpretation of Dreams," in *The Basic Writings of Sigmund Freud* (New York: Random House, Modern Library Ed., 1938), p. 307.

his master to buy some provisions in the marketplace at Baghdad, returned in a state of fright. He had been jostled by someone in the crowd, and when he turned, he saw it was Death who appeared to be threatening him. The servant begged his master for a horse so he could flee to Samarra to avoid his fate. The master gave him the horse and the servant took off in all haste. Then the master went to the marketplace, where he saw Death. He approached and asked why he had threatened his servant. I didn't threaten him, said Death. My arm went up in surprise to see him here in Baghdad because I have an appointment with him tonight in Samarra.

We often say that fate overtakes a person or that a person's fate catches up with him. I have said that such actions ensure one's fate. But *ensure* may be too strong a word. *Invite* seems more appropriate. For example, if a person walks about with a chip on his shoulder, someone is sure to try to knock it off. Certain attitudes naturally invite certain responses from others. Here is a simple clinical example. I had a woman patient who complained that she was never able to "get a man." Her relationships with men all proved to be temporary. One day in the course of a session, she remarked, "My mother constantly told me, 'No man would ever want you.'" It was as if her mother had laid a curse upon her that determined her fate, for she had reached middle age without having found a man who would make a commitment to her. But my patient played an active, if unconscious, role in creating her fate. Believing what her mother said, she clutched and clung to any man who showed an interest in her. She didn't do this in an obvious way, but by being very attentive and helpful to the man. The result, however, was always the same, for she could not hide her desperation. The man would become wary of being trapped and back away. Thus, it turned out that her mother's prophecy seemed to come true.

There is another way of looking at the operation of fate. The defenses we erect to protect us create the very condition we are trying to avoid. Thus, when someone builds a castle to protect his liberty, he ends up as a prisoner in his own castle because he dares not leave it. Similarly, one cannot assure peace by amassing arms, because armies by their very nature lead to war. This concept is particularly evident in the psychological defenses people develop. For example, the person who out of fear of rejection defends himself by not opening up or reaching out to people isolates himself and ensures by this maneuver that he will always feel rejected. No person is free who is tied to a defensive position. This is true of the neurotic character who erects psychological walls and armors himself muscularly as a protection against possible hurt, only to find that the hurt he feared is locked into his being by this very process.

I had a patient who was humiliated as a child by his father because he wasn't strong enough or athletic enough to compete with his cousins. He was afraid of his father, and he was afraid of the tough kids in his neighborhood. As a result, he felt like a coward. To overcome this feeling he engaged in a strenuous program of body building. He developed and even overdeveloped his muscles until he looked like a strong man. But the effect was to make him muscle-bound—with the emphasis upon the word *bound*. He was so bound he couldn't express himself. He didn't know how to relate to people. In company he felt awkward and humiliated because he didn't have anything to say. Thus, the humiliation he felt as a child persisted into adulthood. He complained about a lack of feeling, but he had suppressed all feeling in the effort to overcome his fear. Only by accepting his fear and expressing his sadness could he become a real person in his relations with others. This is what therapy helped him do. The attempt to overcome a personality problem by denying it ("I am not going to be afraid") internalizes the problem and ensures its continuance.

And yet, don't we all try to overcome our weaknesses, our fears, and our guilts? We mobilize our will in the attempt to surmount the inner obstacles that block us from the fulfillment of our dream. We say, "Where there is a will, there is a way." With enough willpower one can almost do the impossible. The will is potent in doing or performing, but it is impotent in changing the inner state of our being. Our feelings are not subject to our will. We can't change them by conscious action, but we can suppress them. However, suppressing a feeling doesn't make it go away; it only pushes it deeper into the unconscious. By this action we internalize the problem. It then becomes necessary to have therapy to bring the conflict back to consciousness so that it can be worked out in a nonneurotic way. In the case of the patient described above, this meant becoming aware that he was afraid to say to his father, "I don't want to compete. I don't want to be what you want." Having suppressed his rebellion, he has nothing to say.

My thesis is that one can't overcome a problem that is part of one's personality. The key word in the statement is *overcome*. The attempt to do that turns one part of the self against the other; the ego, through the will, is set against the body and its feelings. Instead of harmony between these two antithetical aspects of human nature, a conflict is created that must ultimately destroy the person. This is what all neurotics do, locking themselves into the fate they are trying to avoid. The alternative, and the healthy way, is through understanding, which leads to self-acceptance, self-expression, and self-possession.

There are, then, two ways in which we program our fate. First, by our attitude and behavior, that is, by our character, we invite certain responses from others. If, out of fear of rejection, we are aloof and withdrawn, we should not be surprised if people keep their distance. Or if we are paranoid, our distrust will antagonize people, and we will experience their hostility. The second way is by perpetrating within ourselves the fate we fear. We create our own inner emptiness by suppressing our feeling; we trap ourselves with tensions that develop as a resistance to yielding out of fear of being trapped. But these two ways are not unrelated. The person who feels empty within himself lives a life that is empty of meaning in terms of relationships and involvement. The person who feels trapped in himself does get trapped by life situations. The outer situation has to match the inner condition. A square peg doesn't fit in a round hole. Generally speaking, each person finds his appropriate niche in the world. Of course, it is also true, though it may seem like a contradiction, that the outer situation produces the inner situation. Through its influence upon the family, culture molds the character of children. If we live in an alienated world, we become alienated from our bodies and ourselves.

An understanding of the correspondence between the inner condition and the outer situation is essential to an understanding of human nature and fate. People are extremely uncomfortable when they find themselves in situations other than those they are accustomed to. Place a beggar in a fine home and he will plead to be allowed to go back to the streets. Dress a bum in gentleman's clothes and he will not know how to move. The reverse is equally true. We are creatures of habit; our bodies and our behavior become structured by situations, making it very difficult for us to adapt to different ones. Regardless of how we are born, it is how we are raised that determines our fate and our destiny. For example, children who grow up with TV can't live without it because they have become habituated to its kind of stimulation.

Changing the neurotic character is the essential therapeutic task and the most difficult. The case of Sam is a good example. He was a young man, near thirty, whose marriage had just broken up, and he was somewhat depressed. The divorce was mutually desired. Sam felt that his wife was too dependent; she complained, he told me, about his aloofness and unwillingness to share his feelings with her. Sam admitted that he had difficulty in showing or expressing feeling. In other areas of his life he was quite successful.

Characterologically, Sam could be described as having a rigid structure. His body, though well shaped, was tight. His neck was relatively inflexible, his legs were stiff. Despite these handicaps he had good coordination and was competent in many sports. His rigidity represented a need to hold up against collapse, helplessness, and dependency. In his marriage he took the role of the strong one and unconsciously invited his wife to lean on him. At the same time he resented her dependency. He had to be in control of all situations as he was in control of himself, yet he knew that this attitude was self-defeating. Sam needed to learn how to let go and come out with his feelings.

Sam approached this problem of letting go as he approached any other task. He figured it out, then tried to do what was called for. It didn't work. That's not the way to let go. The more he tried to figure it out in his head, the tighter his body became. Even the work on his body to reduce its tension suffered from the same dilemma. He did the bioenergetic exercises as if he was trying to master a skill. The result was that he had very little feeling, though some vibrations did develop in his legs. Sam was characterologically geared for achievement, but letting go is not something one can achieve. Before any genuine feeling would emerge, Sam had to let go of his need to achieve or to be strong.

I have chosen this case to show the difficulty of the therapeutic task. The patient acts unconsciously to defeat the therapeutic undertaking. We call it resistance, but it is, in effect, nothing other than his character structure.

Here is another short example. A woman suffered from severe anxiety, which she sought to allay by finding a man who would protect and take care of her. To gain this end she was sexually seductive, and, since she was an attractive woman, she became involved with many men. All her relationships ended with her feeling betrayed and used. Her anxiety continued to mount. I might add that a previous therapeutic relationship ended with the therapist becoming sexually involved with her.

Mary's father died when she was seven. He had been her support. In all her subsequent relationships she was looking for another father. Since a therapist tries to provide some support for his disturbed patients, it is easy to see a male therapist as a father surrogate. Once Mary made the transference, she became emotionally involved with her therapist. She felt she needed him and was afraid he would die, leave, or not be there for her. Her major effort was directed to assuring his interest in her. Thus, she would be seductive one time, then testing the therapist another time. Needless to say, her maneuvers only increased her anxiety. Her very effort to gain security undermined her security.

Problems of this nature cannot be resolved until their connection with the oedipal situation is traced out and worked through. Sam's need to achieve and to be strong stemmed from his sense of inferiority vis-à-vis his father in that situation and his determination to prove he was a man. But the need to prove one's manhood reinforces the inner feeling of inadequacy and traps the person. Mary was trying to find a father who would accept her sexual feelings. She wanted to be a child and a woman at the same time, which made a real relationship with a man almost impossible.

Struggling against fate only enmeshes one more deeply in its coils. Like an animal caught in a net, the more one struggles, the more tightly bound one becomes. Does this mean we are doomed? We are doomed only when we struggle against ourselves. The main thrust of therapy is to help a person stop struggling against himself. That struggle is self-destructive, and it will exhaust a person's energy and accomplish nothing. Many people want to change. Change is possible, but it must start with self-acceptance. Change is a part of the natural order. Life is not static; it is constantly growing or declining. One doesn't have to *do* anything to grow. Growth happens naturally and spontaneously when energy is available. But when we use our energies in a struggle against our character (fate), we leave no energy for growth or the natural healing process. I have always found that as soon as a patient accepts himself, there is a significant change in his feelings, his behavior, and his personality.

Natural healing is inherent in the structure and function of the living organism. A cut finger will heal, a broken bone will mend, and an infection will clear up spontaneously. A body is not like a bubble, which once it bursts cannot be put together again. Within limits, the body's fate is to restore its integrity and to maintain its process against traumas and injuries from the environment. This should be equally true of the emotional traumas and injuries we receive as children. Why doesn't neurosis heal spontaneously like any other illness or dis-ease? The answer is that the neurotic interferes with this healing process. He keeps picking the scab off the wound. By his defense or resistance, he keeps the injury alive. That is what it means to be neurotic and why we can define neurosis as a struggle against fate.

This idea of fate was never far from Freud's consciousness. He remarked about some people, "The impression they give is of being pursued by some malignant fate or of being possessed by some extraneous power, but psychoanalysis has always taken the view that their fate is for the most part arranged by themsleves and determined by early infantile experiences."[2] Freud illustrated this with the case of the benefactor whose protégés invariably abandon him and "who thus seems doomed to taste all the bitterness of ingratitude," of the man whose friends regularly betray him, and of the lover whose affairs always end the same way. He even mentions the case of a woman whose three husbands had each to be nursed by her on their deathbeds.

Freud believed that such observations indicated the existence of a "compulsion to repeat—something that seems more primitive, more elementary, more instinctual than the pleasure principle."[3] Freud called that something the "death instinct," which he saw as a "compulsion inherent in organic life to restore an earlier state of things."[4] There is much in common between instinct and fate. Both can be described as blind forces inherent

---

2. Sigmund Freud, *Beyond the Pleasure Principle* (New York: Liveright Publishing Co., 1950), p. 23.

3. Ibid., p. 26.

4. Ibid., p. 47.

in the nature of things. Both have the quality of predictability. Both are structured in the organism either genetically or characterologically. There is, however, an important difference between them. Instinct describes an act or a force that furthers the life process. It is an active principle. We speak, for example, of an instinct for survival. Fate, on the other hand, is a passive principle. It describes the way things are.

We have seen that people do not always learn from experience, but repeat self-destructive behavior patterns. In my opinion such behavior reflects the operation of fate, because it is a manifestation of character rather than the expression of an instinctual force. The distinction can be made clear by using the analogy of a record player and comparing life to the music it sends forth. The active force is electricity, which runs the motor, which turns the record, allowing the needle to follow the grooves. When the record come to an end, the music ceases—the equivalent of death. The latter is not a compulsion but a state of being.

In this analogy the compulsion to repeat can be seen as a "broken record." The needle goes round and round in the same groove, repeating the same notes because it is unable to advance. Thus, the repetition compulsion can be seen as the result of a break in the personality, which fixates the individual at a certain pattern of behavior he cannot change. But human beings are not mechanical devices. The repetition compulsion can also be seen as an attempt by the personality to return to the situation where it got stuck, in the hope of someday getting unstuck. However, as long as the break exists, the needle will go round and round in the same groove, the pattern endlessly repeated. That is its fate until the break is healed.

We shall see in a later chapter that when the break in the personality is severe, it gives rise to a death wish in the person. If the wish is conscious it constitutes a suicidal desire or intention. In many cases, however, it is unconscious and severely restricts the individual's ability to live his life fully. Such a wish, though structured in the personality, is not a death instinct, for in most cases it arises from a highly traumatic oedipal situation. To one degree or another that situation breaks the unity of the per- endlessly replaying the conflicts of his oedipal situation. I imagine the woman who nursed three husbands on their deathbeds had been in a similar position with her father when she was a child.

In describing the Oedipus complex Freud revealed the dilemma of modern man, namely, that his success is achieved at the cost of his personal fulfillment and that his power over nature is gained at the expense of his orgiastic potency. But where Freud accepted the inevitability of this dilemma and attempted to jus- tify it biologically in terms of the death instinct, I see the dilemma as a product of this culture and subject, therefore, to change as the culture changes. Pending that change we must find ways to work with that dilemma and the underlying oedipal conflict in the therapeutic endeavor to help a person gain a greater measure of fulfillment in his life.

Few books on psychology today are concerned with the oedipal problem. They don't deny its existence; they simply ignore it. On the thesis that we can be masters of our fate, each offers a recipe for the good life. You are told *how to do it*: how to be successful, how to be aggressive, how to fulfill your potential, how to be happy, etc. On a practical level the advice is sound in most cases. But the effect of these books upon people's lives is almost negligible. The problems of living seem to increase rather than decrease. The misery in people's lives doesn't seem to lessen. There does seem to be a malign fate operating in the lives of many people that psychology is impotent to change, a fate that is tied to the oedipal situation in their childhood.

The Nature of Fate

One of the themes of this book is that character determines fate. Character refers to a person's typical, habitual, or "char- acteristic" way of being and behaving. It defines a set of fixed responses, good or bad, that are independent of conscious mental processes. We cannot change our character through conscious action. It is not subject to our will. Generally, we are not even aware of our character because it has become "second nature" to us.

Fate, like character, can be good or bad. There is nothing in the definition of fate that implies a negative value. Fate is not synonymous with doom. True, it is man's fate to die, but it is also his fate to live. *Webster's New International Dictionary* defines fate as "that principle or determining cause or will by which things in general are supposed to come to be as they are or events to happen as they do; the necessity of nature." Events happen as they do because of nature's laws. Thus, whether we call it fate, a law of nature, or God, we signify by these terms that events are part of a process that is beyond man's control. In Greek mythology, the fates were known as the Moiria. They were named Clotho (the Spinner), who spins the thread of life; Lachesis (Disposer of Lots), who determines its length; and Atropes (Inflexible), who cuts it off.

Destiny is often used as a synonym for fate, but the two words have slightly different meanings. Destiny is related to the word *destination*. It refers to what one becomes, whereas fate describes what one is. Fish are fated to swim as birds are fated to fly, but that is hardly their destiny.

Thus, it would be correct to say that it is my fate to be born as it is my fate to die, but my destiny was to become a psychiatrist. The first two are inherent in the nature of life, but not the third. Whether one becomes a king or a slave, a success or a failure, may be predetermined, but it is certainly not a necessity of nature. The oracle at Delphi did not foretell the destiny of Oedipus, which was to vanish from the earth and find an abode with the gods. He prophesied his fate, which was that he would kill his father and marry his mother. That, as we shall see, is a statement about the nature of things. Under certain conditions it is the fate of all men.

One of the characteristics of fate is its predictability. Those of

us who do not believe in fate or oracles might think that the
future is unpredictable. To some extent this is true, but there is a
greater measure of predictability in life than most people realize.
Prediction is possible wherever there are structures, for structure
determines function or action. This concept is easy to illustrate.
Because of its structure an automobile cannot fly like a plane.
One can safely predict that it will roll on the ground. Because a
human body has a certain structure, it can function in certain
ways and no others. Although we can swim underwater, we cannot breathe underwater like a fish because we do not have any
gills. A structure sets limits, which makes prediction possible.
Thus, knowing the structure of government agencies, we can predict their behavior. Similarly, it would be safe to predict that, all
other factors being equal, a one-legged person cannot run as fast
as a two-legged person. The number of examples is limitless. Since
structure determines behavior, it creates fate.

The important thing about this concept is that it applies equally
to psychic structures and to character structures. If we know a
person's character structure, we can predict his fate. Take the
case of a person with a masochistic character that is structured in
the body mainly as chronic tensions in the flexor muscles.[5] Because
of these tensions it is very difficult for him to express feelings
easily. These tensions are especially severe in the throat and
neck, strongly blocking the utterance of sound. The total pattern
is one of *holding in* both physically and psychologically, with the
result that such a person tends to be submissive. Since such behavior is predictable, we can say that it is his fate to be submissive.

If character determines fate, then we have to know how character develops. In 1906 Freud showed that certain character traits
could be related to a child's experiences in early life. According
to Freud, parsimony, pedantry, and orderliness were the result

5. For a full description of the different character types and how they
are structured in the body by different patterns of muscular tension, see
Alexander Lowen, *Bioenergetics* (New York: Coward, McCann & Geoghegan,
Inc., 1975).

of a toilet-training program that fixated the child on the anal function.[6] Other psychoanalysts established connections between other character traits and certain experiences involving the child's instinctual life. Karl Abraham pointed to an association between ambition and oral eroticism.[7] These studies concerned specific character traits. The understanding of character as a total pattern of response was provided by Reich in his classic work *Character Analysis*.[8] Reich described character as a process of *armoring* on an ego level, which had the function of protecting the ego against internal and external dangers. The internal dangers are unacceptable impulses; the external dangers are threats of punishment from parents or other authority figures for these impulses.

Later, Reich extended the concept of character armor to the somatic realm. In the latter, the armor is expressed in chronic muscular tension, which is the physical mechanism by which dangerous impulses are suppressed. This muscular armoring is the somatic side of the character structure, which has a psychic counterpart in the ego. Since psyche and soma are like the two sides of a coin, head and tail, what goes on in one realm also occurs in the other. Or, one can say that the muscular armor is functionally identical to the psychic character. Therefore, one can read a person's character from the expression of his body. The way a person holds himself and moves tells us who he is. Reich said the various character types needed to be more systematized. I did this in my book *The Physical Dynamics of Character Structure*, retitled *The Language of the Body* in the paperback edition.[9] In this book I showed how the different characters become struc-

6. Sigmund Freud, "Character and Anal Eroticism," 1908 in *Collected Papers*, Vol. II (London: Hogarth Press, 1953), pp. 45-50.

7. Karl Abraham, "Oral Erotism and Character," in *Selected Papers on Psychoanalysis* (New York: Basic Books, 1953), p. 404.

8. Wilhelm Reich, *Character Analysis* (New York: The Orgone Institute Press, 1945), p. 44.

9. Alexander Lowen, *The Physical Dynamics of Character Structure* (New York: Grune & Stratton, 1958). This book is also available in a paperback edition under the title *The Language of the Body* (New York: Collier Books, 1971).

tured in the body through the individual's interaction with the family environment.

Broadly speaking, character forms as a result of the conflict between nature and culture, between the instinctual needs of the child and the demands of the culture acting through the parents. Parents as representatives of the culture have the responsibility of inspiring their children with the values of the culture. They make demands upon the child in terms of attitudes and behavior that are designed to fit the child into the family and the social matrix. The child resists these demands because they amount to a domestication of his animal nature. Therefore, the child must be "broken in" to make him part of the system. This process of adapting a child to the system breaks his spirit. He develops a neurotic character and becomes afraid of life.

The neurotic character is the person's defense against being broken. In effect, he says, "I will do what you want and be what you want. Do not break me." The person doesn't realize that his submission amounts to a break. Once formed, his neurotic character constitutes a denial of the break, while his muscular armoring functions as a splint that doesn't let him feel the break in his spirit. It is like closing the door after the horse is stolen and then believing that the horse is still inside. Of course, one dares not open the door to find out. Then, by repressing the memory of the traumatic event, one can pretend that it didn't happen and that one has not been broken.

The repression jells the character into a structure, like an egg that has been boiled or a pudding that has been chilled. Prior to the act of repression the character is labile; it has not yet hardened into a fixed structure. This repression occurs in the process of resolving the oedipal problem. Thus, Reich says, "Character armoring is, on one hand, a result of the infantile sexual conflict and the mode of solving it."[10] Not only does the repression remove from consciousness all memory of the oedipal situation,

---

10. Reich, *Character Analysis*, p. 148.

but it buries with it almost all the events of early childhood. This is the main reason that most people remember very little of their lives before the age of six.

Let us see how the infantile sexual conflict is solved. Freud observed, "The early efflorescence of infantile sexuality is doomed to come to an end because its wishes are incompatible with reality and with the inadequate stage of development the child has reached. That efflorescence perishes in the most distressing circumstances and to the accompaniment of the most painful feelings."[11] The distressing circumstances are the withdrawal of love and the implied threat of castration. The painful feelings are fear and sadness. As a result, the child *suppresses* its sexual feelings for the parent of the opposite sex, but this is not the same thing as the natural termination of infantile sexuality. Infantile sexuality comes to a natural end if it is not interfered with. The child moves out into the world at about six years of age (going to school is an example) and forms erotic attachments with its peers. Freud conceded that the child's wishes are unrealistic. Reality and normal growth separate a child from his incestuous involvement with his parent. Suppression under the threat of castration is like pulling out a child's baby teeth rather than waiting for them to fall out naturally under pressure from the permanent teeth. The final results may look alike, but the interaction (threat of castration, pulling out teeth) inflicts a severe trauma on the child.

The painful termination of childhood and infantile sexuality forces the child to repress the memory of this period. So few persons can recall the feeling of sexual excitement experienced in relation to the parent of the opposite sex. They will deny that there was any jealousy by the parent of the same sex. However, the experience has become structured in their body. While the repression of a memory is a psychological process, the suppression of feeling is accomplished by deadening a part of the body or reducing its motility so that feeling is diminished. The repression

11. Freud, *Beyond the Pleasure Principle*, p. 22.

of the memory is dependent upon and related to the suppression of feeling, for as long as the feeling persists, the memory remains vivid. Suppression entails the development of chronic muscular tension in those areas of the body where the feeling would be experienced. In the case of sexual feeling, this tension is found in and about the abdomen and pelvis.

Since the experience is different for each individual, the tension will reflect that experience. In some persons the whole lower half of the body is relatively immobilized and held in a passive state; in others the muscular tensions are localized in the pelvic floor and around the genital apparatus. If the latter sort of tension is severe, it constitutes a functional castration; for, although the genitals operate normally, they are dissociated in feeling from the rest of the body. Any reduction of sexual feeling amounts to a psychological castration. Generally the person is unaware of these muscular tensions, but putting pressure upon the muscles in the attempt to release the tension is often experienced as very painful and frightening.

In the attempt to avoid the fate of Oedipus, modern man becomes neurotic. The neurosis consists in the loss of full orgastic potency and in the formation of a character structure that binds the modern individual to a materialistic, power-oriented culture with bourgeois values. If the suppression of sexual feeling is not severe, the individual can make an adjustment to the cultural mores without developing symptoms of emotional illness. This is not to say that such a person is emotionally healthy. His neurosis would be characterological and expressed in rigidity of attitudes. If it is severe, the person will develop symptoms of emotional illness or a state of emotional deadness like Margaret and Robert.

If repression is equated with neurosis, then the price of avoiding Oedipus' fate is to become emotionally ill. But we have to question whether this maneuver is really effective in helping us escape that fate. One result of repression is to fixate part of the personality at the level of the repressed conflict and thus to create an unconscious compulsion to act out the suppressed desire. Further, the loss of orgastic potency undermines an individual's maturity and reduces him to feeling childlike at times. Without being aware of it, many men seek women who remind them of their mothers and toward whom they adopt a juvenile or passive position. Fate acts in strange ways. Do we not, as neurotics, end up marrying our mothers or women who are so much like them that it amounts to the same thing? And if we marry a woman who is not like our mother, do we not treat her like our mother and, in effect, turn her into a mother figure?

The same is true of a woman. If her sexual feelings for her father were suppressed, with a concomitant repression of the memory, the desire remains fixated upon the original love object and can only be transferred to someone who reminds her of that person or to whom she can relate in the same way. This is the basic reason young women marry older men, as we all know. In other cases, though, the acting out of the suppressed desire may not be so evident; but careful analysis shows that the marital situation replicates the oedipal one.

The following case illustrates this principle. I began by re-marking to one patient, Bill, that most men marry their mothers. He immediately countered by saying, "My wife is not at all like my mother."

I answered that often the personalities are different, but we men treat them as if they were the same. And we insist that they treat us as our mothers treated us.

"Oh, no!" Bill said. "My mother was never home to take care of me. She was always out playing cards. One of my problems with my wife stems from the fact that I did demand that she stay home to take care of the kids and of me. She complained that I never allowed her any independent activity. She has started some-thing for herself now, and I am letting her do it. This is a new attitude for me and it seems to be working out better in our relationship."

I should add that Bill and his wife were constantly fighting with each other and their relationship was not a happy one. Each felt deeply frustrated in the relationship, yet Bill assured me that they cared deeply for each other.

It would seem, therefore, that my thesis was not applicable to this case. Bill made demands on his wife that he had never been able to make on his mother. But how did it work out in practice? Did his wife take care of him as he demanded?

"No," Bill said. "She wasn't capable. It turned out to be the other way around. I took care of her." Bill, then, admitted that this was his father's attitude toward his mother and that his own attitude toward his wife was the same. He also admitted that the two women had many personality traits in common. His wife was anxiety ridden as his mother had been. "When I or the children are away, she becomes a nervous wreck just like my mother." And both, as we saw, were relatively helpless—needed taking care of.

"In appearance, however," Bill added, "my wife and my mother are different. I could not have married a woman who looked like my mother because I didn't like the way my mother looked."

Bill made the point that his wife was sexually attractive to him, which his mother wasn't (we know that this last remark isn't true). "She still is attractive to me, but she is afraid of sex. We don't have much sex because she is sexually unresponsive." As a result, his own sexual feelings steadily decreased, causing a further deterioration in the relationship.

What a twist of fate. Bill married his wife thinking it was going to be different because of his strong sexual excitement with her, only to find that it ended on the same note as his first love affair— that with his mother—sexual frustration and the loss of sexual feeling. Symbolically, he had taken his father's place with his mother. His father had had no greater fulfillment.

At this point the discussion turned to his wife, Joan. Bill remarked, "I am the exact opposite of her father. He was five feet, two inches tall, I am six feet, two. He was always broke and never home. I am financially successful and caring. He never touched his daughter, would not permit her to sit on his lap, and was ashamed of showing affection. This is not true of me."

We do not consciously choose mates who are like our parents. If anything, we seem to pick those who, on the surface, are just the opposite. However, as I pointed out earlier on page 37, on the unconscious level each boy marries his mother as each girl marries her father. Unconsciously, we choose as spouses those who have traits or features in common with the loved parents. From what I could determine, Bill's wife and his mother had in common the fact that on an emotional level both were little girls who needed and were looking for a father.

Bill was aware that Joan's fear of sex stemmed from her experience of rejection by her father. That rejection was due to sexual feelings that made her feel guilty. I knew that Bill, too, suffered from sexual guilt. That could be deduced from the severe tension in his pelvic area, which limited the flow of sexual excitation into the pelvis. I asked Bill about his early sexual experiences with his wife.

Bill related the following: "We were very strongly attracted to each other. Joan let herself go with me as she had not done with other men. We engaged in heavy petting, but we did not have intercourse. I did not want to do that until we were married. Joan came from a good family, and I respected her. Strangely, after we got married, all her passion disappeared. We have had problems ever since."

Bill did not realize that in protecting Joan's chastity, he rejected her sexuality just as her father had done. Joan desperately needed to feel that her sexuality was normal and healthy. Bill could not help projecting his own sexual guilt on her. In his mind's eye, he saw Joan as the mother of his children and he unconsciously identified her with his own mother. Having suppressed his sexual feelings for his mother, he could not fully transfer them to his wife. Throughout his marriage, Bill suffered from some degree of erective impotence. He blamed it on his wife's fear of sex and lack of passion. It is not difficult to see that she was disappointed in her marriage by Bill's lack of manhood. At bottom, he proved to be not so different from her father.

At our next session, Bill said, "I realize I am both opposite and similar to Joan's father. She treats me with the same guilt and fear she has toward her father. From time to time I will experience failure in my ability to hold the erection. I feel terrible. I feel impotent. I feel like a *failure*."

We have now uncovered the common factor that identified Bill with Joan's father. Bill had characterized Joan's father as a failure financially. He now recognized that he, too, was a failure, not only because of his difficulties with erection but because his wife had never reached a sexual climax. He blamed himself for this, and he felt guilty toward his wife for his failure. The situation was like a vicious circle, slowly enmeshing the two of them in misery, each outwardly blaming the other but inwardly blaming himself.

Having suppressed much of his sexuality in "resolving" the oedipal situation, Bill could not approach a woman manfully. He was too sexually insecure. His structure only allowed him to pick a girl-woman who needed him. He could then be sure she wouldn't abandon him. In return, he assumed the responsibility to help her, to protect her, and to fulfill her. He played the role of the father, but he was still the boy. As a boy, he had to pick a nonorgasmic woman, which only confirmed his failure to be a man. The harder he tried to overcome his weakness, the more he failed, for he was denying a fate that he had structured in his body.

The idea of fate as body structure is more clearly shown in the following case.

Ruth was a woman about forty years old who complained of depression and a lack of feeling. Her sexual desire was very low. However, she could be excited by a woman, especially when she fantasized kissing a woman with tongue penetration. One other complaint was about severe ulcer-type pains in her stomach. In other areas of her life Ruth was a highly successful person. She had her own very profitable business. She had many friends and was socially active. She was married and had a family. Publicly, Ruth was one kind of person; privately, she was another. This denoted a split in her personality that was also manifested physically.

Ruth's problem was clearly revealed in her body. The upper half of her body was slender and well shaped and had a very girlish quality. Looking at this part of her body, one would have estimated her age to be about twenty-six, whereas she was considerably older. In contrast, her hips and thighs were disproportionately large and heavy, suggesting a more mature woman. The skin in this area had a coarser quality than that on the rest of the body. From the knees down, however, her legs were shapely. The pelvis looked "dead," that is, without much life. Its motility was greatly reduced, and she didn't breathe with her belly. The deadness was also apparent in the masklike expression of her face and in her mechanical smile. This deadness in the face and pelvis was responsible for the lack of feeling about which she complained.

A person's body structure tells us something about his history when interpreted bioenergetically.[12] Each experience leaves its mark on the body. Significant experiences shape the body as they shape the personality. A bioenergetic therapist who is trained in reading the language of the body can make some good guesses about those experiences. Often, these guesses are confirmed by the patient when he senses the conflicts manifested in his chronic muscular tensions.

The marked discrepancy between the two halves of Ruth's body reflected the split in her personality. In the upper half of her body she was a young girl, seemingly innocent about the facts of life. This innocence was belied, however, by the masklike facial expression that reminded me of the Sphinx and suggested that she knew more than she said. The lower half of her body told a different story—of a person who had more than a casual acquaintance with the excitements and frustrations of sex.

Bioenergetically, the heaviness, deadness, and disproportionate bigness of the hips and thighs in a person are the result of a stagnation of energy and sexual excitement. Stagnation occurs when an area of the body that is strongly excited and charged

12. Lowen, *Physical Dynamics of Character Structure*; also, *Language of the Body*.

with feeling is immobilized to hold or contain the feeling because discharge is not possible. If this happens occasionally, it is painful but has no effect upon the body structure. The constant exposure of a young child to sexual stimulation under circumstances that prevent any discharge of the excitation and make the child feel guilty for sexual feelings can result in an overfullness and enlargement of the pelvic area. Since the pain is continuous and intolerable, all feeling in the area must be suppressed. This is accomplished by developing strong tensions about the pelvis, which immobilize it and thereby deaden and numb it.

Ruth was completely out of touch with this area of her body. She had no feeling of it or in it. The respiratory movements did not descend into the lower abdomen. She lived from the waist up.

The interpretation this body dynamic suggests is that the patient had in early life experienced a constant sexual excitation, probably from her father. She, of course, responded to it with sexual feelings as any girl in the oedipal period will. At the same time she was not allowed any expression of her sexuality and was forced to "cut it off." The mechanism she developed to cut off sexual feeling was evident: muscular tension in the waist and diaphragm that blocked the flow of any excitation into the belly. Even such emotional expressions as belly crying or belly laughing were impossible for this patient. In addition, the immobility of the pelvis prevented the buildup of any deep sexual excitation. We can hypothesize that the oedipal period ended in such a painful way that Ruth was forced to repress her memory of the event to avoid feeling the pain. The fear of her mother was so strong that she had to suppress all sexual feeling to protect herself.

Psychologically, Ruth could be described as a "castrated" woman. (The expression "cut off her sexual feelings" says the same thing.) She was terrified of her mother (whom I regard as the castrating person), but this fear was completely denied. In its place there was the submission to penetration of her mouth by another woman's tongue. The displacement of sexuality to the mouth and its inversion allayed her castration anxiety.

If one was to help Ruth get out of her depressed state, it had to be by helping her get some feeling into the lower half of her body. Psychology is relatively helpless in this task. One had to work intensively with her on a physical level to effect some change in her personality. Her breathing had to be deepened, the muscular tensions in the lower abdomen, pelvis, and thighs had to be reduced and released, and the pelvis had to be mobilized. Often the procedures were painful, due to the severity of the tension, but as the tensions let go, the pain diminished. The body work was done in conjunction with a continuing analysis of her relations to her father, her mother, to me, and to a former female therapist.

What emerged from the analysis was the lascivious behavior of her father. She recalled a number of incidents in which her father displayed a prurient interest in her girl friends, at the same time deriding them as dirty and loose. These memories were related without any feeling or emotional charge. The first breakthrough occurred in the form of a dream following the development of some sexual feeling in her pelvis through the body work. She related: "I dreamed that I was in a room with a giant. He was more than nine feet tall. I felt a strong sexual desire for him, and I pressed close against him. My head came just to the level of his pelvis. I wanted to sleep with him, but a woman came into the room and it was impossible."

Ruth couldn't understand why she dreamed of a giant. I had to point out to her that perhaps he wasn't a giant; perhaps she saw him that way because she was only a small child. When I said that, she realized that the man in the dream was her father and that the woman was her mother. The dream dramatized her oedipal situation. But she also recollected that in the dream when she pressed close to the man, she could sense his sexual excitement by the tumescence of his penis.

Ruth then recalled another memory from her childhood. She remembered that her father frequently put his hand on his genitals when he saw her. At the same time he also pursed his lips as if to suggest a kiss. She sensed that she may have had the desire to suck his penis but was very ashamed of that feeling. This desire in the girl underlay the fantasy of a woman's tongue in her mouth.

What kind of man did Ruth marry? Was he like her father? In one important respect the two were similar. Both were sexually excited by young girls and put off by adult female sexuality. I can say this because I saw Ruth's husband in consultation. Because of her experience with her father, Ruth had suppressed much of her sexuality. She made her appeal to men as an innocent young girl, and she attracted a man who would respond to her on that level. Although married and the mother of children, the woman in her was unfulfilled. That was her fate until she came to therapy. To change that fate it was necessary to change the energy dynamics of her body, to make her pelvis come alive. I might add that in the process of doing so her ulcer-type pains disappeared.

The tendency of people to repeat old, established patterns is the main problem in therapy. Here is a simple example. A person complains of a feeling of being "out of it," of holding back, of an inability to move forward. When I look at how this person stands, I see that his knees are locked, the weight of his body is on his heels, and he is leaning backward. Thus, he is doing (unconsciously) just what he is complaining about. This bodily attitude can be reversed. I ask the patient to bend his knees slightly to unlock them and to shift his weight forward to the balls of his feet. He is also instructed to breathe and keep loose. When he does this, he experiences himself differently. He feels himself in the world and ready to act or reach out. His whole body feels more alive. He can sense that the difference involved a change from a passive way of standing and holding himself to a more aggressive one. It is what he wanted and it feels good, but it is uncomfortable. He feels under stress and is afraid that he will fall forward. He can hold himself in the new position by concentrating on it, but as soon as his mind focuses on another subject, he will revert to his old way, which feels natural and comfortable to him.

Why is change for the better so difficult and frightening? We know that in every process of change there is an element of insecurity. The move from a known to an unknown position entails a period of instability. The child learning to stand up and walk is insecure but not frightened. He is not afraid to fall. We cling to the old because we believe it to be safer. We believe the new is dangerous. In the case of neurotic patients, that belief has a certain validity. If one was punished as a child for being aggressive, then it seems safer to take a passive position in life. One can't change one's position or way of standing until the early experience is relived and the feelings associated with it expressed. This is the psychological work of therapy.

The problem of change has another dimension, however. That dimension can be described as a tolerance for excitation. Too little excitation is boredom, depression, or death ("bored to death"). Too much excitation overwhelms the organism, flooding its ego boundaries and wiping out the sense of self. The feeling is one of estrangement and is akin to insanity. Character can be seen as the way we handle excitement, ensuring that it is neither too little nor too much.

As children we learned very early that being quiet and good earned us some love. If we were too active and too noisy, we were disapproved of or punished. Our parents couldn't stand our liveliness. It was too much for them. It drove them crazy. We had to suppress it to survive. Now, our potential for aliveness is too much for *our structures. We* can't stand it. When we are overexcited we become jittery, nervous, and frightened. The therapeutic task here is to expand slowly the person's capacity to tolerate excitation or aliveness.

Summarizing, we can say that once a pattern of behavior is structured in the body it becomes self-perpetuating. It determines how we act, and we must act according to character. Necessarily, then, every effort we make to overcome our character is part of our character and only results in reinforcing its structure. I see this all the time in my office. The compulsive individual compulsively tries to effect a change but only ends by becoming more compulsive. The masochistic individual submits to therapy as he does in all other life situations, and so therapy changes nothing. Even his gestures of rebellion lead to his being more submissive. This has to be understood and accepted before change is possible.

The Fate of Love

We saw in the previous section that much of our behavior is determined by our character structure. We think we choose freely, but it can often be shown that there is a seeming fate at work in our choices. Especially in such important matters as love or marriage, fate seems to play a very large role. People are drawn to each other by inscrutable forces that have some relation to their personalities and character. My wife and I come from different backgrounds and different parts of the country. That we met may be pure chance, but that we married and have stayed married for more than thirty-five years is not due to chance. Our personalities harmonize and our character structures dovetail. Though we vibrate on the same wavelength, we are opposites in many ways. However, we didn't know this when we got married. We acted on our feelings, which is how fate operates. Looking back, we can say that it was fate that drew us together and kept us together. But our marriage could easily have failed. We came close to breaking up many times. Opposite characters clash as often as they complement each other. We had to face our neurotic characters so that we could see and understand how we hurt each other despite our conscious desire not to do so. If one is blind as Oedipus was, one cannot avoid the tragedy of losing one's love.

Like every modern man, I made every effort to avoid marrying my mother. That was one of the forces that drew me to a woman who came from a different "place." And my wife is in very many respects different from my mother. As a child I had resolved my oedipal conflict in such a way that I could not have married any woman who was like my mother. Consciously I had to see my wife as "not my mother" while unconsciously I treated her as if she was my mother and almost destroyed my marriage. Only by recognizing this fact did it become possible for me to respond differently to her.

No more than others could I avoid the fate inherent in the oedipal situation. I have come to recognize that my wife and my mother have certain qualities in common. Aside from their being women, both admire men who are competent, capable, and successful, and both have a strong sense of pride. I am aware that this sense of pride in a woman exercises a strong attraction upon me. Thus, it was the qualities that my wife shares with my mother as well as those that are different that drew me to her so strongly. And, therefore, on one level I did marry my mother.

If, as I believe, we are all destined to marry our mothers, why should this be a prophecy of doom? People often say that getting married is a fatal step, but don't they really mean that it is a fateful one? Which word one uses could depend on the kind of mother one had. If she was a source of joy, pleasure, and satisfaction, one could ask no more than to have a wife who would be like her in every way. If the experience with one's mother was painful and frustrating, one would want to marry a woman who is her opposite. Actually, most mothers are not all good or all bad. Generally there is both pain and pleasure in the relationship, although one or the other may predominate. However, an infant cannot accept that the person who gives him pleasure is also the one who causes him pain. We know that the infant splits the image of his mother into two figures, the "good" mother and the "bad" mother. Although these images become fused later, the initial split persists in the person's unconscious mind.

A man is attracted to a woman who reminds him of his "good" mother because he associates her, unconsciously, with the pleasure he once knew. Throughout courtship and the period of engagement, the man continues to see his lover in the light of his "good" mother. Marriage destroys that vision. After marriage he sees his wife increasingly as his "bad" mother and responds to her in terms of that transference. Why does this happen? For one thing, the responsibilities of marriage create a different relationship. Aside from that, however, there is the taboo against marrying the "good" mother by whom he was sexually excited. He accepted this taboo as part of the deal for resolving his oedipal conflict. Now it prevents him from seeing his *wife* in that light.

What is true for the man is equally true for the woman. She has a split image of her father. The man she is attracted to must remind her of (have some qualities in common with) her father. We may recall Margaret in the first chapter, who said that her heart could open only to a man who was a sufferer like her father. But for the woman, too, marriage demands a renunciation of this relationship. She is not permitted to respond to those aspects of her husband that are sexually exciting to her. She must relate to her husband as if he was not the sexual love of her life. She must suppress her sexual desire for her husband as she had to suppress her sexual love for her father. As the sexual excitement between them diminishes, he literally "fathers" his wife as she "mothers" her husband. That seems to be the fate of love.

In his heart every child loves his mother. She was the life-giver, and if life is loved, the giver of life is loved. I believe this is true regardless of how much pain and hurt the child may have suffered at her hands. Almost all my patients also find that they have much hate against their mothers for having failed them or hurt them in very deep ways. Because it is later in time, the hate covers the love, and it is necessary to discharge the hate before the true love a person has for his mother can be fully experienced. Regardless of how much hate a child may accumulate against his mother, the fire of love in his heart for his mother can never be extinguished. To extinguish this fire is death, for the very heartbeat is love.

For the same reason, every child wants to be close to his mother, to be held in her arms, to be caressed and loved. This desire is part of the living tissue of the child, and no matter how much the child may reject his mother for the pain he knew with her, the longing for closeness to a warm, loving mother figure is never lost. The mother's body is the source of the child's first excitement, of his first conscious experience of pleasure.

Birth is the literal ejection from paradise for each person. For most human creatures the period in the womb is conceived as timeless bliss. All one's needs are fulfilled, and comfort is assured. Life grows and develops without effort. There is not even the need to breathe, for oxygen is supplied from the mother's blood. Then, suddenly, all this ends and the child finds himself out in a cold world where, increasingly, his life depends on his own effort. That effort is not always immediately successful. There is pain and pleasure, the latter always represented in the early days by closeness to the mother, the former by separation.

The joy of love is the feeling of paradise regained. Initially, therefore, it is always the return to the mother, symbolically to the womb. In infancy one is connected to his mother through body contact and nursing. The nursing baby knows the joy of love, its closeness and warmth. This paradise, too, is lost. A separation from the mother occurs when the baby becomes a child able to stand on his own legs as an independent organism. Where breast feeding is the accepted practice, it is carried on for three or more years. Then, somewhere around the ages of three to five, the child is weaned. It is a painful experience, for it represents another loss of love and joy. Fortunately, nature provides another opportunity for the individual to regain paradise or the joy of love. This is through the blooming of infantile sexuality, which enables a child to reestablish a strong connection to the parent in feeling, fantasy, and fact.

The boy sees his mother in a new light. He becomes aware of her sexual charms, and he thrills to the sight and touch of her body. The girl experiences exactly the same emotional excitement with her father or with any man who is fulfilling that function at the time. This is the feeling of pure love. The fantasy is to be married to that person, to be with him forever. This new relationship is sexual in terms of the feeling of erotic excitement and the desire for contact and genital in the image of actual intercourse, but it lacks the conception of discharge. The strong erotic pleasure of body contact actually extends to both parents. This is the age when children love to get into their parents' bed in the morning to feel their bodies and the animal warmth they radiate. The parents, however, are keenly aware of the sexual element in this contact and end the practice, often with the statement, "You are too old for such things now."

This paradise, too, comes to an end. That is our nature and our fate. We lose our first teeth, but a second set is already on its way. We progressively give up our parents as sexual objects as we move into the outer world: going to school, playing with our friends, etc. We grow and mature. And then it happens again. We are now adolescents having passed through puberty. Suddenly we become infatuated with a person our own age and of the opposite sex. Fulfilled adolescent love is heaven on earth. Unfulfilled, it can be hell. Generally, there is only one such intense experience in adolescence.

We leave this paradise, too, with luck to find another in a love affair with the person we will marry. This time it is not forever, but "until death do us part." Only in fairy tales do people live happily ever after. In the romantic movies of the thirties and forties, this was the assumption, too. Unfortunately, it rarely lasts that long. Disillusionment soon sets in, love dims, and sexual excitement fades. Is happiness or paradise an illusion? I suppose so, but love isn't. Rare as it is, there are couples who have known the joy of love for more than fifty years. What goes wrong?

If a person's early experiences of love are fulfilling ones, his or her marriage would, I believe, follow that pattern. But only in very rare cases does this happen in our culture. Each love affair from infancy on ends painfully (as Freud said about one's first sexual love). As a result, a pattern is established that becomes structured in the body as a defense against the pain. And so one's fate is set. I often compare love to a game of baseball because in both the same rule applies, namely, three strikes mean the person is out. Most of us have had two strikes called on us by the time we reach puberty. The first strike was the failure of our love relationship with our mother on the oral level. The pain of rejection and unfulfilled longing was heartbreaking. This is what patients feel who in the course of therapy regress and are able to recapture those early experiences. "Where were you? Why weren't you there for me?" is the sentiment expressed. The premature weaning from the mother, from her breast or her body, is experienced as a betrayal of love. We are shocked, but we go on. This first strike is a blow to our hearts, but we can take it. We move into the genital stage at about the age of three and establish a new love relationship with the parent of the opposite sex. Because this new relationship is heir to all the unfulfilled longing of the earlier oral phase, it is very intense.

But we have seen that this relationship also ends in pain. Again we feel rejected and betrayed. Our hearts are "broken" again, sometimes smashed by this new blow. A second strike has been called against us. One more and we are out—meaning dead. We feel that our hearts would not survive a third heartbreaking experience. We do not think we have a choice but to close our hearts to love. We lock our hearts in a strongbox, the armored thoracic cage. We protect ourselves against heartbreak by not loving, and against death by not living. But by this process we also lock our heartbreak into our being, and so our pain persists although we are no longer conscious of it. We become afraid to love and to live, though we desperately want to do both. We can momentarily open our hearts, but we dare not keep them open. We can feel love, but we cannot express it.

What is there about the oedipal situation that makes it so horrendous? Why are we so horrified by the sexual love of a child for the parent? The idea of incest evokes horror in the human mind for a number of reasons. It denotes that human beings are behaving like animals, since sexual relations between parents and offspring are common in the animal kingdom. It violates our conception of the natural order of life. We are committed to a forward movement—from parent to child, who in turn parents another child. Incest is a reversal of that flow; it evokes the same horror in us that we would feel if time ran backward or water ran uphill. In addition, there are the social dangers that incest creates, namely, the jealousies, hurts, and violence that could erupt in a family where incest occurs.

However, the danger of incest is unreal before puberty. We are talking about a five- or six-year-old child whose sexual activities are not different from his other play activities. They are a necessary preparation for living. Although they are serious, we describe them as play because they are not intended to have any real consequences. Of course, a boy desires to sleep with his mother, but he has no intention to do so in actuality and may not even know how it is done. But by their rejection of the child's sexuality, the parents imply that the danger is real and so add a note of reality to fantasies and feelings that would otherwise remain on the level of play.

As a matter of fact, parents often do more than reject the child's sexuality. They threaten with looks and with voices. When a mother sees her young daughter lift her dress, as little girls will, to expose her body and her sexuality, not infrequently she turns on the child with hostility. She may say to the child, "That's bad," meaning whorish, but generally it is the look that freezes the child. Little girls play with their sexuality as little boys play with toy guns (also a sexual symbol). But no mother would accuse the boy of being a murderer. Why is the little girl a "whore"? The mother is projecting her own feelings on her daughter, and this projection charges the scene with adult emotions that the child cannot handle.

The oedipal problem is further complicated by the fact that parents often respond emotionally to the sexuality of their children. They become sexually aroused by their child's sexual interest and are titillated by this play. And they are also seductive in the sense of initiating and inviting the child's sexual interest. Fenichel notes, "Very often the mother loves the son and the father loves the daughter. The parents' unconscious sexual love for their children is greater when their real sexual satisfaction, due to external circumstances or to their own neuroses, is insufficient."[13] When this happens, the parent generally blames the child. This projection of the parent's guilt on the child makes the latter feel that he is the responsible and guilty party. In this way what was originally an innocent and natural expression of love in the child becomes associated with guilt and pain.

In the same way the child develops a sense of guilt for his hostility toward the parent of the same sex. That hostility arises in response to the behavior of the parent, who sees the child as a rival. It is true that children want the exclusive possession of the love object and see the other parent as a rival, but this desire is not an expression of hostility. The first act of hostility in the oedipal situation is the threat of castration by the parent. It is not generally overt but is expressed by looks, attitudes, or negative comments. The child reacts with a death wish against the parent, creating an internal conflict between this wish and his love for the parent. Since the parents insist that it is the child who is wrong (always so), the latter ends with a double sense of guilt.

The Oedipus legend tells the same story. The fate of Oedipus was conditioned by his early rejection. He was staked out to die by his father; the initial hostile act stemmed from the parent. If patricide is a crime, why not infanticide? The potential sexuality of Oedipus was seen as a threat by his father. The name, Oedipus, means "swollen foot," and is an obvious reference to the penis, which swells up to become erect. Thus, I would relate the rejection by the parents to Oedipus' swollen foot (erect penis) rather than following the myth according to which the swollen foot is seen to be a result of the rejection. In interpreting a myth, which talks in symbolic language as do dreams, we can reverse the chronological order when to do so promotes our understanding.

13. Otto Fenichel, *The Psychoanalytic Theory of Neurosis* (New York: W. W. Norton & Co., 1945), p. 91.

If fate impels us to marry our mothers, like Oedipus but symbolically, does it also decree the killing of our fathers? I am referring to the fate that results from the oedipal conflict, namely, the suppression of sexual desire because of the threat of castration. If we think psychologically, not literally, my answer is yes. The myth itself is not a historical account but reflects the operation of psychological forces. We kill our fathers emotionally, not just in the death wish of a child for the feared and hated rival but in our hearts. We kill the love and respect for the father and the tradition and authority he represents. We oppose ourselves to him as we oppose ourselves to the past. This is the generation gap that is so evident in our times. In rejecting our fathers and our past, we lose the wisdom that the accumulated experience of mankind can provide.

In the next chapter we will examine in detail some of the personality problems that people present. These problems revolve around modern man's difficulty to be himself. Having suppressed his feelings, he wears a mask and adopts a role in conformity with the demands, spoken or unspoken, of his family and society. In the process he loses authenticity.

3 / Being and Fate

Being as Authenticity

Few people in our culture have the courage to be themselves. Most people adopt roles, play games, wear masks, or put up façades. They do not believe that their genuine self is acceptable. It wasn't accepted by their parents. "Don't look so sad," Mother says. "No one will love you. Put a smile on your face." And so the child puts on a smiling mask to be lovable. "Pull your shoulders back, stick out your chest," Dad says to his young son, who proceeds to adopt this façade of manliness. The roles and games generally develop more subtly in response to unspoken demands and pressures from the parents. The masks, façades, and roles become structured in the body because the child believes that this pose will gain the parent's approval and love. Our bodies are molded by the social forces in the family that shape our character and determine our fate . . . which is that we must try to please to gain approval and love.

It didn't work then, and it doesn't work now. Love can't be won or earned, for it is a spontaneous expression of affection and warmth in response to another person's being. It's "I love you," not "I love what you are doing." Love implies an acceptance that was denied the child. Once we give up our true self to play a role, we are fated to be rejected because we have already rejected ourselves. Yet we will struggle to make the role more successful, hoping to overcome our fate but finding ourselves more enmeshed in it. We are caught in a vicious cycle that keeps closing in, diminishing our life and being.

Why don't we give up the role, stop the game, drop the façade, or take off the mask? The answer is that we aren't aware that our appearance and behavior are not fully genuine. The mask or façade has become part of our being. The role has become second nature to us, and we have forgotten what our primary nature was. We have become so identified with the role and the game that we cannot conceive the possibility to be otherwise.

The average person comes to therapy because of some disturbance in his personality or behavior, such as depression, anxiety, or frustration. His desire is to get rid of this disturbing symptom. He does not want to change in a radical way, that is, characterologically. Probably, he doesn't see the necessity for such change. He senses that he is not successful, that his character isn't working, and he wants to learn how to make it work. The broad range of psychology books on the market that tell or teach How To Do It are responses to this desire. One is given advice on how to win friends, influence people, be more self-assertive or more sexually responsive, etc. On a superficial level these books may provide some help to people. But they do not touch the real problem, which denies the person a sense of fulfillment and a feeling of peace and joyfulness. That problem is the fear of being himself, the fear that his true self is tainted, inadequate, and unacceptable. This fear forces him to hide his genuine feelings, to mask his expression, and to accept the role that was demanded of him. Most people go along with the idea that life is a game and that to be successful one has to learn how to play the game. With this attitude, one is prepared to modify the role he plays. What he is not prepared to do is give up role playing and be fully himself. That seems too frightening, for reasons that we will examine in the next chapter. However, if one does not confront his character, the fate it determines cannot be avoided.

The first step in therapy, therefore, is to discover the role a person plays in life. Or we can say that therapy begins with an analysis of the person's character. Until this is done we cannot get behind the façade to the real person. But it is only the first step. One has to understand why the role was adopted in the past and what function it serves in the present. The relation of the role to sexuality and to the oedipal problem should also be clarified. One function of the role or mask is to hide from the person himself those aspects of his personality that are too painful or too frightening to be seen and confronted. The person with a a smiling mask doesn't want to feel the sadness that is hidden from view. The manly person doesn't want to feel his fear. Of course, these aspects of one's personality don't disappear simply because they are hidden from one's consciousness. Buried in the depths of the personality, they influence our behavior and dictate our fate.

Another aspect of this problem is the cost in energy of playing a role or supporting an image. So much energy is required to maintain a role or façade that little is left for pleasure or creativity. Imagine an actor playing a role constantly, both offstage and on, and you will get some idea of the energy it takes to do that. Being is effortless because it is spontaneous and natural. That is why children can be so creative. However, most people do not sense the effort or the energetic drain of the role they play. What they do feel is chronic fatigue, irritability, and frustration. When one plays a role, the end result is always depression.

Since the role is structured in the body, it is possible to tell the role a person is playing or the image he is trying to project from the expression of his body. At a recent bioenergetic workshop, a young man stood before the group with such rigidity and immobility that he looked like a wooden soldier. That was my immediate impression. His face, too, was immobile as befits a soldier at a dress parade. But this young man was not conscious of the impression he created. It was his normal way of holding himself.

Members of the group were doing a falling exercise as a maneuver to break through the individual's defenses. The exercise involves putting all the weight on one leg with the other held out to the side for balance. The knee of the first leg is bent so that the leg muscles are doing all the work to hold the person up. The person is directed not to let himself fall. Eventually the muscles will tire and the leg will collapse. The person will then fall onto the mattress, but the fall must happen against the will of the individual so that it is spontaneous. In that way the experience comes as a slight shock to the person, opening his feelings.[1] It took quite a while for this patient to fall, but when he did there was a cry and he fell forward as if he had been shot through the heart. The manner of his falling brought a gasp from the group. They saw its significance.

In the discussion that followed, Frank, the subject of this exercise, revealed that his father was an ex-army man who had been very strict with him as a boy and of whom he had been frightened. Frank himself was an engineer in a large company, but he behaved like a soldier. He did what he was told and neither felt nor expressed any feeling. That was his problem. One could guess that beneath the façade of the soldier there seethed a rebellion that was rigidly and strictly kept under control. Disobedience carried the risk of court-martial. Even the failure to maintain the pose (the wooden soldier) meant the

---

1. For a fuller discussion of this exercise with examples, see my book *Bioenergetics* (New York: Coward, McCann & Geoghegan, Inc., 1975), pp. 199-210.

firing squad. For Frank to dare to be himself was to die—or to kill. He strongly suppressed any impulse to attack and destroy the authority (father) who had dictated his fate.

In one respect Frank's fate was the opposite of Oedipus'. Frank didn't kill his father and marry his mother. Instead, he was killed, psychologically speaking, by the father as Laius tried to kill Oedipus. There was no kind shepherd to save Frank. The acceptance of his death was structured into Frank's character and being. Without considerable therapy (therapist = shepherd of his flock), no rebellion could occur.

A common role that people assume is that of helper. This role was mentioned on the first page of this book. The helper is a person who is structured characterwise to be "there" for others, that is, to respond to their needs even at the expense of his own. Many therapists play this role, and they have probably chosen this profession because it provides an opportunity for them to live out their fate. The role applies to me, and so I know it well. The body structure of the helper also has considerable rigidity. He cannot afford to collapse because others depend on him. The shoulders are rigidly held to carry the weight or burden of other people's problems. One characteristic aspect of this personality type is an inability to ask for help, because that implies weakness and need. The helper doesn't cry easily because his pain is subordinated to that of the people he is trying to help.

My mother set me up for this role by making me conscious of her suffering. She turned to me rather than to my father as the one who could save her. He was not particularly interested in saving her but in having sex with her, which she could not accept. Thus she enticed me into an intimate relationship with her at the same time that she rejected my sexuality. Having made me feel ashamed and guilty about my sexual feelings for her, she used my guilt to harness me into the role of her savior. It was a perfect oedipal situation, and I would have been destroyed if my father had overreacted. He wasn't jealous of or hostile to me. I am deeply indebted to him for his support.

However, in relation to women, I was trapped. I could not

dissociate my sexuality from the sense of guilt or the feeling of obligation toward them. I wanted to be free, and I knew I had to do it through my body. I owe this realization to my father, who was oriented toward sexuality and the body. But he, too, suffered from sexual guilt related to his own oedipal situation. Nevertheless, my identification with him in these areas led me eventually to Wilhelm Reich. I have written elsewhere about my therapy with Reich.[2] It resulted in my going to medical school and becoming a psychiatrist. So here I am, saving people as a justification for my sexuality. Fate!

If I saved women, I could be sexual. But what kind of sexuality is that! As long as I was trying to save women, I had no real sexuality. I had to stop being a helper, that is, a person who helps in order to feel entitled to pleasure and sexuality. To do that required the recognition that in being a helper I was denying my own needs.

What did I need? I needed my legs so I could walk away from my mother and the guilt she laid on me. But to get my legs I had to feel that I didn't have them. As long as my legs held me up, I could play at being the strong one. I had to fall and to fail. I had to reach the point where I could both feel and say "I can't." As long as I believed I could succeed, I had no right to ask for help. What arrogance to think that I "can" when I see all about me that none of us can.

As I recover the full use of my legs I also regain my full sexuality. At the same time I can give up being a helper. This doesn't affect my ability to do therapy. But perhaps it does. It makes me a better therapist for having found my faith in my body and its sexuality. I can help others find theirs.

There are many roles that people play and many images that they project. There is, for example, the "nice" man who is always smiling and agreeable. "Such a nice man," people say. "He never gets angry." The façade always covers its opposite expression.

2. Ibid., pp. 17–25.

Inside, such a person is full of rage that he dares not acknowledge or show. Some men put up a tough exterior to hide a very sensitive, childlike quality. Even failure can be a role. Many masochistic characters engage in the game of failure to cover an inner feeling of superiority. An outward show of superiority could bring down on them the jealous wrath of the father and the threat of castration. As long as they act like failures they can retain some sexuality, since they are not a threat to the father.

Women put on masks and play games, too. There is the girl who is the life of the party but who, alone at home, is the saddest person. In company she lights up like an electric bulb. As a child she put on a gay face to win her father's love and approval, perhaps to cheer him up. She continues to play the role as a mature woman because it seems to her the only way a man would accept her femininity and her sexuality. Then there is the woman who puts on a show of sexual sophistication but who is inwardly frightened of sexual feeling. Her sophistication is a means of control. Through it, she can act sexual without having to be sexual.

People have always adopted social roles. In every society where work was specialized, people followed patterns of behavior that were appropriate to their social position or activity. A ruler carried himself in such a way as to manifest his superiority and importance. In dress and bearing he projected a regal image. A soldier could be distinguished by different clothes and a different comportment, a priest by still other garments and another way of holding himself.

What is the difference between these social roles and the neurotic ones I described above? In the past there was a person behind the role. The role and the person were not the same. The role was not intended to substitute for or hide the person. It was not adopted as a defense against being or feeling. Social roles served to maintain the hierarchical structure of society. They distinguished between individuals and between generations. The distinctions were respected. That situation changed in the twentieth century. Barriers have broken down, personal space has become narrower, the distance between the generations has decreased. Many mothers take the role of girl friends of their daughters, while fathers often act like companions to their sons. This situation tends to increase the competitiveness between parent and child of the same sex and, therefore, also the jealousy. The result is a more highly charged oedipal situation and a greater castration anxiety on the part of the child. As we saw, the implied threat of castration forces the child to submit to the demands of the parents, which always means the adoption of a neurotic role and the surrender of authenticity.

The loss of authenticity also occurs on the social level. Personal values are sacrificed for money and power. Mass production robs the products of labor of their authenticity, while publicity makes a mockery of virtue. In a technological culture, the only recognized values are money, power, and success. Authenticity is a thing of the past, represented today by genuine antiques. Hence their worth.

With the loss of authenticity, we lose the sense of being. Its place is taken by the image, which has gained an unbelievable importance. Any person who can arrive at creating a public image, regardless of what it is, is considered a success, for he has been singled out from the mass. By the same token, success is the important image. The image of success is behind the success of the image. People strive to be number one or special. But what is the reality of the person's life behind his image of success? Here are some notes from the journal of a well-known and successful actress.

I have loved. Who has ever loved me? Too much pain, too much nothing left of me only pain, fear, hate and despair. Tried so hard, tried so hard. Tired. Don't care. Leave me alone. I want to be free to die.

Tired, tried, tired, tried, tired, trudge, trod upon.

I trudge through life. What am I paying for? When will the debt be paid?

I feel diseased to my very soul. Pain and despair my only reality—no hope, no strength, no will. I wake up choking, filled with dread despair, self-loathing. What do I loathe? There is no me. I am trapped in my own emotional hell. Nothing is real. I float aimlessly through the darkness touching nothing but pain. Unendurable sadness, lostness, loneliness. I feel like a corpse, intact on the outside, decayed and rotting within.

Does anyone love me? If so, why can't I feel it? Why am I not nourished by it?

I keep knocking my head, to knock myself out or to knock my head off. Must I accept the anguish? Yes, it's what there is.

I hurt too much to be afraid. It's like the final dying, like a terminal illness—the torment, not the fear of death. Death brings relief, the torment is living.

When I start feeling better, I get busy like I have to save the world. When strength returns, uptightness comes with it. Maybe despair is kinder to me. At least I can sleep.

The face this person presents to the world would never be connected with the feelings expressed above. She comes out smiling, poised, sophisticated, a woman of the world, but the image is unreal. Her inner being is full of pain and despair. She is tormented by the contradiction between the inner reality and the outer façade.

But it isn't all pretense. The fact that my patient is very successful may be her problem. She made a great effort to achieve that success, and an equally large effort is required to maintain it. She is, as she says, tired—tired of trying, yet she must trudge on. The price of success is never fully paid. The moment one stops trying, one falls and fails.

Why is success so important for my patient that she must commit all her energies to achieve it? Why can't she just *be*? She tells us that the world (her world) depends upon her achievement. She is driven by her need for love, which she hopes to get through her achievement. But then she isn't sure she is loved, since love cannot be earned. If she is loved, she cannot feel it, since she is so exhausted from her efforts to achieve that all she can feel is fatigue and pain. She needs to rest more than she needs the nourishment of love, but rest is possible for her only through the admission of failure and the acceptance of despair. Only by stopping her doing can she reach her being.

The only way out I could see for this woman when she told me her story was for her to accept her despair, to accept what she believed to be her fate—that she would never be loved. I suggested that she stop struggling against fate, since she could not overcome it and the only result of her struggles was a tiredness unto death. One thing was certain: The more she struggled, the harder she strove for success, the closer she came to the fate she dreaded. She had nothing to lose by giving up except her images, her façades, and her illusions.

The logic of this argument impressed my patient. She let down and began to cry softly and deeply. Strangely, it was not a cry of frustration or despair. Having given up the struggle momentarily to realize her illusions, she felt neither frustration nor despair. She cried from a sense of deep hurt, from a deep well of sadness. The pain inside was real, but when she gave in to it and cried, the pain diminished. Crying is the most primitive mechanism the body has to relieve tension and pain.

For this woman, being meant being the unloved child. That was her early life experience, and it has continued to be her inner reality. It has persisted into the present, more than forty years later, because it was denied and suppressed. It was denied by her parents who claimed they loved her—when she was good, that is, productive, outstanding, successful. And although she was successful at school, they always demanded more. "You can try harder and do better." Her parents put the blame for their lack of love upon the child by requiring that she earn it. But despite her achievement she never got the reward of love they promised because they had no love to give. If they had, it would have been offered without conditions, for that is the nature of love. The child, however, had to believe in the possibility of earning love, for without that hope life would have been unbearable. She had no choice but to deny the reality of the lack of love and to bury the experience in her unconscious, where it became a psychological abscess draining pain. This is what she described as the dis-ease within her. By trying to overcome her despair through achievement and success, she became unable to vent or discharge the painful sadness of her being. The pain remained in her body, therefore, which only intensified her efforts to overcome her condition. The result was that she could not let herself be and, lacking true being and authenticity, she continued to feel unloved.

Accepting one's despair or one's fate is not resignation. It acknowledges that one cannot overcome what is within the self, but it does not preclude a protest. My patient had remarked that she woke up often with a sensation of choking. I had the thought that she was choking off her protest. She had not been able to protest her parents' attitude when she was young. She had not dared scream at them, "Why don't you love me? You brought me into the world." Such behavior would have been viewed as "bad" and would have brought the rejection she dreaded. She choked off the scream, but in the process she closed her throat, making it impossible for her to take in and be nourished by the love that became available later.

Another way of describing this patient's problem is to say that the scream was stuck in her throat. But she couldn't get it out, she couldn't scream. The tension in her throat was so severe that it was almost impossible for her to scream. In this situation a therapist has to work directly with the body problem. I do this by pressing with my fingers upon the anterior scalene muscles at the sides of the neck. These are extremely tight in most people, and pressure on them, even with the fingertips, can be very painful. The muscles have to relax because of the pain. Frequently the person will scream spontaneously when this pressure is applied. In other cases the person makes a loud sound voluntarily, which then rises to a scream as the pressure is continued. It is interesting that once the patient starts to scream, the pain disappears although the pressure is maintained. This is because the muscles have relaxed. Often, the screaming will continue after the pressure has been withdrawn.

Using this procedure, I helped this patient scream for the first time in her life—at least, as far back as she could remember. It opened her throat, it deepened her breathing, and it cleared her head. Following the screaming she sobbed very deeply with a sense of relief. When the crying subsided, I asked the patient to kick the bed with extended legs and to scream "Why?" Kicking is another form of protest that mobilizes the body and serves to discharge some of its tensions. In this exercise the "why" sound is prolonged until it rises to a scream. Now this patient kicked and screamed her protest about her lack of love. By making this protest, a person accepts the *fact* that the rejection occurred and realizes that all efforts to deny it are a waste of energy. One is bound to the past only if the memory and feelings associated with it are repressed.

Authenticity is closely related to the voice. The word personality has two different meanings. It is derived from *the persona*, a mask Greek actors wore to dramatize more clearly the role they were playing. On the other hand, the word persona means "by sound," *per sona*. The authentic person can be recognized behind the mask by the sound of his voice. The voice is a major avenue of self-expression, and its quality reflects the richness and resonance of the inner being. When one's voice is limited because of neck and throat tensions, one's self-expression is restricted and one's being is reduced. The voice is also related to sexuality, at least in the male. The thin, feminine voice of a castrated man is well known. Energetically, the scream is similar to an orgasm in that it is an intense discharge. In the scream one "blows one's top," and in the orgasm the same thing happens in the bottom. Both should be fully available to the person. Any diminution of either is a loss of being.

Being as Sexuality

How does the self-perception of an organism develop? Dr. Frank Hladky, one of my associates, offered some observations about this development at a recent conference on bioenergetics. He said that the first expression in language of the sense of self is the use of the word *me*. It is the first word a child uses when referring to the self, and its use begins at about one and a half to two years of age. When saying this word the child generally points his finger at his chest. Adults often use the same gesture when they use the word *me*. He concluded that the sense of the *me* is referred to the chest. At about the age of four or five the child begins to use the personal pronoun *I*. When using that word he will frequently point a finger at his temple or head. Hladky believed that the locus for the sense of the *I* is the head.

Our language provides a third term of reference to our being and that is the word *self*. Dr. Hladky suggested that the point of reference for the self is in the belly, about two inches below the navel. He was influenced in so thinking by the fact that the body disciplines associated with Oriental religions place the center of the self in that area. According to the Japanese system of Zen, if a person is centered at this point, he is said to have *hara*. This means that he is in harmony with both the inner and the outer world. In T'ai Chi, the same point is referred to as T'an Tien. Through this center a person establishes contact with the ground below and the sky above. The individual is then part of the whole, and all his relationships are harmonious.

The three words, *me, myself,* and *I* refer to three different aspects of a person's being. The me expresses the passive state of being. In English it is frequently used as the object of a preposition: "to me," "from me," "of me," etc. The I, on the other hand, denotes an active state. It is a subject pronoun and is generally used when we wish to describe a deliberate action. "I went," "I did," etc. The word *self* designates an aspect of being that is neither object nor subject, neither passive nor active. The dictionary gives the word *self* a number of meanings. It is used to define one's complete individuality, as in "my own self." In *Webster's New International Dictionary*, I found the self defined as "the individual as the object of his own reflective consciousness." An example is the remark "I felt myself go cold." Actually we experience the self most vividly in emotional states. When we are angry, we experience the self in a state of anger. It is not something that is done to the me. It is not something the I does. Anger, or fear, or love, or hate is a state of being. The self is, therefore, equivalent to being. It is the perception of being.

Self-perception or self-awareness is the consciousness of the body in its alive or spontaneously responsive state. The self is the body including the brain. It is the body reacting independently of the ego or the I. Thus I am most aware of myself when I am hungry, tired, sleepy, or excited, or when I am feeling pain or pleasure. I am least aware of myself when my body is unalive and unresponsive. The concept of the self is sophisticated. It develops when the ego has reached the stage where it can observe what is happening in the body and reflect upon it. The I observes its self. The I observes the "It."[3]

We are interested to know why the self is supposed to be centered in the belly. One's first thought is that the belly is the locus of certain feelings. Crying and laughter originate in the belly. When we laugh or cry from the belly, it is a deep experience. We describe such intense experiences as "gut feelings." The most important of these gut sensations is sexual feeling, which is experienced in the belly as melting, heat, and glow. From the belly the excitation flows into the genitals, the organs of discharge. The sexual feeling is related to the movement of blood into the pelvic area and genital apparatus.

At the conference mentioned above, I asked the people present at Dr. Hladky's presentation how many had experienced the self

3. George Groddeck, *The Book of the It* (London: Vision Press, 1956).

as sexual excitement. Quite a number raised their hands. Now, every adult has experienced genital sensation and excitement, but this is not the same as the experience of sexual excitement described above. The experience of genital excitation parallels the experience of the I in that it has a somewhat detached quality. The I as the commanding officer of the personality is like the general of an army. The self is like the army. To observe and command, one has to be somewhat detached. In men the penis is often given a name to indicate that it has a degree of independence from the self. It may be called "John," or *le petit homme*, or "Peter," to denote this independence from the self. On the other hand, when the ego surrenders its control and the body takes over in the moment of orgasm, there is neither an observing I nor a separate genital function. The self is experienced in its unity and totality as complete being. Persons who experience genitality as a function of body sexuality identify the self with sexual feelings.

This view of sexuality is based on Reich's ideas about the nature and function of the orgasm. He described the orgasm as a total body convulsion that is felt as extremely pleasurable and satisfying. Its function is to discharge all the excess excitation or energy in the orgasm. Such a discharge leaves the person in a state of complete relaxation and peace. Reich called the capacity for such a release "orgastic potency" and equated it with emotional health. I would like to describe another aspect of the orgastic response that is relevant to an understanding of the self.

When the orgastic response has the quality of totality, that is, when the whole body is completely involved in the orgastic release, the person has the sensation of being part of a cosmic process. This fullness of sexual response is rare among people in our culture, whose sexuality is generally limited to the genital organ, but it has been described by some writers. Hemingway in *For Whom the Bell Tolls* describes an orgasm in which the sensation is that of the earth moving. In *Lady Chatterley's Lover*, D. H. Lawrence speaks of the orgasm in this way: "and then began again the unspeakable motion that was not really motion, but pure deepening whirlpools of sensation swirling deeper and deeper through all her tissue and consciousness till she was one perfect concentric fluid of feeling."[4] At the moment of orgasm there is a clouding of the ego and a loss of ego boundaries. One has the impression that the self is merged with the partner. At that moment the two are one; the boundary between them disappears. One can also have the impression that the self is merged with the cosmos, that one is part of the whole pulsating universe. In these experiences there is no sense of the I. The ego dies (*la petite mort*), but, strangely, one has a most heightened sense of self. This consciousness of self does not arise from an observing I but is inherent in the nature of the self-experience. Thus, the self is also defined in *Webster's New International Dictionary* as "the subject of consciousness."

This experience illuminates another of the basic contradictions in human nature. The development of the ego as an I (eye) that observes the self as object diminishes the sense of self as being. But this development is necessary to bring the self into consciousness. Only then does it become possible for the self to swallow the ego in the transcendental experience of being as sexuality. When a child is born and during its first year of life, the I and the me are undifferentiated aspects of an inchoate self. Being is a unitary experience with very little self-consciousness. The differentiation of the I, the me, from the inchoate self splits the unity of the experience of being, which must then be sought on a higher level of consciousness. When the self is experienced as sexuality, the unity of being is restored. We have here another example of unity splitting into antithetical aspects that reunite as synthesis on a higher level. It recapitulates the sun cycle of birth, death, and rebirth, the latter being closely associated with sexuality.

Oriental thinking has long recognized this contradiction in

---

4. D. H. Lawrence, *Lady Chatterley's Lover* (New York: Grove Press, Inc., 1957), p. 158.

thinking. The goal of both the T'ai Chi and Zen disciplines is to find the self through its identity with universal or cosmic processes. This identity is achieved when the individual is centered in his belly. A person so centered is a master, because every action he takes is in harmony with the universal and, therefore, right and proper. Every move is effortless because it flows in harmony with the universal flow. This is no small achievement, as anyone who has attempted to become a master of these Oriental disciplines knows. Yet, on a lower level, it is the natural state of an animal or young child whose ego or I has not developed to the point where the unity of being is split or the harmony with nature disrupted. When one regains this unity one becomes a master, a person of wisdom.

It is interesting that these Oriental disciplines, which aim at the full realization of self and being, depend upon a body approach to achieve their aim. T'ai Chi involves a series of exercises that are similar to those we use in bioenergetics. The goal of these exercises is to get out of the mind and into the body, that is, to let go of the I to find the self. This concept is basic to both bioenergetics and the Oriental disciplines of T'ai Chi and Zen. It might be asked, then, What is the difference between them? My answer is that the Oriental disciplines were not designed to deal with the problems of modern man in the Western world, who is subjected to an oedipal situation in childhood that leaves him partially castrated. In my opinion that problem can only be worked out through an analytic therapy that incorporates a body discipline.

Until recently, most Oriental peoples lived in an Eastern world that had little in common with Western ideas of power and progress. Their philosophy of life was to maintain a balance between nature and culture, man and woman, yin and yang. They sought harmony, not progress. Unfortunately this philosophy did not equip or prepare them to cope with Western power. The big threat to their way of life and their freedom came from Japanese imperialism, which had identified with Western technology. In self-defense these people were forced to make a commitment to power and, therefore, also to progress. They are becoming Westernized. This commitment will require the sacrifice of balance and harmony in their lives. And it can be predicted that oedipal problems and concomitant sexual difficulties will become more common. They will share the fate of modern man in the Western world.

I strongly believe that sexuality is the key to being. The pelvis is the keystone bone in the body arch. Any chronic tension in the muscles of and around the pelvis disturbs the motility of the pelvis and upsets the balance and harmony of the whole body. Such tensions are the physical counterpart of castration anxiety, which has a similar disturbing effect upon the personality. Since sexuality is the key to being, it is also the key to personality. To understand this statement, one must distinguish sexuality from sexual activity. The former refers to feeling, the latter to doing. Too often, sexual activity is engaged in to gain sexual feeling. People who lack sexual feeling are often obsessed with sex and sexual activity. Here, too, it is important to keep the distinction between sexual feeling and genital excitation clear. The former describes the feeling in the whole body, not just in the genital organs.

In my view, sexual describes a person who is conscious of his or her sexuality but not self-conscious about it. Such a person has a sense of himself or herself as a man or a woman, since sex refers to the differences between male and female. A sexual person has no need to exaggerate these differences or to deny them. Simply said, a sexual person is proud to be a man or woman.

Sexuality also goes with a pride in one's body and in one's animal nature. The natural functions of the body are not a source of shame or embarrassment. The person feels good about his body and identifies with it. For example, a sexual person will accept his feelings as natural and right. If he is tired, that will be accepted. A lack of identification is expressed by remarks such as "I don't know why I feel tired," or "I shouldn't be tired." The same thing is true of sexual feeling. A sexual person will accept his bodily response as indicative of feeling or not. A neurotic individual, whose orientation is toward performance, regards the lack of genital excitation as a sign of failure and cannot accept that the body always expresses for the self.

An identification with the body implies that one lives with regard for the body. One does not abuse it with drugs, alcohol, excess food, lack of exercise or rest, etc. And one dresses in such a way as to make the body more attractive. A person can see himself as more than a body, more than an animal, more than a sexual being; but body, animality, and sexuality are the foundation upon which the mind and the ego with all their pretensions rest. Without that base, the ego is only a cloud in the sky or an image in smoke. In some respects culture does arise out of the sublimation of sexuality, but without sexuality there would be no culture at all. Without the feeling of sexuality in the body, there would be no dance, no music, no poetry. A sexuality that is limited to genital excitation can produce only pornography.

Having made these few general remarks, I'd like to show how being is conditioned by sexuality in the patients I work with. The first case is a man in his middle forties, attractive and successful in his career, whom I will call Jack. Jack had had considerable therapy before coming to me. He had done two years of "primaling," which involved his regression to an infantile state and wailing, crying, or screaming to release the pain he associated with that state. He said that he felt better after these sessions, but they had no effect upon his character structure. When he consulted me, he still complained of a lack of pleasure and joy in his life.

People responded positively to Jack. He was highly respected in his work, and women found him interesting and exciting. However, he could not accept these positive feelings toward him. He could not let the praise or love that were offered to him enter into his being. He did not see himself as others saw him. His words were, "I'm X and they see me as Y." The X is black, the Y is white, or the X is bad and the Y good.

Jack said that for much of his life he suffered from what he called a "tunnel feeling." He experienced himself as living in a tunnel and out of contact with himself and people.

While other people were enjoying the brightness and warmth of the sun, the feeling of relatedness to people and a sense of growth, Jack felt himself alone and buried in a dark tunnel underground. He described the ground above the tunnel as "birth," signifying that he needed to be born or reborn. It would be logical to equate the tunnel with the birth canal and to see Jack's problem as due to some birth trauma that he would then need to reexperience in order to come out into the world and the sunshine. This had been his objective during his previous therapy, and, though it had not worked out then, he was still pushing in this direction.

However, there was nothing in Jack's personality to support this view of his problem. He was out in the world and functioning well. True, he was unable to enjoy the sunshine and the warmth about him, but it was there. We must ask why Jack was unable to accept the love and praise that were offered him. His answer was that he felt unworthy of it but he didn't know why.

In following up this lead, I asked Jack, "What do you think your basic sin is?"

He said, "Just being me. People have no right to like me. My father was convinced I was bad. Now my parents like me because I'm successful. Some years ago, I saw an image of my father pointing his finger at me and saying, 'Don't be proud of him. He's bad, he's bad.' He used to spank me, to cane me. [Caning is beating a boy across the buttocks with a cane. It is a typically English punishment. Jack was raised in England of British parentage.] I have to believe what he says rather than what I think. He would convince the whole world that I'm bad."

I remarked, "He convinced you."

"Yes," Jack said. "The only way out is to die, run away, or hide."

In the tunnel, I thought.

Jack continued. "Last night I felt tortured. I was with a very beautiful woman, but I couldn't touch her sexually although she wanted me. When I fell asleep, I thought I might as well die as be tortured. Women fall in love with me and desire me sexually. But I find it hard to look at a woman's body. If I have to make a move toward them sexually, I become terrified. However, when we're in bed together, the fear passes."

Then Jack aded, "I've always been attracted to older women, plain women. My mother is very plain." The shadow of Oedipus is very clear here.

There is enough in this statement to show that Jack's problem is related to sexuality and not to some unknown birth trauma. This deduction is strongly supported by the structure of his body, which is well developed but with marked constriction and tension in the pelvic area. Jack is fascinated, excited, and terrified of sexuality. This amounts to being tortured, a situation from which he sees no way out. And, in consequence, a situation he would like to avoid.

Jack avoided the sexual issue by regressing to an infantile level. His wailing, crying, and screaming like a baby was largely a smoke screen to hide his fear of sexuality. I am not suggesting that Jack had no birth trauma or that there were no significant problems in the oral stage (age one to three years) of his life. But these problems cannot be tackled effectively until the later, sexual or oedipal, problem is faced and worked through. This is a basic rule in character analysis. Failure to follow this rule leads to chaos in the treatment. In analysis the chaos takes the form of a mass of infantile material, which the analyst interprets without producing any change in the patient's behavior or attitude. In other forms of therapy, the chaos is in the form of an emotional outpouring (wails, cries, screams) that has no relationship to the patient's immediate life situation.

Jack had said, "My sin is being me." The me is seen as bad. As a boy, Jack remembers "always being in trouble, always feeling guilty." He wondered, "Why was I so bad?"

The me is bad because it is sexual. Being originates in sex. An infant is sexual, without being aware of it, through his mouth and skin eroticism. Then, as he develops, he becomes consciously sexual during the oedipal period. This sexuality is very innocent, very much part of the child's animal nature, very much part of its being. And as we all know, the child is very curious about sexual things. However this innocence doesn't last very long in our culture. The child is threatened for infantile masturbation, shamed into covering itself, and punished for peeping and playing sexually. Since the sexual feelings and impulses are so much a part of its being, the child feels guilty and bad in its very being.

I asked Jack about his childhood, and this is his story. There were five children in the family. Jack was the third child. He had two older sisters and a younger brother and sister. The family lived in a small house, yet Jack does not remember ever seeing his mother or his sisters naked. He doesn't recall even trying to peep. He has no recollection of having masturbated before the age of sixteen. We must assume that he was sexually excited by the presence of his sisters but that he dared not look, he dared not touch himself or them. The threat of the cane put a fear of castration into him that blocked any overt sexual move or expression. He still has difficulty in looking at or touching a woman's body. It was a torture for him as a child and it still is. The tunnel is also a sexual symbol, namely, the vagina. He is in it because he is obsessed with it, but he cannot get out because he cannot move to discharge his excitation. Orgasm eludes him. For only one short period in his life did Jack have a sexual relationship that was fulfilling.

Here is another case, very different from Jack's, but which also shows the key role of sexuality in being. Jane was a woman in her late thirties who had worked with me previously for several years. She had a schizoid character structure, a rather severe personality disturbance.[5] Through the therapy she made a great improvement in her functioning and in her sense of self. She ended

5. See A. Lowen, *The Betrayal of the Body* for description of this character problem (New York: Collier Books, 1969).

the therapy when she felt she could stand on her own feet, although there was much room for further progress.

Jane had gone back to school to get a degree in counseling. Her children were old enough not to need her full time. In school she encountered a teacher who, she felt, was critical and negative toward her, and she became paralyzed. She returned to therapy to work on this problem.

The main aspect of the paralysis in Jane's personality was an inability to speak up in some situations. Her throat became severely constricted, and she had trouble with her voice. In fact, the whole upper half of her body was very tight and constricted, so much so that it was quite narrow. In contrast, her hips and thighs were large and full. This discordance between the upper and lower halves of her body denoted some splitting in the personality between the ego and sexuality. The lower half of the body reflects the person's relationship to the parent of the opposite sex, that is, the sexual feelings that existed in the oedipal period. The upper half of the body reflects the relationship to the parent of the same sex, the ego identification with that parent. Jane had been close to her father; on a feeling level, there was an incestuous involvement between them. She had been terrified of her mother.

In this session, she remarked, "I have difficulty expressing myself in my voice and in words. I could never stand up to my mother. She didn't approve of me. She didn't accept my being, my essence."

I asked Jane, "What is your being? What is the essence of you that she didn't accept?"

Jane replied, "She wanted me to be sexually sophisticated and popular, as she saw herself. But I couldn't be that way!"

In fact, Jane was the exact opposite of that picture. She was a plain Jane. I pointed out that we must assume that her mother did everything necessary unconsciously to make sure that Jane wouldn't be like her regardless of what she said or consciously intended.

Jane said, "There was no room for two women in that house." The implication of this statement is that Jane had to give up her womanhood and her sexuality so as not to be a threat to her mother. Then Jane added, "Strangely, in life I can stand up to women. It is only a man who can destroy me as my mother did."

That does seem strange, but the answer was clear. Jane was not energetically connected to her pelvis, she was not fully identified with her sexuality. Therefore, she lacked a solid base for her being. This weakness in her personality undermined her ability to express herself. She tried to compensate for this weakness by turning to men sexually, hoping that they would affirm her being by accepting her sexuality. She had done this with her father and it had saved her, though, at the same time, it made her vulnerable to her mother's jealousy and hostility. When a man responded to Jane's sexuality, she had a sense of security. It was only temporary because Jane did not accept her own sexuality, but if she was rejected by the man, she felt destroyed.

This is a common problem. Many women turn to men seeking an acceptance of their sexuality, which would include an affirmation of their being. If they get it, they feel good for the moment; but they are dependent on the man and vulnerable to feeling destroyed by his rejection, as Jane was. The other day a patient remarked about her date, "He made me feel like a woman." The implication was that without his interest she didn't feel like a woman. Her sense of self and being was deficient because she was not fully connected to and identified with her sexuality. When a woman is secure in her womanhood, a man's recognition of it is like icing on a cake.

Men have a similar problem. They turn to women for an affirmation of their manhood, and, when it is not forthcoming, they accuse them of being castrators. But a man who is unsure of his masculinity and needs the support of a woman is a partially castrated man, psychologically speaking. Most women are perceptive in these matters and resent being used in this way. When a man goes to a woman with a full measure of his sexuality, he will always meet with a warm response. If he needs to have his masculinity affirmed, he should get it from other men, just as a boy gets affirmation from his father, not his mother. However, a man may find it difficult to turn to other men when his unconscious Oedipus complex is too threatening. In that case therapy is the answer.

All my patients complain of some weakness or lack in their sense of being. In every case there is a corresponding weakness or lack in the person's identification with his sexuality. Being is more than sexuality, and the problems of being cannot be worked out on the sexual level alone. Difficulties in self-expression on an ego level must be given the same care and attention that are given to the sexual problem. But these difficulties can never be fully resolved unless the underlying sexual guilts and anxieties are understood and analyzed in terms of the Oedipus complex. We must keep our focus upon sexuality as the basis of self and being.

Being as Not-Doing

In a recent book, Erich Fromm advances the hypothesis that being is reduced by having. He says, "Only to the extent that we decrease the mode of having, that is, nonbeing—i.e., stop finding security and identity by clinging to what we have, by 'sitting on it,' by holding on to our ego and our possessions—can the mode of being emerge."[6] According to Fromm, the two terms, being and having, represent two very different attitudes to life. The having mode is based on possessive relationships. The self is seen as the I that has a wife, a home, a car, a job, even a body. Since the I that has a body is the ego, the having mode is an egocentric position. This mode developed from and depends upon private property, power, and profit. Its focus is upon the individual rather than the community. The being mode, on the other hand, is based

6. Erich Fromm, *To Have or To Be* (New York: Harper & Row, Publishers, 1976), p. 89.

on loving, giving, and sharing relationships. In this mode the measure of the self is not in terms of what one owns but how much one gives or loves. In the being mode, the individual finds his identity through his responsibility to the community.

Fromm's exposition of the differences between these two attitudes to life is insightful. The possessive mode not only reduces being, it restricts freedom. The things we own, own us. We are possessed by our possessions in the sense that we must think about them, worry about them, and take care of them. We are not free to walk away and leave them because for many of us they represent our identity, our security, and even our sanity. We would not hesitate to describe a person as crazy if he gave away a fortune just to be free. We think one can't be free unless one has a fortune, so we spend our lives trying to make a fortune, and we discover too late that we sacrificed our freedom. We do not realize that freedom is worth more than a fortune, for without freedom one cannot *be*.

There is another antithesis besides the one described above that helps explain the human dilemma. It is between being and doing, an antithesis that also reflects the two sides of man's nature, the body and the mind or ego. On the ego level man expresses himself as a creator, on the body level he is the created. As a creator his focus is upon doing. As a creature created by God, his role is simply to be. All of God's creatures except man just exist. Man is not content just to be; he has to do something, achieve something, create something. This ego drive to create produces culture, which is the glory of mankind; but it can also be the means of his destruction when, for example, it leads to the creation of nuclear weapons.

The antithesis between being and doing is recognized by our language. When we say, "Let it be," for example, we mean, "Don't do anything." Doing something is not letting it be. Doing represents an attempt to change a situation, which is all right when the situation is an external one. However, when the situation is internal, that is, a state of being, trying to change this state by doing results in a reduction of one's being. This can be explained by the fact that to act upon the self one part of the personality must turn against another part. The ego or the I turns against the body by using the will against the feelings of the body. In this process being is split and, therefore, reduced. Such an action may be necessary in the face of real danger, in which case it is not neurotic. It becomes a neurotic reaction when the maneuver persists beyond the point of danger. Neurotics are always trying to change themselves by using willpower, but this only serves to make them more neurotic. Emotional health can be gained only through self-awareness and self-acceptance. Struggling to change one's being only enmeshes the person more deeply in the fate he is trying to avoid.

Does this mean that change is inconsistent with being? The answer depends upon which kind of change one is talking about. Change produced by the application of a force from without is the product of doing and affects being adversely. However, there is a process of change that takes place from within and requires no conscious effort. It is called growth, and it enhances being. It is not something one can do, and it is not, therefore, a function of the ego but of the body. Therapeutic change, which means a change in character, is similar to growth in that it is an inner process that cannot be accomplished by conscious effort. This is not to say that doing plays no role in the growth process. In acquiring a skill it is necessary to repeat certain actions consciously so that learning can occur, but the learning itself takes place on the unconscious level.

Let us examine some other aspects of the being-doing antithesis. I have said that doing is an ego function that involves the conscious application of one's energies to a task. The ego is engaged in setting the goal and in controlling the actions to achieve it. On the other hand an activity in which there is a notable absence of ego involvement belongs to the realm of being. This means that if the goal is secondary to the action, the activity would qualify as being more than doing. For example, strolling down the avenue belongs to the mode of being, whereas walking quickly to the station to catch a train is doing. All productive activities, such as preparing a meal, writing a book, or plowing a field, are aspects of doing. However, where pleasure is the dominant motivation, as in dancing or listening to music, the activity is in the being mode.

Another important distinction concerns the focus of the activity. Where the focus is upon what is happening in the outer world, the activity can be characterized as doing. When the focus is upon what is happening on the inside, that is, upon the feeling one has during the activity, it partakes of being. This distinction is particularly relevant to sex. Some people do sex, that is, they are performers and their interest is in the effect their sexual activity has upon the other person. It's an ego trip for them. For others, sexual activity starts from a strong feeling of desire and ends with a strong feeling of pleasure and satisfaction. When feeling dominates one's sexual activity, it is in the being mode. If the mind, the will, or the ego dominates the activity, it is doing. When feeling inspires and guides an activity, it belongs to one's being.

Being is equated with feeling. One cannot make or produce a feeling any more than one can make being. To be genuine, a feeling must arise spontaneously; otherwise one can be accused of pretending. Further, feelings do not accomplish or produce anything. There is neither goal nor purpose to feelings; in other words, we do not feel *in order to*. We can give reasons for our feelings, but our feelings do not arise in response to the dictates of our reason. They often occur in opposition to reason. They are our involuntary bodily responses to the world about us, and their function is to promote the living process.

It is important to recognize that doing does not involve or lead to feelings and may actually inhibit or block feeling. For example, when I walk from my office to the railroad station with the idea of getting there as quickly as possible, I do not experience any feeling other than a sense of pressure about catching the train.

All my movements are dominated by the goal, and feelings are irrelevant. In fact, they may handicap an efficient performance. For the sake of efficiency I transform myself into a machine until the goal is achieved. Machines have no feelings and no sense of being, but they can do things.

On the other hand, it is possible to do or to produce something with feeling. To have feeling, the process or action must be at least as important as the goal. In the above example, should I walk to the station in a leisurely manner because I have plenty of time, I experience the pleasure of walking and I enjoy looking at the people and at the stores. This happens occasionally, but generally I have too much to *do*. Isn't this a rather universal complaint? Too much to do and too little time to do it! People are so rushed that they don't have time to breathe or to be. Being takes time: time to breathe, and time to feel. When we drive ourselves to produce or accomplish, we become like machines, and our being is reduced. However, if we pay at least as much attention to the process as to the goal, doing becomes a creative or self-expressive action and increases the sense of being. As far as being is concerned, what counts is not *what* one does, but *how* one does it. The reverse is true for doing.

When an activity has the quality of *flow*, it belongs to being. When it has the quality of *push*, it belongs to doing. One pushes when the goal or end becomes more important than the process or the means. An activity that flows is always experienced pleasurably because it stems directly from a desire and leads to the satisfaction of the need. An activity in which push is required is painful because it is against one's desire and so requires a conscious effort through the use of the will. Most times writing is a very pleasurable process for me. When I have something I want to say, the writing flows and is easy. When I use my will to write, it is because I don't have anything exciting to say. The writing is painful and poor. I always have to do it over. This distinction between flow and push applies equally to those activities we call play, games, or sport. When winning is more important than playing, the sport or activity is no longer a game but a job. Thus, we can say that for some people work is play because it is pleasurable (flow), while for others play is work because it is painful (push). Unfortunately, too many of our activities are in the doing mode. This is particularly true of the educational process. The emphasis upon achievement and the disregard for feeling make children resistant to school because they sense that their being is denied by the system.

Since being is related to feeling, it is also related to those spontaneous and involuntary movements and gestures that constitute true self-expression. In our spontaneous movements and utterances, we experience directly the life force within us. We do not get the same sense from our reasoned and deliberate actions. Spontaneous responses bypass the ego and, therefore, are regarded as authentic or genuine responses of the self. When we respond spontaneously, we do not say, "I did it." Since the action is not willed by the ego, we tend to adopt the passive tense. We would say, "I was moved to anger," or "I became angry." These two expressions suggest that some force independent of the ego or the I acted in the person to produce the feeling. All emotional experiences are of this nature. They are "moving" experiences. We relish them because they make us feel so alive, so full of the sense of being.

It should be pointed out that emotional responses or moving experiences are different from hysterical reactions. A hysterical outburst, though spontaneous and involuntary, is not the same as an emotion. The latter is a total response of the individual; the whole being is moved; both mind and body, thinking and feeling, ego and id are involved and coordinated in the emotional response. The hysterical reaction is a release phenomenon in which the outburst occurs against the ego. The ego is trying to suppress the feeling, which breaks out despite the conscious intention.

Normally, the actions of a healthy person show a fine balance of being and doing, of feeling and thinking, of spontaneity and deliberated response. Full harmony between ego and body, I and "it,"[7] leads to movements that are both spontaneous and controlled. This may sound like a contradiction, but only this combination produces actions that are graceful and efficient, that are completely natural yet totally appropriate to the situation. The individual in whom these forces are harmonized possesses poise, grace, and dignity. In such a person, being is raised to its highest state.

Doing can be superimposed upon being, but it cannot substitute for being. If one is a person, one can do and produce as a self-expressive activity. One isn't defined by what one does, but one can be enhanced by it. But if one isn't a person, the doing or producing will not remedy the lack. One cannot become a person by doing. Doing is like putting on clothes, which can dress up the body, but which cannot substitute for it.

And yet we all attempt to seek our identity in terms of what we do. We are familiar with this concept from the fact that we identify people with their vocation or profession. We say of a person, for example, that "he is a banker." In using the verb *to be*, we confuse doing with being. Of course, he isn't a banker, that's only his work. He can change his occupation without changing his being; man is not determined by *what* he does.

There is another, more subtle way in which we attempt to create an identity by doing. We shape our bodies to the image we wish to create. For example, a man will puff out his chest, pull his shoulders back, and suck in his belly to make himself look more manly, and he will believe that as long as he can maintain the pose, he is manly. Women do similar things with their bodies to appear more feminine. Wearing a corset was such a doing. Today the same result is achieved by dieting and tension: holding the shoulders up, tightening the abdomen, etc.

Much of this kind of doing is unconscious. The roles we adopt

7. The word "it" is used in George Groddeck's sense of the self viewed objectively by the I. "It" represents the vital force of the body.

in life become structured into our bodies as our way of being in the world. But they become the only way we can be and thus severely limit our being. This is another way of stating that *a person's fate is determined by his character, which is structured in the body by chronic muscular tensions.* These tensions constitute "holding patterns." We hold ourselves up, hold ourselves in, hold ourselves back, etc. Holding is a form of control. By holding we do not allow the flow of excitation to occur naturally, we control it. This holding against the flow develops gradually and insidiously and ends by being unconscious. Our character structure then becomes second nature to us, and we are no longer aware that we are blocking the natural flow of our feelings into responses and movements.

Though the holding is unconscious, we are "doing" it. The voluntary or striated muscles are under the control of the ego. Chronic tensions in these muscles reflect superego inhibition against the expression of certain feelings. In the beginning the tension was consciously created to block the expression of an impulse that could evoke a hostile response from our parents. In time, however, the tension becomes chronic and we are no longer aware of it, but it still remains a function of the ego. We are not letting ourselves be; we are not letting the flow of excitation move fully through our bodies into expression. We hold against our anger, our sadness, and our fear. We hold in our crying and our screaming. We hold back our love. We do this because we are afraid to let go, afraid to be, afraid to live.

The therapeutic process, which aims at furthering or enlarging the patient's being or self, involves a "letting go" of these holding actions, allowing the flow of excitation to occur freely. In therapy the patient learns to "undo" the doing that blocks the flow. It is not a matter of learning *how to be* but of learning *how not to do*.

Let us take breathing as an example of what I mean by letting go. When I was in therapy with Wilhelm Reich, the therapeutic process involved deep breathing. Reich directed me to breathe while I was lying on the bed, and, like the "good" boy I was, proceeded to do so. Nothing happened because I wasn't "letting go." Reich would then say, "Don't do it." In the beginning I replied, "But you told me to breathe." "Yes," he would say. "You are to let go to the breathing, not do it." It took me some time to learn that my not breathing was a doing. If I "let go" or did nothing, I would breathe easily and deeply like any child or animal. When I let my body breathe, a number of very significant reactions developed spontaneously in my body. One of these was the body movement that Reich called the orgasm reflex.

All neurotic and schizoid patients breathe poorly. In most cases the breathing is shallow and segmental in that it is limited to thoracic or abdominal regions and does not involve the total body. In order to help the patient become aware of his breathing disturbance, the therapist encourages him to make a conscious effort to breathe more deeply and more fully. This deeper breathing brings more oxygen into the body and so increases its energy, but it is still a doing and as such it does not further the sense of being. However, the effort to breathe more deeply makes one conscious of the fact that one is *holding* one's breath. One senses that the deeper breathing activates feelings that have lain buried in the unconscious through suppression, and one realizes that holding the breath is an effective way of reducing feeling. This is necessary when the feelings are too painful or too threatening. As long as the person is frightened of these feelings, he will not let himself breathe naturally, that is, easily and deeply. He will control his breathing consciously or unconsciously. But breathing exercises do not help in this situation since they are a form of control. The person will stop breathing when the threatening feelings arise.

"Holding," though unconscious, is an ego defense against feelings that have been perceived as dangerous in the past. For example, a person might be afraid of his sadness, sensing that if he gave in to it, he could fall into a despair so deep that he might not survive it. Or, the feeling could be a fear so great that it becomes a paralyzing terror, or an anger so intense one would want to kill. The sexual feelings can be very frightening because they are associated with the fear of castration. On the other hand, the conscious holding back of an impulse because its expression in a given situation would be inappropriate or inadvisable is not neurotic. The neurotic is afraid of the feelíng, whereas a healthy person can accept and identify with his feelings though he may refrain from the action. For this reason neurosis should be seen as a fear of being or a fear of life.

The therapeutic task, then, is to help a person get in touch with his feelings, accept them, and under the proper conditions allow them to move him into action. The therapeutic situation is the proper place for a patient to experience being and life without fear. With the support of the therapist he may be encouraged to give in to his rage and to express it by hitting the bed with his fists or a tennis racquet. As he does this he discovers that he won't kill anybody, though he may feel like doing so. He learns that he can give in to the feeling and control the action. Since the hitting is always done against a bed or mattress, never a person, the patient can let go fully to his feeling. And by giving up the unconscious control of feeling (holding), he gains an effective conscious control over his actions. Thus, his ego strength is increased. He also gains a greater understanding of his feelings by sensing their relation to early life experiences.

Only by venting feelings in the controlled setting of the therapeutic situation can the chronic muscular tensions that "hold" unconsciously against feelings be released. In this way feelings that could be explosive or hysterical become integrated into the personality and extend the range of the person's emotional responsiveness. What I have said about anger is equally true of the other feelings. With help, a patient can find the courage to give in to his sadness even if it seems to lead to the depths of despair. By venting that despair he will discover that opening the wound to the fresh air may result in a healing that he didn't believe possible.

Every time a patient makes contact with and releases a suppressed feeling, he decreases the tension that held the feeling in suppression. This increases his energy, because his breathing now becomes deeper and fuller. He can afford to let his body be more alive, because aliveness, being, and feeling no longer pose the danger they formerly did.

Being is the state of aliveness of the body. The more alive, the greater the being. Being is reduced by every chronic tension that restricts the motility of the body, that decreases its respiration and blocks its expressiveness. It is enhanced every time we allow ourselves to feel deeply and to express our feelings in appropriate action.

There is one further aspect of the antithesis between being and doing that needs some discussion. If we are afraid of being, of life, we can mask this fear by increasing our doing. The busier we become, the less time we will have available for feeling, being, and living. And we can delude ourselves into believing that doing *is* being and living. We can measure our life by what we accomplish rather than by the richness and fullness of our experience. In my opinion the hectic and almost frantic pace of modern living is a clear sign of the fear we have of being and of life. And as long as this fear exists in a person's unconscious, he will run faster and do more so as not to feel his fear. What, specifically, is the fear of life and of being?

4/ The Fear of Being

The Fear of Living and of Dying

If being is what life is all about, why are we so afraid of it? Why is it so difficult for us to "let go and just be"? People spend years in therapy (as I have done) striving to discover themselves, to find the truth of their being. Yet every animal knows instinctively what it is and how to be itself. Being is the natural state of the animal. Each human being starts life as an animal with a full sense of being. And, like an animal, a child just is. His ego is essentially a body ego fully identified with the natural processes of the body. That identification gets broken as his parents impose a civilized way of behavior upon the child in opposition to his animal nature. That upbringing, in association with the oedipal situation, forces the ego to take a position anti-thetical to the body and sexuality. In the preceding chapter we saw how this develops. The question here is, Why is it so difficult to reestablish the original connection later in life? What fears stand in the way of recovering one's innocence? We know that it is not so simple as showing someone the way home. The way traverses hidden valleys with unknown dangers that we discover only as we make the journey back to our childhood and infancy.

The first case I will present is a man in his fiftieth year who had been in therapy off and on for about twenty years. I had known Arthur for most of that time, and I worked with him on an irregular basis for much of it. He suffered from insecurity, anxiety, and depression. He was not financially insecure, since he was independently wealthy. His insecurity was with women. His anxiety stemmed from difficulty in self-expression and self-assertion. His depression was low-grade and chronic; it did not incapacitate him, but it left him joyless. These symptoms had been greatly ameliorated in the course of his therapy, and for the first time in his life he was supporting himself financially by his own efforts. His relationships with women had also improved considerably.

Recently, Arthur came to a session with this comment: "More and more I find myself half in love with the idea of dying." I must say that at first I was surprised by this statement. In view of his substantial progress, I did not expect this remark. However, it did not fully surprise me. I had learned some years before that the idea of death is in the background of all my patients' thoughts and is connected with their neurosis.

Arthur continued, "A phrase from one of Keats's sonnets keeps running through my head: 'To be half in love with easeful death.' I think it wouldn't be so bad to lie down and die, and I really don't care. I actually feel myself dying and it doesn't upset me. I find myself spending long periods of time doing nothing, lying in bed for several hours with no interest and no desire. I know this is a depressed state of being. On the other hand, my life is more active, my sexual desire is greater, and I am more into life than ever before."

After Arthur made these remarks, he added, "I realize now that I have lived my life in a low-grade chronic depression. As I become more alive, I feel this depressive tendency in me. Each morning I do fifteen to twenty minutes of body work and the feeling of depression disappears. But it comes back when my work is done."

There is an apparent contradiction in Arthur's statements that needs some clarification. How is it that the more alive and active he is, the more conscious he is of death and the desire to die? One can easily surmise that the wish to die was present all along but blocked out by numbness and busyness. Arthur was busier before than he is now, although, as he says, he is more active now. He was occupied before with countless chores that allowed him no time to be or to feel. He was constantly doing, even though the doing never achieved much of anything. Now that he lets himself be (being in the world) and is doing less, he can sense himself (his problems, his fears, his resignation, etc.).

I asked Arthur what association he had to the idea of dying, and he recounted the following memory almost as if he were experiencing it now: "I feel myself lying in my own sleeping quarters in the cold. I slept in an unheated sleeping porch all year. The idea was to toughen me up. It was at the opposite end of our large house from my parents' quarters. I was about three. I remember that at the time I was proud that I could take it, but I was really out in the cold."

Arthur explained that he felt out in the cold both physically and emotionally. He was so far removed from his parents that if he cried, they couldn't hear him. He felt that he had no way to reach them. He understood now how he had reacted to that situation. He remarked, "As a child I cut off the pain of 'being out in the cold' by numbing myself. I sense that I pinched off the blood supply to my brain."

Arthur was numbed by the cold, but he also numbed himself

not to feel the pain of his longing to be close to his mother and father, not to feel his need of their warmth. He said, "I sense that the longing is so intense I've got to have it [warmth] or I'll die. Since I can't get it, I might as well die."

This last statement holds an important key to the understanding of neurosis. The neurotic is as much afraid to live as to die. Arthur's being half in love with death means that he is only half in love with life. His fear of life is connected with his fear of death. He doesn't dare reach out for warmth because the pain of his longing would be almost intolerable. He cannot risk opening his heart because he feels that if he is rejected, he will die. Thus, his neurotic attitude of being able to take the cold (lack of a warm human relationship) and "holding" against the longing for love is experienced as a means of survival. To live fully is to risk death. The belief that being open to life is dangerous has some validity. When, as a child, Arthur suppressed his longing and held back his reaching out, he may actually have saved his life. I believe that a child can die if the pain of an unfulfilled longing for contact and warmth becomes intolerable. He will give up the desire to live. Such deaths are known.

Consider the child who is put to bed in a dark room alone and cries for his mother. If she doesn't respond, the child will continue to cry as long as he has any strength left. He is in a state of pain, which steadily increases. Such a child could die, but nature interferes to protect his life. At the point of exhaustion, he falls asleep. In the morning his mother is there again and hope is renewed. One lets the child cry himself out again on the second night. He doesn't cry as long; he doesn't have the energy after his previous defeat. He falls asleep sooner because he is exhausted sooner. No child can afford this game. To save his life he must surrender, and that means suppressing his longing for his parent. Letting a child cry himself out is an effective tactic for getting a child to submit to being put to bed alone, but it breaks the spirit of the child. To restore his faith in life and being will be a herculean task.

Let's return to Arthur's case and ask why he wishes to die. The answer is easy. Because he doesn't really believe that the love and warmth he wants will be there for him. And it won't be. It is difficult to respond with love to someone who prides himself on his ability to take the cold and who has numbed himself to his need for love. Arthur became numb by being frozen. Emotionally, he is like a "cold fish" and half dead already. The numbness that saved his life determined his fate. He could survive, but he would have to remain out in the cold the rest of his life.

Of course, Arthur won't die. His wish to die was only half a desire and one that had lain buried in his unconscious since he was little. He is letting himself be, and that means experiencing the truth of his inner life, which includes the wish to die. He has to experience this truth before he can let himself fully be. Many years ago, when Arthur first came into therapy with me, he had suicidal thoughts and impulses. But suicide is not just a wish to die, it is a will to die. Wishes and feelings are part of being; actions belong to doing. In suicide one takes destructive action against the self and others. The action stems in large part from repressed anger, which is turned against the self to hurt others. "You'll be sorry when I'm dead." Suicide represents a rejection of one's being. Arthur's perception of his wish to die amounted to self-acceptance. Through therapy he had gained the courage to recognize that he had been engaged in an empty struggle: surviving in a cold world. He was beginning to sense that life under those conditions wasn't worth the effort. Instead of putting his energy into the struggle for survival as he had done previously, he was ready now to invest it in the search for warmth and joy.

I could tell Arthur to take the risk of reaching out to women, since he is aware that they respond to him and he knows that he won't die. But in making this recommendation I am saying to Arthur, "Do it." With enough willpower he might be able to do it, but would this increase his state of being? I don't believe so. In my opinion, such a therapeutic approach may modify behavior, but it does not affect being. It overlooks an essential fact. Arthur's problem is no longer on the outside or in the external world. It is now within him in his quality of being. Doing only creates an illusion that one's being has changed.

You may recall that Arthur said he had numbed himself to the pain of being in the cold. The therapeutic task, then, is to restore his aliveness, to warm up his body, and to animate his sensitivity. But in the process of restoring his aliveness, he will reenter the state of pain that he had suppressed through his numbness. There is no way to avoid that. It is like restoring the circulation to a finger that has been frostbitten. It hurts, and so one proceeds very gradually in both situations. But to avoid the pain is to risk the loss of the finger. If Arthur does not reexperience the pain in his body from the hurts suffered as a child, he risks perpetuating the loss of his being.

Arthur also said that he had pinched off the circulation to his brain. The day of this session he had come in with a headache and tension in the back of the neck at the base of the skull. He asked me to work on this tension. Arthur bent over, and I put my knuckles against the base of his skull and pushed his head down, in effect, to force him to submit. He resisted, strongly forcing his head up against the pressure. When he lifted his head, forcing me to release the pressure, the tension had diminished greatly and his eyes were flashing. He was angry, and the headache was gone.

I had hurt him physically as his parents had hurt him emotionally by making him submit. But this time he was able to fight back and not take it.

Although Arthur had been my patient for many years, this was the first time I had the story of his being put out in the cold. Why it had not come up sooner, I don't know. It wasn't as if Arthur had repressed the memory—I am sure that he had known it all along—but I believe he wasn't able to face it until the issue of life or death arose again.

Arthur's story reminded me of Oedipus, who was also put out in the cold. One could believe there were other resemblances to the Oedipus story. Arthur didn't literally kill his father and marry his mother, but his father died when Arthur was a young man and Arthur inherited a considerable fortune. Further, the woman he married proved to be very much like his mother. And as a man he found himself as much out in the cold as he had been when a child. It seemed to be his fate. Why?

From our previous analytic work it was clear that Arthur's mother had been seductive with him. He knew that he had supplanted his father in her affections, and he felt guilty about it. He described his father as an impotent man who, he felt, was jealous of him and yet lived through and depended upon him. His father had inherited his money from his own father and had never worked in his life. I suspect that Arthur's oedipal situation was a repeat of the one his father had experienced.

Arthur was out in the cold emotionally as well as physically. He did not have any real contact with his mother or with his father. His relationship with his mother was too sexual, and he felt used by her. Her sexual involvement with him was a substitute for real maternal care and warmth, which she could not give. But Arthur could not establish a real relationship with his father either. He felt contempt for his father's weakness, but he also felt sorry for him. He was afraid of his father and he hated him. Such a situation allows only two possible outcomes. One is for the son to outdo his father and prove his superiority, thus acting out the Oedipus story. This was the direction chosen by Robert, whose case we studied in the first chapter. To do this the son must surrender a large part of his sexuality. The other outcome is for the son to withdraw from the competition and identify with his father. Arthur took the latter course. Father and son developed a relationship in which Arthur reported all his activities to his father, allowing his father to share his life. I believe that this contact with his father prevented Arthur from becoming a homosexual, but it did not otherwise change his fate.

Arthur's identification with his father in this situation was made possible by the cutting off of his sexual feelings for his mother. Like all victims of the oedipal conflict, he was psychologically castrated. He suffered from severe castration anxiety related to extreme tension about the genital area. His pelvis was tightly held and his pelvic floor was pulled up. This tension immobilized the pelvis so that very little pelvic movement was possible. The resulting reduction in his sexual potency made Arthur feel insecure with women and among men. He was afraid that women would use him if he had any strong sexual feelings for them. Toward men he felt both superior and inferior, as with his father. And he was worried about possible homosexual tendencies if he let any closeness to men occur.

Arthur did not consciously choose this outcome. He reacted to the oedipal situation in such a way as to minimize its traumatic effect upon him. His character structure developed as a defense against possible incest with his mother and possible castration by his father. If it required that he give up part of his life (the wish to die), it enabled him to retain another part and to function somewhat as a man, albeit with the feeling of being "out in the cold."

Therapy cannot eradicate the past. It deals with the past in terms of its effect on the present. The lack of warmth in Arthur's infancy cannot be remedied by loving Arthur as a baby now. He can be warmed as an adult only by his sexual passion and the love of a woman. For Arthur to be a man, the oedipal problem has to be worked through and his sexual anxiety alleviated. This means that the patient has to confront his fear of castration physically. Since women, too, suffer from the same oedipal problem, they have a fear of castration that has to be handled similarly.

The second case concerns a very successful man in his middle forties whom I will call Frank, who also complained of being depressed. In addition, he had a very disturbing hypochondriacal fear of death; he felt he was going to die, and every ache and pain in his body confirmed his fear. He was constantly worried about the possibility of a heart attack or a stroke, but his blood pressure was normal and his pulse slower than normal. Actually, he suffered from an orthostatic problem; when he stood up from a lying down position he bcame dizzy and felt faint. Although Frank was obsessed with the idea of dying, he had other problems.

His home life was unhappy. He was afraid of his wife and women in general. His sexual drive was depressed.

Frank's case offers a good opportunity to study the pathological fear of death and its relation to the personality. Frank was a doer, that is, his focus was upon achievement, success, and power. Starting from a poor financial situation in childhood, he made his way up in the world by pushing and competitive striving. The higher he rose in his profession, the more responsibility he assumed and the more stress was placed on him. When he came to see me for a consultation, he was in a very vulnerable position. He was being considered for another important promotion, and it scared him to death.

Why should a person be afraid of success? We can easily understand the fear of failure, which is rather common, but what threat does success pose?

To understand this problem we must think in terms of the oedipal situation. Each boy in our culture is in a competitive struggle with his father for the love of his mother. Since women in our culture feel themselves to be in an inferior position vis-à-vis men, the mother looks to her son as her champion who will vindicate her honor. The boy is expected to outshine his father and in this way to bring honor to her. Arthur had been caught in this same situation, and he, too, dared not succeed. Because of their guilt, most fathers support the son's ambition and applaud his success while inwardly they resent the implied put-down, namely, that the boy is a better man than the father.

The boy is in a real trap. To fail is to risk the loss of his mother's love. It would also displease his father, who also hopes to attain some honor through his son's success. But success means the displacement of the father and marriage to the mother. No child can take that route, much as he may wish it in fantasy. He is too small. He senses that his mother would possess him and he would lose his independence. Without his father he would be swallowed by her. And though the father can accept the son's victory over him on a theoretical level, inwardly he feels betrayed and is furious at both his wife and son. He may not acknowledge or be conscious of this feeling, but the child is sensitive to his parents' inner states and is frightened of his father's unexpressed anger.

Obviously the boy has to act in such a way as to avoid being destroyed by his father or sexually overwhelmed by his mother. If the pressure to achieve is strong enough, he will suppress his sexual feelings for his mother and devote his energies to the struggle for success. He will sacrifice his being to become a doer. The suppression of his sexuality removes all danger because it amounts to a psychological castration. This is how Freud saw the solution to the oedipal situation. But repression does not solve emotional conflicts.

Let me say that not every child is affected by the oedipal situation to the same degree. Much depends on the relationship between the parents, on the love and respect each has for the other, and on the importance attached to success. However, there are very few families in our culture that are not caught up in the striving for success and in which the children are spared the effects of the oedipal conflict.

Success and power are the ego's answer to the oedipal problem. Their achievement compensates for the castration. It assures one of admiration and respect. It promises love for fulfilling the parents' demands, and it proclaims the superiority of the son over the father. But by the same token, success evokes the threat of castration. Admiration brings envy. Power leads to fear, not love. Victory over the father brings back the fear of being destroyed or devoured.

The higher one rises, the greater is the excitement, and so is the danger. What goes up has to come down. Down is the direction to discharge excitement and to obtain release. Without the ability to come down, the person is hung up and unable to find surcease from his struggle and toil. Normally, coming down or letting down occurs through sex and pleasure. After a satisfactory sexual experience the person feels let down and relaxed in a contented way. But this avenue was blocked for Frank; he had never allowed himself much pleasure, and he was afraid of women. Sensing that he had to come down, Frank was afraid that he would fall down, which would take the form of illness or death.

This analysis of Frank's situation led to a surprising conclusion, namely, that Frank was more afraid of living than of dying. His statement that he was afraid to die is also true because if a person is afraid to live, he is asking to die, and that is frightening. One could see in Frank's body the tightness in his chest, which severely restricted his breathing. He couldn't cry, he couldn't scream, and he couldn't reach out for love despite his evident emotional deprivation. His pelvis was tightly held, and its muscles were markedly contracted. The fear of castration was clearly discernible in this tension, yet Frank was unaware of this aspect of his problem because of his hypochondriacal preoccupation with death. He knew about his oedipal problem through many years of psychoanalysis, but he had never experienced the fear of castration, and so it was only words to him. When a chest pain gripped him for a moment and stopped his breathing, he panicked and all he could think of was that he would die. I offered Frank my assurance that I did not think it would happen soon. He had consulted all kinds of specialists, none of whom found any organic reason for his anxiety. I told him that it was not the fate of hypochondriacs to find an "easeful death." Their fate seems to be to suffer the torments of the doomed without the release that death offers. However, Frank was not much reassured by my statement.

I could make Frank aware that his breathing was very shallow. Lying over the bioenergetic stool[1] he became aware of the tension in his throat and chest and of how difficult it was for him to breathe deeply. I was also able to show him how pulled up he was in his body. He was over six feet tall, and rather thin. He appeared very weak, and his legs didn't look as if they would

---

1. See Alexander and Leslie Lowen, *The Way to Vibrant Health* (New York: Harper & Row, Publishers, 1977) for a description and pictures of how the bioenergetic stool is used.

hold him up. The arches of his feet were collapsed, his ankles were thin, and his knees were locked to give him some support. His shoulders were raised as if he were holding himself up by them. He reminded me of a scarecrow, only he was the one who was frightened.

Frank was tired. He wanted to let down, but he couldn't. Down represented failure and death. Still, he couldn't stay up indefinitely, either. That was impossible. I could understand his anxiety; it was real.

Frank was holding himself up for dear life. No wonder he was terrified of dying! How long can one stay up? But every tension is literally a holding on "for dear life." It doesn't matter what muscles are involved. Each tension is part of a total pattern, which constitutes the character structure and which is intended to ensure the survival of the individual. To step out of character is too frightening. It is experienced as a loss of identity, a momentary nonbeing or death.[2] But death is also the way out—from the trap, from the struggle, from the pain of living. Frank desperately wanted to give up, to let down, to die, and this unacknowledged wish to die scared him to death.

I have found this wish to die in every patient I have treated. In some it is weak, in others it is strong. Its strength is directly proportional to the degree that one is afraid to live. The inhibition of life is death. Every chronic tension in the body is a fear of life, a fear of letting go, a fear of being. It can be interpreted as a wish to die. This is different, however, from Freud's concept of a death instinct. An instinct is inherent in the organism, whereas the wish to die develops only when life becomes too painful. I worked with a person some years ago in a bioenergetic workshop for therapists. He was lying over the bioenergetic stool and let-

2. Reuven Bar-Levav, "Behavior Change—Insignificant and Significant, Apparent and Real," in *What Makes Behavior Change Possible?* ed. Arthur Burton (New York: Brunner-Maisel, 1976), p. 288. "The giving up of personality traits that have always been considered essential for survival is a frightening and painful process."

ting go to his breathing. This was his first experience with the stool. All of a sudden he exclaimed, "I am so tired, I want to die!" He collapsed onto the floor and broke into deep sobs.

I recall experiencing something similar while swimming in a pool. I was floating with my head underwater, quite relaxed. The thought entered my mind, "Why not just lie here? How nice it would be not to have to make the effort to lift my head out of the water to breathe." Of course, I did make the effort. It was an effort because I had to counter the wish to do nothing. That effort expressed my will to live, which I mobilized against some deep-seated wish to die. So many of us are like Arthur, struggling to survive in a "cold" world and denying the desire to give up the struggle. We use our wills in order to keep going on, which means that the living process is a doing, not a being. We are afraid, then, to give up the "willing," the doing, because we are afraid we might die. If we are afraid to die, we are afraid to live or to be. And if we are afraid to live, we are afraid we might die.

The fear of death is one of the valleys we must cross on the journey back into childhood and infancy. We must confront the fear of death in us and recognize that it stems from a wish to die. The wish, in turn, stems from the struggle we all engage in to prove we are worthy of love, to overcome our vulnerability, and to deny our fear. But these are goals that can never be achieved, and, indeed, there is no real need to achieve them. We can afford to give up the struggle. In fact, if we don't, we will find ourselves in Frank's situation: pushing ourselves to the point where death seems the only way out. Giving up the struggle removes the wish to die and eliminates the fear of dying. It opens the door to full living and being.

The Fear of Sex

Saying that people are afraid of sex sounds only a little less absurd than saying they are afraid of life. Yet the reality is that both life and sex have frightening aspects for people. Both are unpredictable, beyond ego control, and inherently explosive by nature. The orgasm isn't just a flow of feeling. It starts as a flow and ends as a burst. It is like riding on a horse and suddenly being catapulted into space. There are many ways to describe the orgastic response, but common to all is the idea of bursting through barriers, of exploding, of transcending. A scream is similar. When it occurs spontaneously, it bursts forth. Even the reaction of sobbing has this quality. We say a person breaks into tears.

Not all sexual activity leads to orgastic release. If it doesn't, the sex or the foreplay can still be pleasurable. But without the orgastic release one misses the ecstatic or joyful experience that sex can offer. To have that experience is to know what life is about. But not only in sex does life burst forth in its glory and splendor to add significance to living. The bursting forth of spring in a field of flowers is the magic of creation filling us with awe and making us feel the wonder and magnificence of life. It is not the gradual transformation that excites us so. The mystery lies in the explosive nature of the phenomenon. For van Gogh the explosion occurred not only in nature but in his brain and in his pictures.

We know, of course, that the bursting forth of life is preceded by a long period of preparation. A baby bursts into the world at birth, but it was slowly being prepared for this event. A flower seems to open overnight, but it, too, had a long development. The bursting is always the breaking into light of a process that previously went on in the dark, and it is this aspect that seems magical. There is a sense of liberation, as if a force previously bound breaks free. There is also a sense of creation, as if a new being or new state of being is suddenly there.

Yet it is this very quality of life, this magic, creativity, joyfulness, exuberance, this explosive aspect that our culture is trying to suppress. We seek to control the life process to guard us against its vicissitudes, to protect us from illness and death, little realizing that to do this one must transform life into a mechanical operation. In our attempt to prevent the valleys of experience we must eliminate the peaks. We must flatten life out so that it rolls like an assembly line in a manufacturing plant. At no point should it burst through its barriers, overwhelm its guardians, or confront them with a new creation. We talk creativity, but all our energies go into productive work rather than creativity. We worship doing, not being.

The flattening of life is achieved by sexual suppression. Of course, sex cannot be fully suppressed, since this would stop all reproductive activity. What is suppressed is the bursting, explosive, enchanting aspect of sexuality. In the past this was done by a moral code that limited its expression. The implicit command of this code was that one should not "give in" fully to the sexual urge. Such codes that restrict life are ignored as much as they are observed, but their effect is to inhibit the natural and spontaneous expression of sexual feeling. We have largely discarded this code of morality today by removing all limits and barriers to the expression of sex, but we have done this in such a way that life has become even flatter. By commercially exploiting sex, by vulgar and pornographic display, by throwing the cold light of knowledge upon the mysteries of sex, we prevent the buildup of excitement to where any bursting or explosion can occur. Sex in our time has become a production, not a creation.

Sex is the most intense manifestation of the living process. By controlling sex one controls life. We do not want to stop the life process; what we want is for it to run smoothly, in ordained and regular channels, predictable, like a machine. We are afraid of the ebullient, bursting quality. We are afraid that if it explodes, it may cease to be; if it rises like a fountain, it will fall like a cascade. We can play with sex in the most sensual ways, but we are scared to death to explode in an orgasm of joy and ecstasy. Reich called this fear "orgasm anxiety." In his view and mine it underlies all neurotic behavior.

The close association of sex and death is well known. The French call the orgasm *la petite mort*, the little death. Since the ego is extinguished in the full orgasm, it is experienced by the ego as a little death. In *Love and Orgasm*[3] I wrote, "The intimate

3. Alexander Lowen, *Love and Orgasm* (New York: Collier Books, 1965), p. 44.

psychological connection between sex and death is the symbol of the round or the cave, which represents both the womb and the tomb. Orgasm anxiety, that is, the fear of ego dissolution that overwhelms the neurotic individual at the approach of the full sexual climax, is perceived as the fear of dying."

Most of us do not experience a fear of death at the approach of the full orgasm because we unconsciously hold back the discharge, allowing only a partial release to occur. Thus we do not die, but neither are we reborn. The full orgastic release is blocked by tensions in the pelvis. I related these tensions to castration anxiety, which is also closely associated with the idea of death. This association is shown in the following report by a patient whom I will call Mike. He told me, "You worked on my pelvis in the last session, and I felt that the bottom fell out of me. It was like an energy release. All the energy drained out of me, and I felt as if I was dead, a little death. Then I came down with a virus, feeling the weakest I've been for a long time. I had no sexual feelings. I became frightened that I wouldn't get better, that I would die, that I was going down the drain. I became very depressed. It lasted three weeks; my energy has been coming back very slowly."

This experience made Mike conscious that death was somehow tied up with his sexual fears. He remarked, "The dark circles that look like death under my eyes developed at puberty. My pictures show that I looked like a happy child. Puberty was my lowest state. I was exhausted, depressed, isolated, and suicidal then. I felt lost. I was always looking for a girl who would save me, who would love me, who would make me feel alive."

From other material that Mike presented it was clear that he equated sexual excitement with life. This is a common equation, because most people feel very alive when they are sexually excited. For this reason the discharge of the excitation can be experienced as dying. This would be true if the person failed to reach an explosive climax and, instead, felt the excitation fade out or drain away. And that can happen if one is frightened of the orgastic release and "freezes" just before climax. On the other hand, the orgasm leaves one with a feeling of satisfaction and a sense of being fulfilled (full, not empty). *La petite mort* merely describes the clouding of consciousness that occurs with the full orgasm. Following orgasm one feels a deep sense of peace and quiet. At night it brings on a very restful slumber. Sooner or later, depending on the person, the sexual excitement builds again, and one is ready for another act of creation. In sex, the eternal cycle of birth, death, and rebirth is repeated regularly.

At another session some time later, Mike reported that the tensions in his neck and shoulders were becoming unbearable. He remarked, "If I let go of my head, bend it down, I feel weak, helpless, and frightened. I have to hold myself up." The back of the neck especially at its junction with the head is one of the most important "holding" areas of the body. There is hardly a person who does not have strong tensions in this area. We are all afraid to let go of our heads, which is tantamount to being out of control. "Don't lose your head" is common advice. Being in control means that the body is subject to the ego's will and that there will be no movements without the ego's consent. The will is in command. In Mike's case this meant the will to live. Letting go of the head signified collapse, defeat, and death.

That day was heavy with rain. Mike remembered such days as a boy at home with his mother. He recalled, "I used to feel so heavy. It was so black." His mother was a very depressed person who always seemed to be dying. She clung to Mike as if this little boy could save her. And he felt that he had to save her. It was really too much for him, yet if he let go, she would die and he, too, since he was also dependent on her. He had to hold on for her sake and his.

I applied some pressure with my fingers to the muscles at the junction of the skull and neck, at the same time encouraging Mike to breathe deeply. He felt a buzzing in his head, and then a darkness as if he were going to pass out. I have seen this happen to a number of patients, who instead of letting go to the pressure, resist it by increasing the tension and reducing the blood supply to the brain. But Mike had experienced this feeling before when I had tried the same maneuver, and he told me later, "I didn't die then. I won't die now, I don't have to be afraid to let go." And he let go of his head.

Lying on the bed after it was over, Mike felt a great sense of peace. He cried deeply. There was no need to hold on anymore. He let his jaw drop and remarked, "I feel like a corpse. If people could see me now, they would say, 'Look at death.' The muscles at the back of my neck are like the strings of a marionette. If they let go, I would collapse into being nothing."

In Mike's character being is equated with emptiness or nothingness. This is not an existential problem. Although quite common in our culture, it is not the natural condition of human existence. The suppression of feeling, especially sexual feeling, produces an inner emptiness in the personality, which is then filled with doing. For Mike, doing was protecting others. He said, "I am a protector. I'll protect anybody." We saw how important Mike was to his mother. This created a triangle situation in which Mike felt superior to his father. He remarked, "I think he felt *put out*. I had to sacrifice my sexuality not to threaten him. I made the sacrifice, hoping he would give it back to me later. But he didn't appreciate me."

Mike had made the sacrifice during the oedipal phase at about six or seven years of age. He hoped to regain his sexuality at puberty. When this failed to occur, he became severely depressed and suicidal. In our culture the oedipal conflict does not lead to the death of the father but to that of the son. The father has too much power. However, the death of the son, symbolically speaking (castration = death), means that the father also dies, symbolically speaking. The son becomes a father in his turn, but, having been psychologically castrated earlier, he is now the "dead" father who compensates for his sexual impotence by position and power. And, in turn, he will castrate his own sons, not deliberately, but by his weakness as a man.

Mike's therapy was focused upon helping him get past the feelings of weakness, tiredness, and helplessness that undermined his manhood. There was no way he could overcome these feelings by an effort of will, since he was using all his willpower just to survive. Moreover, that would not be desirable even if it were possible, since it would increase the "holding" and with that the fear of letting go. There was no alternative but for Mike to give in to these feelings. Whenever I worked on the tensions in his pelvis or in his jaw, he collapsed into crying. This had the effect of deepening his breathing and giving him more energy. Strangely, every time he let himself feel weak, he became stronger. Every time he let himself feel his tiredness, he rested and recuperated. Every time he felt frightened, it turned into anger, which diminished his fear.

Mike had to make some adjustments in his life. He could not continue to act like a man in order to save his mother, his wife, or his patients. I mention this because Mike was a therapist himself. He cut down on his work and backed away from new challenges or demands. And he asserted his own needs. All of this took time. I saw him only half a dozen times a year, but he knew he had my support.

The big change came when he let me work strongly on his pelvic tension. He became very frightened and started to shake violently. Then he cried very deeply. He felt "wiped out" by the experience. He went home after the session and slept for twelve hours. When he awoke, he felt much better. He told me that since then he felt himself slowly becoming stronger. The old weakness seemed to have disappeared, and his fear seemed to have diminished correspondingly. He had hit bottom and was now on his way up. Once earlier I had worked on his pelvic tensions and he had felt "wiped out." He used the words "drained of energy." This time was different. He let go, and his body went into a convulsive response that suggested an orgasmic release. He had let down fully, and as a result he could rebound.

In the next case to be presented, the fear of the sexual release is seen through a woman's eyes. Martha had been in therapy for a number of years prior to consulting me. She was an attractive woman about thirty, very alive with much feeling, yet unable to transform her energy into a satisfying life. Her main difficulty was her relation to men. Her problems were clearly portrayed in her dreams.

Martha reported that she had some clearly sexual dreams. One was repeated three times, which had never happened before. This is the dream in Martha's words: "I was lying nude on a couch open and ready for sex. My father was near a wall. He had his clothes off. He came toward me, but just then my mother came into the room and stood several feet from my head. She didn't acknowledge his presence. He turned his back to me and stood there saying nothing. The feeling I got from him was 'I'm not here. I don't have anything to do with this.'

"My mother's look was very stern and scowling, like 'How could you do this?' But nothing was said. I remember looking up at her in disbelief as if 'It's not my fault. Don't you see him? It's not my fault.' I looked at him with the feeling 'Why don't you say something? You're part of this, too.' She didn't acknowledge his part, and I was left with the feeling that it's all on me. I'm the responsible party."

The dream depicts her problem with men. She has strong sexual desires but also guilt that she is the seducer. As a consequence there is resentment of the man and an inability to give in to him sexually. In the end she is frustrated and angry.

About a year later another dream revealed her conflict with her mother. She said, "I dreamt that my parents were having sex, and I had the understanding that I was to be next. I was very excited, but I couldn't give in to the feeling. Once when I was twenty-eight years old I was with my parents at a resort. They were having sex, thinking I was asleep. I was very excited.

"In the dream I thought that if I had sex with my father I would be better than my mother. I also thought she would be watching me, and I couldn't enjoy it. I felt angry with her. If I let go to him and she couldn't, she would be hurt. I felt sorry for her. I could have taken him away from her, but she would be all alone. She needed him more than I did."

Here again, we have the theme of sacrifice of sexual fulfillment.

However, the fantasy of superiority over the mother was countered by the reality that the father did have sex with the mother.

Shortly after this dream there was another. "I'm lying in bed ready to go to sleep. The scene is my parents' bedroom. There is a very loud banging on the door. Someone is breaking in. I don't scream. I expect my parents to hear and come to protect me. But I realize no one is coming.

"A man breaks in and stands in the middle of the room looking at me, and I know he is going to attack me. I say, 'Don't hurt me, I am just a little girl.' However, I was my present size. The man becomes two men. One stands near my bed. I feel terrified. I plead with him, 'I am just a little girl.' I feel paralyzed from the waist down. I was flailing with my arms, but I couldn't reach him because the lower part of my body wouldn't move.

"I lunged and grabbed him. I felt his ass against me and I got sexually excited. Then I turned him around and saw it was my father. I shouted, 'It's my father. He wants me.' I was shouting at the other man. In my father's eyes was a look of rage because I had exposed him. I was stunned. I felt he was going to kill me, and I awoke with the feeling of his hand on my throat and another hand over my mouth."

This dream was significant for Martha because it made her realize that her sexual problems stemmed from her father's interest in her. Although she was highly excited, she dared not respond overtly (move her pelvis), for she would be blamed by her mother and threatened by her father. He would attack her for the very sexual feelings that he projected onto her. Martha still suffers from some degree of paralysis of the lower part of the body when she is sexually excited. The reduction in pelvic motility is a form of castration.

This dream brought up some important material from Martha's early life. She related, "I used to go to bed with a hunting knife under my pillow and a baseball bat under the bed. I heard sounds as if someone was coming to get me, but I couldn't tell my parents because I dared not go into their room and I was ashamed since no one else heard them. I was so terrified I used to crawl out of the window and go up to the local school, where I sat on the swings all night singing until the sun came up. Then I went back home and crawled into bed. This happened several times a week until I was eleven. I realize now how terrified I was as a child . . . and still am.

"I started dating at eleven or twelve. I engaged in a lot of sexual play with my brother when I was fourteen. However, I was a prude with the other boys. I didn't masturbate until I was sixteen, but I used to rock myself. I felt incredibly guilty about my sexuality. I felt terribly ashamed when my parents told their friends about my breasts developing and my period coming. I felt horribly exposed.

"I also realize there was something lascivious about my parents. In my family sexuality was all over the place, ready to explode, but never acknowledged, never admitted, covered up. It was all innuendo. Dirty jokes and remarks were common, and my father walked around naked but you weren't supposed to see. It was 'Look, look but don't look.' Even now he lies naked on his bed with the door open, but one is not supposed to look. It was enough to drive me crazy."

Martha didn't dare be because that meant being sexually responsive, which posed the threat of death. On the other hand, she was tormented by sexual feelings that she could not release and by guilt that she could not assuage. She was trapped. She tried to get out of the trap by doing the right things, what her parents wanted. But that didn't work, and she ended up feeling hopeless. This she could not accept, so she continued to try and to do. Martha described her situation as follows:

"I feel hopeless, so I think I've got to do something. But doing it doesn't help, so I feel more hopeless. Then I've got to try to do something again. [Doing is an action designed to win someone's approval and acceptance.] I feel in a vicious circle unable to get out."

One can never get out of a trap by struggling, which is what

Martha did. One only becomes more tightly bound. One has to stop the struggle, the trying, the doing. For Martha to do that meant to accept her feeling of hopelessness, not to struggle against it. And the situation was hopeless. She could never get her parents to accept and approve of her, since they did not accept her sexuality. If she accepted that fact, she would have two very powerful feelings, one of sadness and the other of rage. The sadness verges on despair, with thoughts of suicide. The rage is demonic. Given the despair and rage, she would either kill herself or kill her father. To do either, she would have to be mad—crazy mad with anger. She could keep her sanity only by doing and hoping, even though that course must fail.

The Fear of Insanity

Insanity poses as great a threat to the human personality as does death. It is a kind of death, since the self as it is normally experienced is lost in the psychotic state. In this section, we will see how the fear of insanity prevents many people from "letting go" to their feelings and blocks them from discovering their being. I shall illustrate this problem with a case.

Alice was a woman about fifty years old who came to therapy because she was depressed. On the surface of things she saw no reason to be depressed. In her own eyes and those of her friends, she seemed to have a successful life. About eight months previously she had been in an automobile accident through no fault of hers. Although no one was badly hurt, the accident upset her and led to a rather severe depression. She lost the desire to go out and abandoned her former activities. The accident made her realize she was frightened, something she had not been aware of before.

Alice had a well-developed, youthful-looking body. As a young woman, she had been a model, and her body still showed that quality. She held herself tightly together: belly in, bosom presented, lips smiling in a sexually seductive manner, but not breathing much. Her body was a model of sexuality, but only a model. It lacked the inner passion of sexuality. And there was no passion in her sexual life, though she had had many affairs.

The therapeutic task was to get her body alive and to find out why it went dead. One can accomplish the first part by deepening the breathing, involving the patient in movement, and releasing some of the tension in the tight muscles. At the same time, the patient and I are engaged in the analytic work of uncovering the past. As the body becomes more alive, memories are recalled with the feelings and emotions that surrounded the events. Expressing these feelings in the therapeutic setting releases the body from the muscular tension of holding these feelings suppressed, and so promotes aliveness. Thus, the body work and the analytic work go hand in hand to help the person regain self or being.

Early in the therapy, Alice related a traumatic experience from early childhood. When she was about six years old, her father told her to clean the spitoon. This had been her mother's chore, but the mother refused to do it anymore. The girl was repelled by the thought of handling this dirty object and refused. Her father became enraged and struck her with his fists, knocking her across the room. She was injured badly enough for her mother to take her to the hospital. Seeing the injuries, the doctors told her mother that if her father struck her again, they would report him to the police for child abuse.

One would imagine that the recital of this incident would evoke a feeling of intense anger. But Alice felt no anger toward her father or any fear of him. She was still in a state of shock and numbness. Her father was a violent man who not infrequently beat her mother. After the above incident, Alice never confronted him or challenged him. She became a good girl and a good student; in fact, a perfect model of a child. Later she became a real model, married a rich man, and was a model wife—all without feeling, however.

Alice responded very well to the therapy. She enjoyed the body work, since it made her feel alive and diminished her depression. Little by little she allowed more feeling to develop as she allowed herself to relate to me as a person. The men in her life were mainly figures such as father, husband, lover, son. She had little feeling for any of them except her children. Slowly she let herself be more of a woman and less of a model.

Again and again in the course of therapy I focused upon the issue of her feelings toward her father. Generally she said that she felt neither fear nor anger toward him. He was an old man now, and she was concerned about his health. When he was ill, he stayed in her home and she took care of him. Then one day Alice said to me, "I cannot even wish him dead because that would be equivalent to his dying. The thought is the same as the fact for me." Equating the thought with the action is typical of both infantile and schizophrenic thinking. Alice wasn't schizophrenic. She knew that her belief in the power of thought was unrealistic, yet it had the power to control her behavior. One could surmise that there was a strong schizoid element in Alice's personality. I asked her if she had been afraid that she could go crazy, and her answer was yes. She told me that her brother had been diagnosed as schizophrenic.

To help Alice overcome the fear of insanity so she could get in touch with her anger toward her father, I asked her to pretend that she was mad, to roll her eyes and act crazy. Then I told her to take the tennis racquet and hit the bed. She followed my instructions, and as she hit the bed the rage against her father erupted. She called him a bastard and said that she could smash him. She was so mad her body was shaking. But she wasn't frightened, nor did she feel crazy. She knew, however, that her fear of being mad meant both becoming furious and going crazy. The two were identified in her mind.

The identification between the two states, anger and insanity, is expressed in the common word *mad*. To go mad means to lose one's head or to be so angry that one loses one's head. Disorientation occurs when the mind is overwhelmed by a feeling[4] that it is trying to control. As the feeling bursts through the protective

4. See A. Lowen, *Betrayal of the Body* (New York: Collier Books, 1969), for a fuller discussion of the process underlying the psychotic break.

barriers, the mind is swept off its foundations in reality. The person feels confused, estranged, and unable to orient himself. This disorientation may be momentary if, as the feeling subsides, the person recovers his footing, that is, his orientation in reality. Or, in cases where the individual is vulnerable because of inadequate grounding in reality—the schizoid character structure, for example—the effect may be longer lasting. The person would then experience what we call a nervous breakdown.

Theoretically, any feeling can overwhelm the ego if it explodes with sufficient force to destroy the boundaries of the self. We say the organism is flooded, similar to the flooding that occurs when a river overruns its banks and eradicates the familiar outlines of the land. Practically, the two feelings that most threaten the personality are anger and sex, because both of these feelings are closely linked to fear and guilt. If a surge of anger evokes a corresponding amount of fear, one will attempt to control the anger. Should the anger break through the control, one would be in the position of a rider who has lost control of his horse. The person could be thrown into confusion just as easily as the rider could be thrown off his horse. The same thing would be true of a powerful sex urge if it is associated with an equal quantity of guilt.

Alice was actually threatened by both of these feelings. She was furious with her father, but there was no way she could have expressed that feeling without risking her life. That he would have killed her is unlikely, but she had every reason to believe that he might. She had no choice but to suppress her anger. It guaranteed her survival. She would have had to be "mad" to attack her father. In one sense, then, the denial of her anger protected her sanity. However, it also made her vulnerable to a psychotic break, because the anger was latent within her and she could never be fully sure that it would not erupt and drive her "mad." She had to be on guard all the time against her own feelings. Suppressing them as she did left her with only the façade of a personality.

The father's sadistic behavior to Alice and her mother made

Alice afraid of him as a man. This fear became extended later to all men, and while it, too, was suppressed and denied, it forced her to be submissive in her sexual relations. On occasion, however, she would become provocative and goad her husband into making a physical attack upon her. She would then fight with him, but it always ended with her being beaten. He would describe her behavior as crazy, and she would believe him. She never got angry with her husband or questioned his right to beat her. It was her due, her fate. She had married a man who was violent, like her father.

Her excuse for her lack of anger was that she felt guilty. It was a deeply rooted feeling of guilt that pervaded her entire being. But Alice had no idea why she felt guilty. I had no doubt that the guilt stemmed from the suppression of sexual feelings toward her father during the oedipal period, which was also the time of the trauma. It was very difficult for her to accept this idea. However, when she tried to move her pelvis in the sexual exercises,[5] she became very disturbed. She thought of herself as a sexually sophisticated woman, and she was distressed when she found that she could move her pelvis only with difficulty. This made her aware of how sexually repressed she was. She also became aware of how happy she felt in taking care of her father, and this made her realize she had taken her mother's place.

Without going into Alice's therapy in any detailed way, let me say that she improved in proportion to the degree she faced her oedipal problem. As her guilt diminished, she was able to identify with her anger without feeling that she was mad-crazy. She learned how to express her anger without provoking a fight that ended with her being beaten. She sensed that she had far to go to reclaim fully her being, but she would no longer settle for being a model-mannequin.

Children can be driven to the edge of sanity by parents who are sexually seductive and rejecting at the same time. It is a

5. See Lowen, *The Way to Vibrant Health*.

typical double-bind situation. The child is given two opposite messages at the same time, and the conflict is enough to drive one crazy.

The story as Bill tells it is not atypical. "When I am on my back and my girl friend haunches over me tenderly, my body begins to melt and I become absolutely terrified. I couldn't stand my mother touching me. I have the feeling that she was 'getting off' by touching me. [By getting off, he meant she was becoming sexually excited.] But if I got excited, she turned away. I couldn't stand it. I felt I would go out of my mind and explode if I did not block the charge. As a child I used to beat my mother until she was black and blue, but she never told me to stop."

A child cannot contain and handle adult sexuality. His body is not mature enough for such intense excitation, which threatens to overwhelm his ego. Whenever a child is overstimulated sexually by adults, he must find some way to reduce the excitation. Bill was an overeater. Through the therapy he was able to see the connection between eating and sexuality. He described his problems as follows:

"Feeding and eating are expressions of love. Food was the most important thing to my mother. We thought about food, talked about it, were obsessed with it. At the same time that my desire for and interest in food was stimulated, I was told that I was ugly and repulsive because I was fat and liked to eat. My mother would say, 'Your overeating makes me miserable. It shows you have no feelings for me, that you are a cruel, insensitive creature.' If I didn't eat what she gave me, she would accuse me in the same tone and with the same words for not eating. I was in a double bind; no matter what I did I couldn't win.

"The double bind about sexual matters occurred in the same way on a more subtle plane. On the one hand, there was the stimulation. My mother would tell me to make her bed or scratch her back while she was wearing only a nightgown. Or she would walk around in a diaphanous nightgown with her breasts, pubic hair, and buttocks clearly visible. My father would say,

'Not in front of the boy.' He would be furious, but he let it go on.

"I slept in the same bedroom with my sexy sister, who is eight years older, until I was eleven years old. I masturbated with obsessive regularity from age five through the so-called latency period and into adulthood. My mother and sister caught me in the act with some frequency, and I believe this was deliberately if unconsciously arranged. My mother would tell me with characteristic ferocity that masturbation would make me a gorilla, a monster, an unspeakably disgusting creature, a grotesque and unthinkably abnormal person. She would say, 'Masturbation is an evil distortion of what is natural and beautiful.'

"So in being overstimulated and disapproved of for trying to respond, I frantically played out a circular no-win scenario, trying to satisfy the conflicting messages from my mother.

"Stimulus—desire to respond—guilt for wanting to respond—rage at being judged bad for responding—feeling overwhelmed—responding defiantly while feeling anxiety—remorse at having responded—punish self or self-punishment to alleviate guilt and assuage remorse."

Self-punishment took the form of overeating, so that Bill was heavy with pendulous breasts and a massive accumulation of fat under the skin. He really did look grotesque, and so he despised himself. Overeating also seemed to reduce sexual excitation in the body, though it left the genital excitation undiminished. Bill kept the latter within bounds through his excessive masturbation. By these two means—eating and masturbation—Bill was able to keep his sanity. Knowing this relation between overeating and sexuality helps us understand why many fat people find it so difficult to lose weight and why in some cases, a too rapid loss of weight can result in a psychotic break.

Here is another case, that of a thirty-year-old woman named Sally, who was a lesbian. She was an only child. "My father," she said, "was deeply involved with me. He got his excitement through me. He would tease me and stimulate me. He would pat my behind, saying how nice it was. He used to tickle me till I cried. He talked to me as if we were equals. I was excited by him, and though I wanted to go with my friends, I would often stay with him. I felt he needed me.

"He used to compare me with my mother to her detriment. For example, if she prepared the meal and I made the salad, he would praise my salad but dismiss her meal as somewhat lacking. She felt rejected and would withdraw. I guess this is what he wanted, because he would then say, 'Let's go to the movies.' My mother would answer, 'I can't go. Take Sally.' And he and I would go to the movies alone. He was paranoid. He insisted everything had to be happy and exciting. My mother finally committed suicide."

In this case the oedipal story was acted out to the bitter end. With the death of her mother, Sally was alone with her father. He wanted her to stay and live with him, but she found the situation intolerable. She got out, but without her sexuality. She cut off her sexual feelings as Oedipus had cut off his eyesight.

As the therapy progressed, Sally found that she was losing the desire for sexual contact with women. She realized that her lesbian activities represented both an appeasement of her mother and a way to block any sexual feelings for her father or any man. She had kept her sanity as a child by a massive denial of the reality of the situation, of her role in it, and of her sexual feelings for her father. When I first saw her she presented the happy, excited appearance that her father wanted, though her life was chaotic. There was much that was insane about her life then, but she did not sense it. She had to act out the charade and to pretend it was real. Reality had been too much for her. It was still very frightening. She remarked, "If I let go of my head and give in to my sexual feelings, I'll go crazy."

The cases described in this section may seem extreme, but I have become convinced that they are not as uncommon as one would think. Beneath the seemingly rational exterior of our lives is a fear of insanity. We dare not question the values by which we live or rebel against the roles we play for fear of putting our sanity into doubt. We are like the inmates of a mental institution who must accept its inhumanity and insensitivity as caring and knowledgeableness if they hope to be regarded as sane enough to leave. The question who is sane and who is crazy was the theme of the novel *One Flew Over the Cuckoo's Nest*. The question, what is sanity? was clearly asked in the play *Equus*.

The idea that much of what we do is insane and that if we want to be sane, we must let ourselves go crazy has been strongly advanced by R. D. Laing. In the preface to the Pelican edition of his book *The Divided Self*, Laing writes: "In the context of our present pervasive madness that we call normality, sanity, freedom, all of our frames of reference are ambiguous and equivocal." And in the same preface: "Thus I would wish to emphasize that our 'normal' 'adjusted' state is too often the abdication of ecstasy, the betrayal of our true potentialities; that many of us are only too successful in acquiring a false self to adapt to false realities."[6]

Wilhelm Reich had a somewhat similar view of present-day human behavior. Thus Reich says, "Homo normalis blocks off entirely the perception of basic orgonotic functioning by means of rigid armoring; in the schizophrenic, on the other hand, the armoring practically breaks down and thus the biosystem is flooded with deep experiences from the biophysical core with which it cannot cope."[7] The "deep experiences" to which Reich refers are the pleasurable streaming sensations associated with intense excitation that is mainly sexual in nature. The schizophrenic cannot cope with these sensations because his body is too contracted to tolerate the charge. Unable to "block" the excitation or reduce it as a neurotic can, and unable to "stand" the charge, the schizophrenic is literally "driven crazy."

But the neurotic does not escape so easily either. He avoids

6. R. D. Laing, *The Divided Self*, Preface to Pelican edition (London: Penguin Books, Ltd., 1965).

7. Wilhelm Reich, *Character Analysis*, 3d ed. (New York: The Orgone Institute Press, 1949), p. 401.

insanity by blocking the excitation, that is, by reducing it to a point where there is no danger of explosion, or bursting. In effect the neurotic undergoes a psychological castration. However, the potential for explosive release is still present in his body, although it is rigidly guarded as if it were a bomb. The neurotic is on guard against himself, terrified to let go of his defenses and allow his feelings free expression. Having become, as Reich calls him, "homo normalis," having bartered his freedom and ecstasy for the security of being "well adjusted," he sees the alternative as "crazy." And in a sense he is right. Without going "crazy," without becoming "mad," so mad that he could kill, it is impossible to give up the defenses that protect him in the same way that a mental institution protects its inmates from self-destruction and the destruction of others.

5 / A Therapy for Being

The Spiral of Growth

When I was a young therapist, I was enthusiastic about therapy and optimistic about what it could do. I believed we could free an individual from his repressions and restore him to a state of harmony with himself and with nature. I was firmly convinced that Reich was correct in claiming that the suppression of sexuality was the cause of all our difficulties. The therapeutic aim, therefore, was to reestablish the capacity for full surrender to sexual feeling, which Reich called orgastic potency. This was to be accomplished by a combination of character analysis and body work. The latter was designed to reduce or eliminate the muscular tensions that blocked the giving in to the body and its feelings. As a patient of Reich, I had experienced the effectiveness of this therapeutic approach.[1]

It is now thirty-five years since I began my own personal therapy with Reich, which lasted three years. I have also had therapy with my former associate, Dr. John Pierrakos, for about three years, in addition to which I have consistently worked with myself to free my being from the inhibitions and repressions stemming from my upbringing. It would be nice to say that I have succeeded, but, though I have changed in significant ways, I am still aware of tensions and difficulties that disturb me and limit my being. This makes me sad. However, there is nothing to stop me from continuing to work with my body to expand my being, and I am committed to this undertaking for the rest of my life. The idea that I haven't "made it" yet is not depressing. Rather, it is exciting to think that I could improve in areas where I sense a lack in my being.

What about my sexual potency? It has changed with the change in my being. To the degree that I as a person have grown and matured, my sexual feelings have become deeper and fuller. However, as I became older my sexual drive lost some of its intensity. Sexuality is an expression of a person's being, and it reflects, therefore, the state of his being. So I haven't "made it" on the sexual level either. I am not totally potent orgastically in Reich's sense of that term. I have had some great experiences, which I can credit to therapy. And, most important, the feelings of pleasure and satisfaction that I derive from my sexuality have increased greatly.

I believe that therapy has helped me enormously, but it has not brought me to paradise or elevated me to a state of transcendence, though I have spent the major part of my life engaged in the process. I also believe that I have helped most of my patients, but none of them have been totally freed from repres-

---

1. I have described some of my experiences as Reich's patient in *Bioenergetics*.

sion or inhibition. Therapy is not a panacea for human ills; it is not the answer to the human dilemma. That most people need help today to function with some measure of ease and pleasure is a sad reflection of our culture, but it is true. The more industrialized and sophisticated a culture becomes, the more problems it poses for people and the more help they need simply to cope. Therapy is a necessary adjunct to modern living as, it seems, are sedative and tranquilizing pills. It is a sign of "progress."

The limitation of therapy arises to some extent from the fact that it belongs to the culture that produces the problems it aims to resolve. Therapy has to help an individual adapt to his culture; it has to help him live and work within that culture. Isolating a person from his culture or setting him up against it can be more destructive. Thus, we are trying to help a person reduce the stress in his life within a cultural situation that subjects him daily to similar stress. It's like telling a person to be calm and relaxed while the guns of war are booming around him, or to stay sane and rational while living in an insane asylum.

In this respect, the modern therapist cannot be compared with the medicine man or witch doctor of primitive society. The latter treated the aberrant individual, one who through witchcraft or the violation of a taboo had become contaminated or possessed by an evil spirit. Restoring his purity allowed him to return to the tribe or community. But how can we therapists restore the purity or innocence of a person when living in his culture exposes him to constant contamination?

To understand contamination in modern terms we should think of purity as innocence. The antithetical relationships are purity-contamination, innocence-guilt. Guilt is the modern equivalent of contamination. The child, like the primitive, lives in the condition of innocence or purity. And, like the primitive, he loses his purity by violating a taboo—the taboo against incestuous feelings for the parent. He is made to feel guilty for having these feelings and the feelings of hostility toward the parent of the same sex. He has no choice but to suppress these feelings and disown them. But feelings that are suppressed continue to exist in the unconscious as dissociated and alien forces. In this sense one can speak of these suppressed impulses as evil spirits. And when we realize that the child's sexual feeling is further contaminated by the input of adult sexuality through the parent's seductive behavior, it is not difficult to understand the connection between contamination-guilt and the loss of innocence-purity.

In one sense the therapeutic undertaking aims to remove guilt and restore innocence or purity. In this respect we therapists are like the medicine man and our methods have much in common with his. The witch doctor recognized that evil spirits are bad feelings (hostility and malevolence) and that these can make a person ill. Bringing these feelings out into the open and discharging them through the maneuvers of the shaman or witch doctor freed the individual and the community from a negative force that had disturbed their well-being. As therapists we try to do the same thing, but since we are unable to bring the community itself directly into the therapeutic process, there is no final resolution of the conflict.

There is also a significant difference between the problem facing the shaman or witch doctor and that confronting the modern therapist. The former dealt with an acute and current situation. The person was sick because an immediate negative or evil force was operating upon him that he could not discharge. He could, however, confront the situation and thereby effectuate a release of his bad feelings indirectly through the medium of the shaman. The therapist has to deal with an old conflict, so old that it has become structured into the personality. The person is not even aware of the conflict; it has become repressed. His dis-ease is chronic. He is no longer even aware of its nature and senses only that he is not well. Almost all the conflicts that create the problems that bring people to therapy occur in infancy and early childhood and are buried in the unconscious. To unearth them we must delve into the unconscious. In contrast, the conflicts with which the shaman dealt were current.

All unconscious emotional conflicts are structured in the body in the form of chronic muscular tensions. These tensions have both a quantitative and a qualitative effect. Qualitatively, they determine how a person will act or behave, with what feelings he will respond to situations. Quantitatively, they determine how much feeling or excitation a person can bring to bear in a given situation. For example, some people have difficulty feeling and expressing anger, while crying is a more available response. Their need is to become aware of their suppressed anger and to express it.

But how much anger does a person have to release before we can say that he has discharged all the repressed anger in his personality? Certainly the experience of anger for a person who has not let himself feel it before is therapeutically helpful. It does not, however, constitute a cure of this problem. One can still discover depths of suppressed anger that remain to be opened up and released. The same thing holds true for the other suppressed feelings. The patient who has not been able to give in to his sadness and through therapy discovers the ability to cry feels an immeasurable expansion of his being. It is as if a door to life has opened for him. But how wide is the opening? How much sadness has he released, and how much sadness remains to be expressed? Fear is another emotion that is strongly suppressed. We cannot afford to be afraid, and so we don't allow ourselves to sense and feel the fear within us. We lower our brows to deny it, set our jaws to defy it, and smile to deceive ourselves. But inwardly we remain scared to death. A therapist can help a patient experience and release some of his fear. To scream in terror, for example, may seem to shatter one's world, but what it really shatters are the shells that enclose and isolate us. Still, one scream doesn't fully free a person, any more than one swallow constitutes springtime. Both are harbingers of more to come. One can ask how deep is the sadness, how pervasive is the fear, how engulfing the anger?

The best answer to this question follows from another set of questions. Why are we sad? What is causing our fear? What is the basis for our anger? To attribute these emotions to past experience is a historical explanation, not a dynamic one. Feelings stem directly from present-day experiences; however, these experiences are conditioned by the past to the degree that the latter has become structured into one's way of being. In this way the past is part of the present. Thus, it is not fully correct to attribute a feeling of sadness to a loss of love in childhood. The sadness stems directly from the experience of a lack of love in the present. If one is fulfilled in the present, the loss of love in childhood would be a memory without an emotional charge. But a loss of love in childhood may cause us, in self-defense, to close our hearts, and so, not able to love, we remain unloved. Are we not really sad because our hearts are closed? In the same way our anger, insofar as it is not connected to a present-day situation, is our reaction to the frustration we experience now because we have been forced to close our hearts and our being. And we are also frightened of our anger because we sense that it could erupt in a destructive rage. It is the limitation of our being that makes us sad and angry and constitutes our fear.

But when an experience in the present is similar to one in the past that we have never worked through, we are in trouble. For example, if we suffer a loss of love as young children, the grief may still be in us. Children cannot properly mourn such losses because they cannot conceive of a replacement. Such a loss could be caused by the death of a parent, by loss of contact with one parent through divorce, or by parental rejection. Such a loss is devastating to a young child unless there is a replacement. The child can only react by denying the loss and living in the fantasy that the parent will return with love. Thus, there is no way to vent the grief and the pain, which become buried in the body. The experience is like a wound that never healed. Perhaps it is better described as an abscess in the personality, which the individual does not feel but which drains his energy. A rejection or disappointment in love in the present touches the wound, resulting in a pain that is both new and old. It seems like the operation of fate.

Such an early trauma that becomes encapsulated in the personality as a chronic abscess is manifested and experienced as despair. It affects the body. One sees it in lackluster eyes, drawn or drooping facial features, hanging shoulders, collapsed chest, contracted abdomen, and overall unaliveness. The loss of love results in a person who feels unlovable and looks unlovely. That's something to be sad about. Until that bodily condition changes, the person has every reason to feel sad and to cry. But in crying for the present, one is also crying about the past. If, as a result of analysis, the present sadness becomes connected to the early loss, the expression of grief through crying and sobbing discharges the abscess and cleans the wound. Healing can now occur.

Feeling unlovable and unlovely, we are afraid to reach out with love, to ask for or demand respect. Fearing a hostile response from people, we do not allow ourselves to speak up freely and be assertive. We hold our natural aggression in check. We shrink back from affirming our being. Or we may become counterphobic and overaggressive to hide our fears. But whether we withdraw or overaggress, our bodies manifest our fear. In the withdrawn state the body is contracted and shrunk inward; in the compensated state it is hard and tight. Both are defensive positions, which by their very nature lead to fear. As long as we are defensive, we are going to be frightened. While it is true that the defensive attitude developed as a result of early life experiences, it is the continued persistence of defensiveness that is causing our present-day fear. Not until the body is freed up from its defensive posture, represented by chronically tight and contracted muscles, can we speak of a release from fear.

We are angry because our being is diminished. We are angry because we feel frightened and unlovely. And our anger is proportionate to our fear, our pain, and the loss of self. Just as we have every reason to be sad about this state of affairs, so we have every reason to be angry. We can lock this anger up in our jaws, shoulders, back, and legs; that is, in all the muscles that can express our anger through biting, hitting, and kicking. But if we do this, we only make ourselves more miserable and thereby increase our anger, which we then have to work hard to keep suppressed. That is the typical vicious circle that closes tighter and tighter upon the life of the person until it kills him. The alternative is to open up and express the suppressed feelings progressively until the body is freed from its tensions and restored to its natural state of grace and loveliness.

Every chronic muscular tension in the body has associated with it sadness, fear, and anger. Since tension is a restriction of our being, it makes us sad. It also makes us angry to be so limited. And we are frightened to show our sadness or express our anger, so we stay locked in a diminished state of being and tied to our fate.

A therapy that aims at enlarging or expanding the state of being must take cognizance of the dynamic or energetic factor. More feeling means more aliveness, more excitation, and more energy in the organism. Tight, contracted bodies cannot tolerate the increased charge or excitation. It threatens the integrity of the personality. Like too much air blown into a small balloon, the charge poses the risk of explosion or bursting, which the person will experience as a fear of dying or going crazy. In the next section I will discuss how we can handle this fear. At this point I want to emphasize that a therapy for being involves a constant working out of the muscular tensions and working through of the underlying emotional conflicts with release of associated feelings.

The pattern of therapy is the reverse of the vicious circle. Each breakthrough of feeling increases the energy or excitation in the organism, which the individual must now learn to tolerate. This is done by integrating the experience into the personality and life of the individual, so that his being is expanded as a result. Thus, each time the person cries or becomes angry, the feeling is deeper and more charged. There is a corresponding enlargement of awareness, even though the problem confronted is not a new one. In fact, we will confront the same problems over and over again, hoping each time to increase the amount of energy and feeling in the process.

In the therapeutic process we go round and round the circle of the individual's life from the past to the present and back to the past again. Each circuit opens up the patient's memories and feelings about the people and events of his past and relates them to his present behavior and situation. When a circuit is completed, the result is greater awareness, deeper feelings, and a higher level of energy. Then the next circuit is undertaken with more energy and awareness. The gradually enlarging circles represent the growth of the personality through the expansion of being. But the process is never completed. One cannot work through all the problems or work out all the tensions. The wounds produced by the traumas of our life may heal, but the scars remain. We cannot return to our original state of innocence. There will always be some limitation upon our being. The human being is an imperfect animal and an inferior god. Nevertheless, the body's tolerance for excitation, especially sexual excitation, and its ability to discharge that excitation through pleasure, specifically, the orgasm, can be significantly increased.

There is another way of looking at the therapeutic process— as if it were an attempt to solve a jigsaw puzzle. We therapists are trying to help a patient make sense out of his life, to see it as a whole. I have said earlier that therapy is a voyage in self-discovery. Unlike a jigsaw puzzle, we don't have all the pieces to start with, but as the therapy progresses, more and more memories become available. Whenever a bit of information fits and locks with neighboring pieces to make the picture clearer, the patient gains insight. He begins to know himself. Although the puzzle is never fully completed, the picture grows in clarity as the therapy proceeds. Knowing his past, a person is in touch with himself, and to be in touch with the self is to be in touch with the body. By reclaiming the past, we reclaim our body. These relationships work in reverse too. Getting in touch with the body gives a person a sense of himself and awakens the memories which have lain dormant in the contracted and immobilized musculature.

Breakthrough and Breakdown

Therapeutic growth does not occur as an upward straight line. There are peaks and valleys in the therapeutic experience. The peak is a breakthrough to a higher level of excitation. The person breaks through one protective shell of his defense and steps forth to a new sense of freedom and light. Or it could be said that the person emerges with a greater awareness of self. The neurosis is a protective shell that insulates but also isolates the individual. Shells don't dissolve. One has to break out of the shell like a newly hatched chick. Similarly, one has to break through the barriers or limits that constrain the self.

A breakthrough may occur in the course of a therapeutic session or as a dream. It is always accompanied by an insight, that is, light is shed upon some dark area of the personality. This light shines through the breach in the shell. In my opinion, therefore, the break comes before the insight, not as a result of the insight. The break is caused by the swelling of life within the container, which is no longer able to hold the excitation or energy and so breaks. In more concrete terms, it is the increased feeling or charge that produces the break, which leads to the insight. No one can predict the time of a breakthrough. It happens spontaneously when sufficient force has been built up inside the self to produce a break in the container. This buildup generally occurs slowly as a result of careful therapeutic work. Here is an example.

Mark is a patient with whom I have been working for two years. Mark is slightly above average height and rather thin. The outstanding features of his expression are deep-set eyes and a lowered brow. His face is sensitive. At times it brightens with a boyish smile; at others the feeling is withdrawn and the eyes look somewhat blank. The tendency to withdraw has been one of Mark's difficulties, and he has made considerable progress in gaining a stronger sense of self. But his being is still quite limited. He has not been able to develop a really satisfactory relationship with any woman. He has been married and divorced twice. I will report two sessions from his therapy because of the breakthroughs that occurred in them.

Mark was standing in front of me. He was aware that he tended to be "in his head" and not enough in his body. He knew that he was afraid to "let go" of his head. He leaned forward on the balls of his feet with his knees slightly bent, and as he let his weight sink into his feet, he could sense his head "letting go." For a moment he felt connected to his body and to the ground. However, his brows did not relax.

I then asked Mark to lie on the bed. I bent over him and with my thumbs pressed moderately under his brows to lift them up. His eyes were focused on mine. When his brows went up, his eyes opened wide and a strong wave of fear went through him. Keeping eye contact with him, I asked Mark what he was afraid of. He said, "I am afraid I am going to break." With these words, he broke into deep sobs and remarked, "I feel connected all over. I feel I am all there."

When his crying was over, we discussed his experience. He said, "It involves my mother and father. I am about three years old. I see my mother in a dressing gown, off-white, shiny like satin. It's like we're in the kitchen, early in the morning. My father has left for work. The scene has the feeling of orange juice and sunshine. I'm in a high chair. I feel very warm, positive, glowing."

I asked Mark, "What is the fear?"

He replied, "I feel something like seductiveness coming from my mother. There's a closeness, an assumption of intimacy. She wants it—a physical intimacy—but I don't. If I reach out, there is nothing there. My mother feels left alone and she's turning to me. I feel her reaching out to me, but if I reach out, I'll get burned, rejected. I'm excited. I would like to touch her, to caress her, to hold her. Then, there's a *gap*. I've been living with this gap all my life. I feel hurt, angry, furious, but I also feel the warmth and the need."

At this point Mark began to sob deeply again, muttering, "Oh, God! Oh, God! Help me."

Mark continued, "By her withdrawal she turns into a witch, that is the feeling of the gap. My God! I just got in touch with my two marriages. I couldn't stand the idea of a woman being fully committed to me, loving. I couldn't stand the closeness and the excitement without any possibility of release or fulfillment. If I could have stood the excitement? But no, I can't stand it. It's too much." And with a look of despair, Mark said, "I had to give it up. It would drive me crazy."

In this session Mark broke through to an awareness of his mother's seductiveness and his sexual excitement in response. He knew that he couldn't stand the excitement because there was no possibility of release. His marriages cracked up on his fear of closeness and intimacy, because these reminded him of the situation with his mother.

When Mark came in for his next session two weeks later, he reported, "The day after our last session, I awoke with a tremendous feeling of liberation. I felt free."

As I looked at him, I noticed that his brows were still down. It seemed that he had a lid on his head and over his eyes, which served to keep his excitement down. "Keep a lid on your feelings." But it also seemed that the lid was a defense against seeing. I asked Mark if he was aware that he didn't want to see.

In response, he related the following dream that he had had two nights before. "I am in a boat going through shallow waters. I go to a beachfront house, where there are many people. I see my mother, who is in the kitchen cooking. She is cutting a lemon.

"The most important part of the dream is her attitude toward me. She is very seductive. Her eyes are bright, and she looks at me with an excitement in them. She peels the lemon and leaves a huge chunk of free lemon [pulp]. I realize that is the way to cook the meal, but I am frightened."

As we discussed the meaning of the dream, Mark realized that the lemon represented his testicles, that his mother was "cutting my balls off."

I asked Mark how his mother related to men. He said:

"She is dependent on them. She makes up to them, but has contempt for them. She wants to trust them, but doesn't. She is furious at them. Feels disappointed by them.

"In the dream I feel cut across my abdomen, eviscerated. I don't know what I am doing at the beach house. I don't see."

The gap referred to an empty space in the jigsaw puzzle. He didn't see the complete picture because one or more pieces was missing. The not seeing is a self-imposed blindness similar to the action of Oedipus in destroying his eyes. A person blocks out a visual scene because it is too frightening or too horrible. Therapy works by getting a patient to see the full picture of his life—we call it gaining insight. What was it my patient didn't see? Strangely, the answer is the same as in the case of Oedipus: the incestuous relationship with the mother.

I asked Mark to describe his feelings toward his mother and, by extension, to all women. He said:

"I keep trying to please them, but I never succeed. I hold myself available, helpful, open, and sensitive to them. I was very trustful of my mother. Then I became afraid of her anger. I have a sense of betrayal. I was furious with her. It was so strong, it immobilized me. My first wife oozed anger like my mother."

After this exchange I had Mark lie over the bioenergetic stool. He began to cry. He felt the pain and rigidity of his lower back. Then he remarked that he felt he could *break* in the region of the lower back.

I asked Mark what thoughts he had about breaking. He said he had two: that he would be lost, and that he would be free. He went on to say that his mother was seductive, but "if you reach out to her with sexual feeling, she would cut you up." That meant evisceration. You lost your guts, your courage. Then Mark added, "Some years ago I felt I had a hole in my belly."

No guts, no balls. Mark now realized that he had been broken. The energetic connections in his body between head and genitals had been broken, and as a result his ego was not grounded in his sexuality. This happened when Mark was little. It made him afraid to reach out to women with his sexuality. To avoid being hurt again, he held back. He immobilized the pelvis by tensing the muscles of the lower back and abdomen. This tension in the muscles of his back produced the rigidity and pain that he felt while lying over the bioenergetic stool. The rigidity in Mark's back was like a splint. His back (spirit) had been broken. Now his back was in a splint to protect it against breaking again, but the defense perpetuated the fear of breaking.

And of women. Since Mark adopts a passive role with women because he dares not be sexually aggressive, he is fated to become involved with women who will assume an overaggressive role in the relationship. But these are angry women who feel they have been betrayed by their fathers, who were, similarly, passive in relation to their mothers. This anger is then projected onto men who are passive. Inevitably, Mark would become involved with women who ooze anger, like his mother.

I described these two sessions with Mark in some detail to show the intimate relationship between breakthrough and breakdown. When Mark confronted his fear of breaking, he was able to see the events in his life that produced the fear. I have heard very many patients express the fear that if they let go, they would break down. In other words, to break through is to risk a breakdown. It is like birth. When a baby is being born, he has no guarantee that he will make it successfully into the world. Some get caught with the umbilical cord coiled around the neck and die. There is always some risk in life, but ordinarily it is minimal. Lying over the bioenergetic stool as Mark did can evoke the fear of breaking in a person with a rigid back, but I have never seen a back break.

However, something does break. The person's resistance to the expression of feeling breaks. Generally, there is a giving in to the pain and sadness, and the person breaks down into tears and sobs. Sometimes the person breaks out with feelings of anger that were long suppressed. In all cases there is a breakdown of the control that the person developed as a defense in those childhood situations where the expression of feeling was dangerous. There is also a breakdown of the façade that was erected to protect the sensitive being of the individual. But since the ego is identified with the control, the will, and the façade, the person sees the breakdown as a danger.

The fear of breakdown is most pronounced whenever the character structure of the patient is challenged. This is because that structure developed as a defense against breakdown. The resistance the patient puts up to this challenge is insurmountable unless one understands the fear that motivates it.

W. D. Winnicott, who studied this problem in his patients, defined the threat to the patient as a fear of the "breakdown of the establishment of the unit self."[2] We would say, in simpler language, a disintegration of ego organization. In lay language, a breakdown means a psychotic break. We should know, therefore, that underlying the fear of letting go is also the fear of insanity.

I pointed out in the preceding chapter that the fear of insanity arises when the ego is flooded or overwhelmed by excitation or feeling. Yet this must happen if expansion of being or growth is to occur. The snake sheds its skin, the crab discards its shell in the process of growth. And we humans must break out of old structures if we are to grow. During the transition the organism is vulnerable. There is a risk. But all organisms accept vulnerability and risk in the nature of the living process. Why are our patients so frightened?

2. W. D. Winnicott, "Fear of Breakdown," *International Review of Psychoanalysis* 1 (1974): 103.

Winnicott has the answer to this question. He says that the "clinical fear of breakdown is *the fear of a breakdown that has already been experienced.*" He then goes on to say, "It is a fact that is carried round hidden away in the unconscious."[3] The significance of this observation becomes apparent when we apply it to all life situations. As the saying goes, "Once burned, twice shy." A child is not afraid of a hot stove until he gets burned. If a birth experience was traumatic in the sense that there was a threat to the child's life, then any situation that calls for birth or emergence would be viewed with terror.

The question, raised at the beginning of this book, is, Why do we learn from some traumatic experiences and not others? No child who has touched a hot stove repeats the experience. Neurotics, as we have seen, repeat the same traumas again and again. If the experience of a breakdown is buried in the unconscious, it is also projected into the future. The ego defense system that was erected in the past to deny the trauma and to serve as a safeguard against a future recurrence of the event becomes the magnet that attracts the experience it is designed to avoid. This is what I described as the operation of fate.

It is easy to explain this with regard to the fear of breakdown. The energy invested in the defense system decreases the body's tolerance for excitation. Defense means structure rather than movement. It represents a frozen state rather than a mobile one. It diminishes the amount of excitation and feeling, hoping thereby to prevent the flooding that could overwhelm the ego and produce a breakdown. It reduces being to protect being. However, this diminution of being evokes the fear of breakdown, because the organism strives to expand its life or being to its full potential. The body is life oriented and seeks to increase its state of excitation even at the risk of overwhelming the frightened ego. This could easily lead to a vicious circle in which every effort to expand is countered by an increase of the defensive structure.

3. Ibid., p. 104.

This is the opposite of the growth cycle described above. Without some change in a person's character, his being, is constantly shrinking to the point where a breakdown is inevitable. The breakdown can be in the form of a somatic illness as well as a mental one.

To be fully alive is to let one's self be carried away by a flood of feeling. It provides a moving or a peak experience. It is an orgastic-type response. But such intense emotional reactions should not be too common. If one is constantly being flooded by an overwhelming excitation, one's boundaries become vague and the self becomes nebulous. One becomes confused about one's identity, and psychosis is near. Weak egos are particularly vulnerable. A stronger ego can support and contain a higher level of excitation without losing its boundaries. But even a relatively strong ego can be flooded or overwhelmed if the intensity of the feeling increases greatly. A healthy ego can allow itself to be momentarily submerged by a flood of feeling without any damage. Every river occasionally floods and overflows its banks. If it does this permanently, the banks are destroyed and we have a lake, not a river. But a lake is static, whereas a river is flowing. It is one of the contradictions of life that a flow has to be contained to maintain the movement.

These considerations suggest that when a patient gives up his defensive position, he will experience some sense of being mad or crazy. Of course going "crazy" on demand isn't real insanity, but it comes close enough to make the patient aware that the fear of breakdown is real, that there are suppressed feelings in the personality that threaten the ego, and that one can cross the line from rationality to irrationality and return again without danger. The arousal of strong feelings in a borderline patient whose ego is weak can result in a temporary "break." He can "flip out" if the excitation becomes too strong. This poses no danger to the patient if the therapist is aware of that possibility, doesn't panic, and can stay with the patient until the excitation subsides. When that happens, the patient becomes fully rational again. Through the experience he has opened up some strong feelings, which can then be integrated into his personality, strengthening his ego and expanding his being. In this way the patient increases his tolerance for excitation and feeling and decreases the likelihood of a future breakdown.

Breakthrough and breakdown are never far apart in therapy, since some breakdown of ego defenses has to occur for the breakthrough to take place. However, the breaking down of ego defenses is not a legitimate aim of therapy. Such defenses are to be respected unless one can help the patient develop a more effective way of coping with life stresses. The breakdown is valid only if it leads to a breakthrough. This involves the development of insight and the integration of the new feelings into the personality. Integration means accepting the feelings and expressing them with full ego cooperation.

One of my patients cannot scream in the sessions. However, she screams at home against her husband and her children. It is a hysterical reaction, expressed against her will, and her ego is dissociated from the action. She doesn't want to scream, but feels provoked into it. She said, "When I scream, I feel like a maniac. It wipes me out." It makes her feel crazy. Yet she needs to scream to release the terror in her being. She was terrorized as a child and thus has every reason to scream. Integration required that she accept the fact that inwardly she was a screaming maniac. She had been overwhelmed by her terror and it had driven her crazy. *The breakdown had occurred.* Once this acceptance was made, she could no longer be "wiped out." She could retain her identity as a person who had been terrorized and driven to the point of being a screaming maniac. What was wiped out previously was her false identity, namely, that of a calm and rational being. This false identity was a denial of her being, which increased her vulnerability to and fear of a breakdown.

In the average neurotic patient, the fear of breakdown is hidden behind a seemingly secure and stable ego. If one asks such a patient if he ever thought he could go crazy, the answer generally is no. But this answer is belied by his problem. Every neurotic has suppressed feelings that could flood and overwhelm his ego if they arose with their full intensity. To put it simply, every patient could go "mad" and is afraid of "going mad" if he "let go" fully to feelings. He retains his sanity by keeping the level of excitation within tolerable limits, and he maintains a close guard upon his feelings to make sure that these limits are not exceeded. Relying upon this control, he may be quite convinced that he has no fear of insanity. But the defense itself betrays the underlying fear. One erects defenses only if one is afraid.

Behavior that is too rational (relatively devoid of feeling) or too controlled (lacking spontaneity) may be suspected of covering an underlying fear of insanity. The person cannot let go fully and freely to his feelings, and so his being is severely limited. In such a case one may have to encourage the patient to act a *little* crazy. That means letting go of the head, losing one's head, or "going out of one's mind."

I use several simple exercises to help a patient approach this state so that he can become aware of the fear. The exercise has to be appropriate to the patient and to his immediate situation. For example, with one young man whose muscular holding pattern expressed the sense of "leave me alone," the exercise involved kicking the bed, banging the fists, and yelling, "Leave me alone." In the course of this exercise, I asked him to shout the words, "You're driving me crazy." After he did so, he turned to me and said, "By God, that's true. She nagged me so much she drove me to the wall." He then went on to describe an aspect of his mother that explained his personality. "She was so confused that I didn't know what was truth. I could never reach her with logic or reason. I armored myself against her insanity and my possible insanity." When I asked him what his possible insanity would be, he said, "I would go mad and kill her, murderously mad. But I was always sure that it would never happen to me." Then he added, sadly, "I know now why I can never let my anger explode. I'm really afraid I'd go crazy."

If we follow Winnicott's argument, the fear of a mental breakdown implies that such a breakdown has happened in the past. One locks the stable door after the horse is stolen, not before. This seeming contradiction is explained by the idea that if no theft has ever occurred, there would be no need, nor even the thought, to lock the door. One does not erect a defense against an inconceivable danger. It is important for the patient to realize that a breakdown has occurred, that his defense is as much a denial of this fact as it is a safeguard against a possible future breakdown. For, as we have seen, the defense itself predisposes the individual to this possibility.

The breakdown as it occurred in the past was overcome by an effort of will. It had been experienced as a sense of confusion, a feeling of being overwhelmed, and a loss of boundaries. The person felt he was falling apart. It was terrifying. He pulled himself together through his will, and he continues to hold himself together as a defense against the fear of falling apart or feeling confused and overwhelmed by life. The will operates through the voluntary musculature contracting the relevant muscles to provide the necessary control. The above patient remarked, "I realize that I struggled to keep my head straight. That helps me understand why my neck muscles are so overdeveloped."

Another exercise is for the patient to bang his head against the bed, using the words, "I can't stand it. You're driving me crazy." Or, "I can't stand it. I'll go out of my mind." These are rather common expressions that one can hear ordinary people say. In my opinion, they reflect the understanding represented by language. Any feeling that is too intense for the organism to tolerate threatens the person's sanity. One can go out of one's mind with pain, fear, sorrow, or even desire. If the ego is flooded and its boundaries destroyed, the result is confusion and a loss of self-possession and orientation As the individual attempts to contain the feeling, the tension becomes unbearable. It has to be relieved, even if sanity is temporarily abandoned. At this point children bang their heads. It is a way of breaking the tension in the back of the neck. When patients do this exercise they sense the tension in the back of the neck and become aware of a feeling that they have to stand it, even though the situation is tormenting. Not to stand it is to go crazy. It often becomes clear to the patient what the torment was.

One young man described the torment as follows: "My mother looked at me with pleading eyes, as if she expected me to save her. At the same time, there was something seductive in her glance. I felt that saving her meant having sex with her. I was excited and terrified. It was a torment. I didn't dare respond to her, but I couldn't get away from her." It almost drove him out of his mind. To prevent this breakdown he went "dead." He is one of the cases I described in the preceding chapter.

To expose this fear in neurotic patients, I often ask them if they ever felt or thought they would go crazy. Some will recall a situation when this fear was conscious. One woman related two such experiences. The second occurred when she was thirty years old. She related: "I fell in love with a priest. The feeling of excitement in my body was very intense. It was a sexual feeling, and I couldn't express it to him. I lay in bed feeling the energy clawing inside my skin trying to get out. I couldn't release it. Then I began to feel very frightened and despairing. I thought I would slip, have a nervous breakdown. I prayed to God for help."

This patient had been brought up with a very strict religious training. She had never touched her body, she said, until she was twenty-two or twenty-three. She was referring to a sensual touch, of course. She didn't know how to masturbate and so had no way of relieving herself. In such conditions a very strong and persistent feeling of sexual love could drive a person out of his mind.

The first incident had happened when she was in a religious school away from home. She remarked that she was hated by both the principal and her superior. She was suffering from chronic appendicitis, but she was forced to stay at her studies. "I was under a great strain. I weighed ninety pounds. It was the lowest point of my life. Then I had an acute attack and got to the hospital, which was run by the sisters. After I was operated on, I stayed in the hospital one month. I wasn't allowed to see anyone. I was frightened and helpless. I couldn't do anything for myself. I felt I could break down."

This patient never did become psychotic, and I doubt that she would. Her ego had a strength that would enable it to hold under the greatest strain. But she was not invulnerable. If she was pushed to the wall, she said she would prefer to die. Death was preferable to insanity. And, in fact, there was a hint of death in the darkness around her eyes. She didn't crack up in the hospital, because she resigned herself to death. Luckily, she wasn't pushed that far. But she was pushed far enough to see death's face.

There is a dynamic relationship between death and insanity, physical death and psychic death. If an organism is overwhelmed by any intense excitation, the boundaries of the self are inundated and dissolve; without boundaries the self does not exist. Insanity may be called a form of psychic death, the death of the self or ego. This also happens at the full height of the orgasm, if one reaches that height. The ego or self disappears momentarily. If we are frightened of being overwhelmed, we will suppress our feeling and our excitement. The greater the fear, the more the suppression. But the suppression of feeling and excitement is death, a death of the body by congelation. We are equally frightened by that specter.

Castration Anxiety

Freud pointed out that we avoid the fate of Oedipus by suppressing our sexual feelings for our mothers and giving up our hostility to our fathers. We take this action because of the threat of castration. Having submitted to this cultural demand, we now become well-adjusted citizens: going to school, marrying the proper girl, and supporting the established order. And we repress our memory of that period, which means that we deny our submission under the threat of castration. If we have children, we will repeat the same process with them to make sure that the culture continues to make progress.

If this system worked well there would be no complaints. But there are complaints. For example, a woman, married about ten years, is unhappy about her relationship with her husband. Their sexual life has deteriorated over the years. She says that when they married, she was eager for the promised sexual intimacy and excited about the sexual pleasure she could now enjoy. They had sexual relations the first night. The next morning when she awoke she turned to her husband with excitement and anticipation, but he rebuffed her, saying, "Don't pressure me." Her honeymoon, she remarked, was a nightmare. From then on, there was always some tension between them about sex.

What anxiety prevented her husband from fully enjoying the sexual pleasure that was available to him? Was it a fear of success? Or, like so many men, did he become frightened when his wife became the sexual aggressor? By taking the initiative, she reminded him of his mother, and suddenly she became the forbidden fruit.

Next, I am consulted by a man who is depressed because he is overweight and his wife is losing her sexual interest in him. Theirs is a second marriage for each. It began on a note of romance and excitement several years ago. The marriage seemed to change their lives. My patient said he lost weight, felt younger and more enthusiastic. But after a few years the excitement dimmed somewhat. He began to overeat and couldn't control it. In this first session he told me that he had had seven years of psychoanalytic treatment previously, five times a week, which he felt had helped him considerably. It had enabled him to terminate a rather unsatisfactory marriage. He believed that it had freed him from his neurosis, and he was somewhat shocked to find himself depressed. To help him get some movement going in his body, I suggested that he throw up each morning.

The idea of throwing up may seem strange to readers unfamiliar with bioenergetic therapy. It is one of our standard procedures. It serves two important purposes. First, it helps a person "get it out." Many people hold in their feelings. They choke off the expression. Throwing up breaks through this "holding in" pattern. Second, it opens the throat and therefore facilitates the expression of feeling. This exercise is done in the morning before breakfast. The person drinks two full glasses of water so that the stomach will have something to contract on. Then he touches the back of his mouth with his thumb to induce the gag reflex, while bending over the toilet bowl. If one breathes out deeply before gagging, the expulsion of the fluid will generally occur easily. It is important to exhale deeply while doing this exercise, since it relaxes the diaphragm. In no event should one force the expulsion. It should come up easily. One shouldn't try to get all the water out. Several good regurgitations are sufficient.

When my patient returned two weeks later, he reported, "I started to do the vomiting that you suggested. Since then I've had many nightmares."

This is not a common consequence of throwing up. I've been using this technique myself off and on for more than thirty years, and it has not affected me that way. I do it regularly even now.

He continued, "In one dream, I was watching a show on TV. It was like a National Geographic special. I was looking at a scene in which a predator captures a prey. The prey is paralyzed with terror before being eaten. As I watch the picture, it keeps getting bigger and bigger as if I were being drawn into it. Then it changed. The predator became a primitive-type Stone Age man about seven or eight feet tall, who had seized a small civilized man. He took a sledgehammer and with some quick blows broke the bones of the man's right arm. The arm hung as if paralyzed. Then the primitive man took out the eyes of his victim and then bit his head as if to bite it off. I had the feeling he wanted to eat his brains. I was horrified. I couldn't scream. I woke myself up in a state of sweat and fear."

My patient recognized immediately that the dream expressed

his castration anxiety. He identified with the small civilized man and realized that the big primitive man was his father. I might add that my patient was himself a psychoanalyst and so was quite familar with these ideas. He remarked that in the course of his previous analysis he had discussed the question of his castration anxiety. However, it had never arisen so vividly as in this dream.

This patient had a lot of tension about his pelvis. The pelvic area was flattened out and tight, while a roll of fat hung over it from above. It appeared as if a ring of constriction encircled the lower abdomen at the level of the iliac crests. No breathing movements entered the lower abdomen, which seemed cut off from the rest of the body.

I had the patient lie on the floor over a rolled-up blanket that was placed under his lower back. With feet placed against each other and knees apart, the pelvic area was exposed. This position will often bring out a patient's fear and shame. My patient felt neither, but when I placed my thumbs in his groin and pressed moderately against the tense muscles, he almost jumped out of his skin. It wasn't that painful, he said, just frightening. Whenever he felt the pressure of my thumbs in that area, especially if I moved them slightly, he yelled as if . . . as if I were going to do some terrible thing to him there.

When we discussed his experience, he said that he was astonished that he had such fear. He thought that he had talked it out during analysis. But he admitted that he had never felt the fear until now. Castration anxiety was just an idea before. He was a little angry at the time that he had lost in analysis, but then he realized that it had served its purpose. He left this session profoundly shaken up.

I saw him again several weeks later. He had continued to overeat due to his anxiety. He did not feel depressed. He was too sad and frightened for that. He knew he had a problem on the body level that had to be worked out physically (reduce the tension in the pelvic area) if he was to fully enjoy his sexuality.

We repeated the exercise described above several times. At the beginning he yelled and jumped as soon as I touched him. But he quickly discovered that if he breathed deeply and relaxed his pelvis, the fear diminished and the pain almost disappeared. He was quite surprised to learn that his panic resulted not from what I did but from what he believed I might do. It became evident that tensing his muscles in anticipation of hurt made them painful to pressure, whereas when they were relaxed, he felt the pressure without any pain. We all have to learn that tension is fear.

Having experienced the great amount of fear he had about being castrated, my patient wondered where it came from. He did not recall his father as a violent man. He had been a good boy, doing everything that was expected of him. He admitted that he and his mother were very close and he saw that his father could have been jealous. Not only my patient but his parents played into the denial of any sexual implication in their relationships, which only increased the child's fear. He could see that such a situation could create a fear of sexual feeling.

As we worked through this problem during the session, my patient began to laugh and feel gleeful. As a result of this and another exercise, his pelvis was becoming charged. His legs were vibrating. The lower part of his body felt alive. He said that he felt as if a great weight had been lifted off him. He felt a sense of liberation. He had broken through to a deeper sense of being.

Working with castration anxiety through this technique is not the answer to all of a patient's problems. However it is the key problem as the oedipal conflict is the key conflict in the arch of the personality. The failure to achieve a breakthrough on this level means that all other work on the personality remains superficial.

I worked with another psychiatrist some years ago who complained of being depressed. He, too, had had many years of psychoanalysis. When his therapy with me was drawing to a close and his depression had completely lifted, he commented on his experience with me. "You were not afraid of my contempt for you. The other analysts were." He felt superior to them. Being one of them, he could see their personal problems, which they tried to hide behind the professional mask. It was a repeat of his oedipal situation in which he felt superior to his father. But the analysts never challenged his attitude and so the analysis failed. For he, too, had been able to hide behind the façade of psycho-analytic language. In the bioenergetic therapy with me, he was undressed. I saw a big fat body with a round face like an over-sized baby. His pelvic area was tight and contracted. In this case, as in many others, contempt is used to cover up one's own sense of inadequacy.

He also said that I had helped him get over his castration anxiety. When I pressed on the insertion of the thigh muscles into his pelvis, it was painful, but he also was aware that he was frightened. He felt the tension and tried to "let go" to my pres-sure. In this position, letting go means breathing deeply and pushing the pelvis downward against the floor. This maneuver relaxes the thigh muscles, and the pain diminishes or disappears. Another part of his comment was, "Through what you did, I was able to feel that you weren't going to hurt me and my anxiety left."

Most men are not aware of having any castration anxiety. In fact, they are not aware of the tension in and around the pelvic floor. The lack of awareness is due to a lack of feeling. The area is relatively dead; only the penis is alive. And as long as they are erectively potent, they assume they have no sexual problems. Performance is their criterion of sexual health. That all their sexual feeling is limited to the penis doesn't strike them as odd because they know no different. The lovely melting sensation in the pelvis that is preorgastic and the streaming sensations follow-ing orgasm are unknown. Their body does not take part in the sexual response. But just this condition constitutes castration, for the feeling in the penis is cut off or not connected to any feeling in the body.

When the sexual excitation is restricted to the penis, the man's sexuality is very limited. His being or masculinity is equally reduced. In his relations with women, he will often complain that they are castrating him. He will accuse them of "cutting off his balls." But the fact is that he is already relatively castrated psychologically. No woman wants to or can castrate a real man. His anxiety in this situation reflects an event that happened in the past. Only by reliving that event emotionally can one become free of the anxiety associated with it.

What about castration anxiety in women? We have seen that the girl child is subject to the same conflicts as her brother. She is part of a triangle that includes her parents and in which she is an object of the sexual interest of the father and the jealousy and hostility of her mother. The castration that results is both psychological and physiological. On the former level it is a sense of guilt and shame about sexual feeling. On the latter level it consists of muscular tensions in the pelvic area that reduce the amount of sexual feeling. Castration consists in the severance of the connection between the ego and sexuality, between the pelvis and the upper half of the body, and in the loss of aliveness and motility in the pelvis.

Here is a case. Claire is a rather heavy girl aged twenty-seven years. She is depressed and feels unable to go out into the world. Yet she is talented and believes she could do quite well. The outstanding feature of her body is the heaviness of her hips and thighs. They look big, even massive, but unalive. Strangely, her lower leg below the knee is shapely. Her face is round and soft, its expression one of weakness and helplessness. However, she is not unattractive. Claire had several years of therapy previously, some of it with a bioenergetic therapist who had failed to touch her problem.

What was her problem? To put it bluntly, it was to get her ass moving. The meaning of this expression is to get up and get going, which she needed to do. But it was also literal. Her heavy ass was like an anchor that prevented her from moving. She was bogged down in her ass. Interpreted bioenergetically, the heaviness and bigness of her ass represented the accumulation and stagnation of energy. Fat is accumulated energy. In her case, it was energy associated with sexual feelings that accumulated over the years and was locked and held in the pelvis. Moving the ass or pelvis is a sexual expression and would, therefore, be possible when the guilts and anxieties attached to such expression were removed.

When I asked Claire about her sexual feelings, she said, "If I look sexual or attractive or show any sexual feelings, it leaves me open to being raped. I feel guilty about my sexuality. People can see that I masturbate, they can tell that I'm dirty, perverse. With men I've never been able to say no, to stand up for what I want." If she goes out with a man, she lets herself be used sexually. At this point she has enough sense to stay away from men.

Where did Claire get such a feeling about herself? What happened in her childhood to put her in this position? It is, of course, the task of therapy to help Claire gain some insight into this problem, to *see* what had transpired in her early life. Since seeing is a function of the eyes, I asked Claire, when she was lying on the bed, to open her eyes wide and look at the ceiling. As she did this, I held her forehead with my left hand and pressed with two fingers on her occiput opposite the visual centers in the brain. This procedure has some effect in releasing visual blocks.[4] Claire reacted dramatically.

She screamed and said she saw her father. "He is bending over me watching me like I am an insect, a thing. I feel that I am a baby lying in the crib. He's looking at my crotch, like he's curious. I don't understand why he is looking at me like that. I am afraid he's going to put his fingers in me, so I lie very still. I won't be able to stop him because he's so big. I feel paralyzed, but I'm also anxious."

This image is significant because it points to the root of her

4. See Alexander Lowen, *Bioenergetics* (New York: Coward, McCann & Geohegan, Inc., 1975), pp. 291–296 for full description.

trouble. Since her infancy she experienced her father as having a sexual interest in her. He regarded her as a sexual object. That became quite obvious later.

Claire was an only child. How did her mother react to her? To learn that answer I then asked Claire to look at me with wide-open eyes. She assumed the expression of fear and said that my eyes looked like her mother's. "What expression do you see in them?" I asked. "Like she wanted to kill me. She was always looking at me like that. I never knew what I did that made her hate me."

In female patients the fear of being killed or destroyed by the mother is quite common. It is the specific form of castration anxiety in the woman, whereas in a man the fear is related to an injury to the genitals by the father. Young girls fear injury to the genitals by the father if he would attempt to have intercourse with them.

Claire continued to describe her home situation. "I caused trouble. When I was older, I felt that I took him away from her. After I was thirteen, my parents never slept together. He dropped my mother and turned to me. I became his mistress. I took care of him." However, there were no sexual relations between father and daughter.

She remarked that her father was unconsciously obsessed with sex. "He looked at me with a leer on his face. Whenever a man looks at my breasts or vagina with that look, I feel like killing him."

I gave Claire a tennis racquet, and she began to hit the bed with it violently. With each blow she said, "I'll smash you, I'll kill you first." I asked who she would kill and she answered, "Both of them."

Claire was as full of suppressed anger as she was of suppressed sexual feeling. Frightened of both these strong feelings, she felt depressed and suicidal. A paralysis seemed to overtake her, which she had to use all her will to fight.

The best way to fight the paralysis was to get some movement going in her body and pelvis. She lay on the floor over a rolled-up blanket. In this position she said she felt vulnerable. "I feel I am going to be gang raped. I never had a boyfriend when I was young."

This was the second time in the session that Claire spoke of being raped. It made me think it might be something she wanted. I asked her about that. She said, "I wish they would get it over with. I want it and I'm afraid of it." She wasn't referring to rape; she was speaking about sex. She was tormented by her sexual feelings and ready to explode, but she was also paralyzed by fear and couldn't move. It had to be done to her so she could get a release. Unconsciously she wanted to be raped.

This was the situation Claire had been in all her life—sexually excited by her father's seductive behavior but terrified and unable to respond. Out of his own guilt her father also rejected her. Whenever she complained to him about her mother's attitude toward her, he would say, "She's your mother and she wouldn't hurt you. But she always hurt me. She was crazy."

When I pressed on the tense muscles at the junction of thigh and pelvis, Claire screamed. Some vibration began in the pelvis. She remarked, "I'm scared. I feel I'm going to melt and I wouldn't be able to hold myself up." I pointed out to her that her fear of the strong sexual excitation was that she would yield and have sexual relations with her father. She understood that anxiety.

We repeated the procedure. Again, she screamed with fear when I first touched her. Then she began to cry, deeply. The sobs went through her body and into her pelvis, which moved upward with each sob spontaneously. Each sob was a pulse of life in her body. She was crying softly and deeply like a mother who finds a lost child. She was crying because she had found her sexuality (for the moment) and with it her being.

The session finished with Claire feeling alive and hopeful. But much more work had to be done in the same vein to maintain the pulse of life in her body so that she would be connected to her sexuality. She had been castrated by the loss of this connection.

Fortunately, she was aware of what had happened, and so it was possible to have such a dramatic session.

Every patient feels good when the pelvis or ass comes alive. By alive, I mean that there is feeling and spontaneous movement in the pelvis with breathing. The more the pelvis comes alive, the stronger is the overall feeling. I recall one young woman patient who had confronted her oedipal problem. We had just completed the exercise described above. She was crying softly, her pelvis flooding with feeling. It was vibrating intensely. Then she exclaimed, "I'm so happy! I'm so happy!" I could understand her joy (her pelvis was literally jumping for joy). She had recovered her sexuality and found her being.

6 / A Heroic Attitude to Life

Regression and Progression

My focus upon the key role of the oedipal conflict in shaping character should not be taken to mean that preoedipal problems are unimportant and ignored in bioenergetic therapy. The events of infancy and early childhood have an enormous influence upon personality development and character formation. For simplicity in discussion I will group these early events under the heading of oral experiences. The term "oral" refers to the period when the mouth is the principal organ of relationship with the world. It also refers to those functions concerned with taking in nourishment, love, support, and excitation. Broadly speaking, the oral period covers the first three years of life.

From the ages of three to six years the focus of personality development is upon the growth of independence and the establishment of genital primacy. Although a six-year-old child is still dependent upon his parents for support and protection, his basic character is pretty much formed. Though an immature organism in many respects, he is ready to take some steps into the outer world with the support of the family. He will go to school or be schooled for his position in society. We can label the years from three to six as the genital period, since they are critical for the development of sexual identity. This period includes the time when the oedipal conflict arises and finds some resolution.

In contrast to psychoanalytic thinking, I don't believe there is an anal stage of personality development. However, most people in our culture have anal problems because of the nature of the training in excremental cleanliness that they underwent as children. Constipation and hemorrhoids are the common physical disturbances that could be produced by tension from traumatic experiences related to this function. On the psychological level character traits such as parsimony, obstinacy, and a compulsion to exaggerated cleanliness have been identified as resulting from a too early and too severe toilet-training program. Anxiety about anal functioning must affect genital functioning, since the two areas are in such close proximity. If the pelvic floor is pulled up and contracted because of a fear of soiling, it will inhibit the person from letting go fully in the sexual act. Also, some people have an anal fixation; the anus and buttocks become an eroticized area because their parents invested too much energy and feeling in the child's anal functioning. None of this, however, justifies the assumption of an anal stage in personality development as a natural or biological fact. Training a child is a cultural problem in those societies and for those people who regard the excretory functions as a source of shame. Together with sexuality these functions are the clearest manifestation of man's basic animal nature.

The character of an individual and his fate are determined by all his experiences. However, those of childhood starting from the moment of conception to the end of the oedipal period between six and seven years of age are most important, because the personality is most impressionable during these early years. The manner in which the oedipal conflict is resolved pretty much "sets" the structure of the person's character. However, the events in the preoedipal period from birth to three years of age are equally important in shaping character, though they do not determine its final form. Actually, the quality of a child's experiences in the oral stage are not very different from the quality of its experiences in the genital stage, since the parents are the same. Loving parents do not become hateful as the child grows, nor do hostile parents become affectionate. In their effect upon a child's character, it is not so much what the parents do as who they are. Children identify with their parents and unconsciously absorb their values and attitudes. The children of sexually healthy parents tend to be sexually healthy themselves.

What happens in the oral stage or preoedipal period foreshadows and conditions the problems that will develop later in the genital stage. The mother who cannot accept an infant's need to nurse will not be able to accept the child's need to express its sexuality. And the mother who becomes genitally excited by her child's nursing may find herself incestuously involved with that child as it grows older.

To understand the relationship between the two periods and how the earlier affects the later, we have to know the dynamics of the oral period. In primitive societies the child is breast fed throughout this period, a minimum of three years. Nursing fulfills all of a child's oral needs, providing it with nourishment, love, support, and excitement. It also satisfies the physiological need of the infant to suck. Sucking the breast stimulates the baby's respiration and promotes a deep breathing that fills the lower abdomen with energy and feeling. Nursing also gives the child the physical contact with the body of its mother that is essential to the child's ability to feel its own body. How many children in our culture have had the opportunity to enjoy this kind of closeness to their mother?

I do not believe that bottle feeding fulfills all the oral needs of a child. Even if babies are held while being bottle fed, they are deprived of the exciting contact between the mouth and the breast. This contact is as important to the young child as sexual contact is to an adult. Reich believed that babies experience a mouth orgasm when the nursing is fully satisfying. Whether this is true or not, the baby who is nursed to sleep shows in its face and body a peace and contentment that are beautiful to see. Many children are not held while they feed, which reduces the time of body contact between mother and baby. As a result of the lack of breast feeding, most children in our culture are orally deprived. This means that there is an emptiness in their bodies and in their personalities. Since their oral needs have not been fulfilled, they are not fully filled.

It may be difficult to see that our babies are inwardly empty when they look so well fed. In fact, they are overfed on solid foods, increasing their mass or bulk but not their energy. Breast-fed infants do not gain weight like babies who are bottle fed and eat solid food in the early months of life. But our pride in the weight gain of our infants changes to chagrin when it continues into their adolescent years. We also take pride in the fact that each freshman class in college is taller and heavier on average than the preceding class. As a people, we Americans are getting bigger and heavier, but I don't believe that this increase in size and weight is a manifestation of more health. Actually, our heaviness is a matter of concern to physicians, for we have become an overweight society. I see a direct relation between heaviness and a lack of energy in people. This lack is manifested in their complaints about chronic fatigue and in their inability to sustain the kind of physical effort in work that our parents and grandparents could.

A severe lack of oral fulfillment leads to the development of an oral character structure; if less severe, to oral tendencies in the personality. The body of a person with an oral character structure is, typically, long and thin with an underdeveloped musculature

(Sheldon's ectomorph type[1]). The legs are always thin and rigid, while the feet are narrow and weak. In most cases the arches of one or both feet are collapsed. Since development in the child is caudalward, that is, from the head downward, a lack of fulfillment is manifested by a weakness or lack of development of the lower part of the body. Psychologically, one finds in this personality a diminished aggressive drive, which correlates with the underdeveloped musculature and dependent needs related to the weakness in the legs. The individual with this character structure seeks to be taken care of, he looks for someone to give him what his mother failed to provide. He does not stand on his own feet psychologically or literally. However, in many cases the weakness in the legs is compensated for by an exaggerated rigidity, which allows the person to assume a position of independence but which collapses under stress or in a crisis. A dominant aspect of the personality is fear of being alone or being abandoned. These traits are less pronounced where the character contains oral tendencies in a different character structure.

An individual with an oral character structure is subject to mood swings of elation and depression. The latter is pathognomic, that is, the typical symptom of oral deprivation in any personality. Elation occurs when the person finds someone who he believes will fulfill his oral needs—be a mother to him. Or he will become elated when he thinks the situation will provide fulfillment. This is an illusion, since no person or situation can fill the inner emptiness of an adult. No amount of sucking on a breast can provide the milk that the person needed as an infant. When the illusion collapses, as it inevitably does, the person becomes depressed. In time he will emerge from his depression with a new hope that will develop into another phase of elation, which, in turn, will collapse into a new depressive reaction.

The effect of oral deprivation is to fixate the individual upon the oral stage of development. This means that he is always look-

1. W. H. Sheldon, *The Varieties of Human Physique* (New York: Harper and Brothers, 1940).

ing to get, to be fulfilled by others. His sexuality will be oriented in the same direction. Most important to him is the feeling of closeness and contact, and the sense of being loved rather than loving. He will, therefore, seek to prolong the sexual act so as not to lose the contact. This maneuver, however, reduces the intensity of a climax that is already weak because of the person's low energy level. In this character, orgastic potency is low. Yet it is only through deep sexual satisfaction that the oral character can be fulfilled as an adult. To achieve such satisfaction, the person's energy level must be raised and his sexual problems worked through.

Unfortunately, oral deprivation in a child leads to a heightened oedipal conflict. When a deprived child turns to the parent of the opposite sex with sexual interest, it is also seeking the fulfillment of its oral needs. The desire for closeness and contact with this parent has a double motivation, oral and sexual. Of the two, the former is the stronger because it is related to survival. So the child, like an adult with unfulfilled oral needs, will use its sexuality to entice the parent into physical closeness to get the warmth and support it needs. But this sexual enticement, done innocently, is effective only if the parent responds.

The fact is that parents do respond with their own sexual feelings and desires. There are several reasons for this parental response. The flirtation between parent and child is exciting to the parent and yet seemingly devoid of serious consequences. No actual sex is contemplated. And the ego of the parent is inflated by the interest and admiration of the child. Such parents were psychologically castrated as children and, therefore, feel a need for this kind of support. Thus, a father will turn to his daughter for an affirmation of his manhood that he does not get from his wife. The wife and mother is put into the position of being the unappreciative and derogatory person against whom father and daughter form an unholy alliance. This, of course, infuriates the woman, increasing her contempt for her husband and her hostility toward her daughter.

The exact same process is acted out by mothers with their sons.

Feeling unappreciated by their husbands, frightened of sexual feelings and unable to have a full orgasm, they turn to their sons for an affirmation of their womanhood and sexuality. How can the boy resist? He was deprived of contact with his mother on the oral level and is now offered it on the sexual level. Of course, it is only an offer. There is no intention on the mother's part to consummate the relationship sexually. Nevertheless, the boy is both terrified and excited at the possibility. With her young son, the mother acts like a little girl again: coquettish, playful, teasing, etc. The father is furious and contemptuous. He knows that his wife is partially frigid, yet he sees her acting with his son like a most erotic female. His fury, however, is directed at the boy. Why doesn't he direct it against his wife? He can't, because he feels guilty about his own lack of manhood, which he senses is partly responsible for his wife's behavior. What a mess!

Because of their guilt, parents can't talk to each other about these things. They blame each other with reason, but each one is responsible for the problem. This is where family therapy can be of help. If through such therapy the parents can face their sexual anxieties and not "act out" with their children, the latter might be spared the fate of the parents. Otherwise, the child will resolve its oedipal problem by cutting off its sexual feelings. Then, as an adult he will suffer from orgastic impotence and will make a marriage that will be no different from his parents'.

Deprivation on the oral level has another effect upon the person's sexuality. There occurs what analysts call a displacement downward. Oral desires and feelings are transferred to the genital function. This means that the vagina becomes like a mouth in that it is used to take in nourishment. For the man, penetration is like the return of a child to the arms and body of its mother. The feeling is one of being held warmly and securely. The trouble with this kind of sexuality is that it reduces the orgastic response. The man may have an ejaculation but not a full orgasm. The woman will probably not reach a climax. Orgasm is the bodily reaction of discharge or ending. It occurs when the organism is filled with excess energy or excitation that has to be released. It does not result from the process of taking in. Oral longing seeks continuous closeness and abhors separation. Sexual longing seeks the closeness of a shared experience that has a natural termination. Thus, to the degree that oral feelings enter into sexual activity, sexuality in the sense of orgastic response is diminished. And while the feeling of closeness is pleasurable, it is not fulfilling. The inner emptiness remains, and the person is forced to repeat the experience again and again.

Displacement also occurs from below upward. Genitality becomes associated with the mouth. This upward displacement stems from a fear of genitality, that is, from castration anxiety, and it helps the person avoid facing his castration. Oral sex is safe. It seems to satisfy the individual's need to suck and to fulfill his oral longing. I believe that is why it has become so common today. But oral sex is not conducive to orgastic response. It does not allow for those pelvic movements that bring the person to the involuntary phase of the orgastic reaction. What a strange trick of fate! By depriving our children of the opportunity to fulfill their oral needs by nursing, we program them to act out their unfulfilled oral desires as adults on the sexual level.

A necessary step in the therapeutic undertaking is to help our patients separate oral elements and sexual elements in their behavior. This is done by getting the patient to become aware of his oral and sexual tensions. The former are located in the upper part of the body and involve the lips, mouth, jaws, throat, chest, shoulders, and arms. Chronic muscular spasticities in these areas limit the person's ability to open up and reach out for love. The inability to reach out is an important manifestation of the fear of life. Sexual tensions are located in and around the pelvis also in the form of spastic muscles that restrict the natural involuntary movements of the pelvis. They reduce the ability of the person to tolerate and contain sexual excitation. Both sets of tensions surround the openings of the body, the mouth above and the genital apertures below. They parallel each other in the sense that the same kind and degree of tension exist at both ends of the body. The constriction on the oral level equals the one on the genital level. For example, the floor of the mouth is as tight as the floor of the pelvis. An equivalent tension is found in the throat and in the lower abdomen. This phenomenon is due to the functional and energetic symmetry of the body A person cannot allow more feeling to come through one opening than through another. This means that sexual problems cannot be resolved unless the corresponding oral problems are also worked through.

My approach to these problems is to work with both areas of the body alternately. Working with the patient to reduce the tension in and about his mouth and throat enables him to breathe more deeply and thus increase the level of excitation. It is necessary, then, to work with the lower part of the body so that this increased excitation can be discharged. This can be done by using the grounding exercises described elsewhere[2] or by diminishing the sexual tensions, or both. This physical work takes place within the context of an analytic working through of the person's history and behavior. When this approach is used, the person's tolerance for excitation is gradually raised and his capacity to experience life increased.

In the previous chapter I described some of the therapeutic procedures I use for castration anxiety. In this chapter I will discuss the treatment of oral deprivation. The oral character is described as being empty and unfulfilled. Since the deprivation occurred when he was an infant, the question arises, What keeps him in that state as an adult? We saw that it was impossible for him to be filled by the love and support of another. The explanation for this situation is that his ability to *take in* this love and support has been reduced by the tensions that develop as a consequence of his early deprivation. He cannot even take in enough air to fulfill his energetic needs because these tensions restrict his breathing. The suppression of sucking impulses means that the

2. See my book *Depression and The Body* (New York: Penguin Books, 1973).

person cannot make a strong inspiratory effort, which is done by sucking air. Unable to take the air in deeply, he cannot let it out fully in expiration or sound (of crying and of screaming). Tensions develop in the arms, shoulders, and chest to inhibit impulses to reach out because of the fear and pain of rejection. In chapter 2 I described this pain as heartbreak.

All tensions serve the function of blocking impulses the expression of which is too painful. It is painful to want to suck a breast when none is available, to reach out when no one is there, to cry when no one cares. By compressing their lips, setting their jaws, and constricting their throats children can block the desire and deaden the pain of a need that will not be fulfilled. But, then, as adults they are similarly blocked in their ability to reach out to another person with feeling. There is no way to regain this ability except by reliving the original experience and expressing all feelings associated with it. This is regression, which is a necessary part of therapy. Freud was aware that his patients tended to relive early experiences. He called this tendency "the compulsion to repeat." He says, "He is obliged to *repeat* the repressed material as a contemporary experience instead of, as the physician would prefer to see, *remembering* it as something belonging to the past."[3]

But if the patient needs to relive the experience, why shouldn't this be done in the therapeutic situation? It would prevent the patient's "acting out" the repressed experience in real life to his detriment. In my opinion, the failure of psychoanalysis to alter character and fate stemmed from Freud's fear of regression, his distrust of the body, and his overvaluation of rationality. If one wants to change character, it is not enough to *talk* about feelings. They must be experienced and expressed. The body must be freed from its chronic tensions and constrictions if the person is to be freed from the fate they represent.

In working with the problems of the preoedipal period, the

3. Sigmund Freud, *Beyond the Pleasure Principle* (New York: Liveright Publishing Co., 1950), p. 19.

patient is encouraged to regress to an infantile level. Here is an example. The person lies on a bed or on the floor and reaches out with both arms for his mother. At the same time, he is directed to say, "Mama, Mama," and to let himself go to the feeling these words suggest. Few patients can do this exercise with any feeling at first. They say, "I don't feel anything." Yet each one has been a baby who wanted his mother with all his heart. That feeling is not gone; it has been suppressed and now cannot be openly expressed.

It can't be expressed because unconsciously the person associates the feeling with an intolerable pain. He dares not regress to that period of his life because the sense of helplessness he had then was too frightening. It was a time of sorrow, not of joy, and so he repressed the memory of it. He survived, and he is not willing to put that survival on the line. He is not prepared to relive those experiences consciously, even though he may act them out unconsciously in his life. Yet another part of his personality wants to clear up the confusion in his relationships and to straighten out the mess of his life. This can be done with the aid of a therapist who will be "there" for him in this need, in contrast to his mother, who wasn't there for him when he was an infant in need.

To break through this unconscious resistance it is often necessary to apply some pressure with one's hand to the tight muscles of the jaw and throat. Because of the tension, this pressure is experienced as painful; but under this pressure, the muscles relax, allowing the voice to become stronger and more alive. It is equally necessary for the patient to breathe deeply so that the suppressed feelings become charged. Generally, I encourage the patient to let go and give in to the feeling. In almost all cases these maneuvers enable the suppressed longing for the mother to come through. It is accompanied by deep sobbing, the crying of an infant for a mother who wasn't there, who didn't respond. When this happens, the person will experience himself in one aspect of his being as an infant. He will not lose consciousness of who he is or where he is. He will know that he is an adult, but he will feel like an infant. This is regression in therapy.

It is also important to get the person to reach out with his lips as if for a breast. It is a very simple movement, yet most people cannot do it correctly. The muscles of the mouth and lips are so tense and contracted that the lips cannot be extended softly. Or the person will thrust the jaw forward in the attempt to extend the lower lip. The forward thrust of the lower jaw expresses defiance and denies the idea of reaching. In most people the stiffness of the upper lip also prevents any meaningful reaching with the mouth. The tension in the muscles of the mouth is supplemented by even stronger tension in the muscles of the jaw, so that any real opening to the world is very limited and guarded. When the tension around the mouth is reduced so that the person can feel his lips reaching, they will go into vibration. They will quiver with excitement, and the person may experience sensations of tingling in his face and mouth. The face and mouth will feel alive, and the person may experience the desire to suck a breast. Sometimes I encourage the patient to suck on the knuckle of his hand or mine to help him feel his lips and his mouth. I am always surprised that so few people know how to suck. They use only their lips but not the inside of the mouth.

Reliving the repressed conflict will involve the expression of strong emotions such as crying, screaming, kicking, hitting, biting, etc. All of these impulses must be allowed full expression in the therapeutic situation if the patient is to release the tensions of the oral conflicts. Since the tensions developed to block these impulses, they can be released only when the person feels free and able to express them. Letting go all the way to his suppressed feelings may bring up the fear of insanity or of death that froze the person into a structured position that became his character and his fate. But by living out his fate in the therapeutic situation, the patient is freed from it in life.

Releasing suppressed emotions in this way is not "acting out." The patient is held to the responsibility of knowing that these emotions stem from the past and are expressed in the present only to free the body. All violent actions are directed against a bed, a towel, or some inanimate object. The therapist's role is to guide and supervise the release of the feeling. It is also his responsibility to avoid any countertransference that could involve him with the patient. Under these conditions the therapeutic situation is the proper setting for the release of these impulses, since there is very little likelihood of injury to the patient or anyone else. For example, my patients will beat upon the bed with their fists or a tennis racquet, twist or bite a towel, or scream their heads off. The office is soundproofed. They can let go because I keep control. If they want to "go crazy," I will become the guardian of their sanity.

Working through the oral problems in this way helps the person open up to life. He can breathe more fully and deeply, and this increases his energy. He can reach out and take in more life, which fills the emptiness caused by his early deprivation. Actually, the very act of opening up and reaching out overcomes the deprivation that, in an adult, consists of the inability to be fully in life. Let me state that idea again because I believe it is essential to an understanding of how therapy works. Although the child was deprived of love and support, the adult is deprived of his ability to function, that is, to love, to give, and to take in. This disturbance in the adult cannot be remedied with love alone. The person needs to gain an understanding of his dysfunction. To that end, love may be helpful but he must realize that no one can live for him, breathe, or reach out for him. He has to know that to be full means to be fully in possession of one's self. He has to be able to breathe deeply, reach out freely, and respond fully.

However, if regression is a necessary part of the therapeutic process because it releases feelings, one has to gain the ability to handle these feelings in a mature way. Being an infant or a screaming maniac is not my idea of the goal of therapy. Regression is in the service of progression. And progress in therapy represents the ability to tolerate increasing levels of excitation without going crazy or cutting off the feeling. The ability to contain excitation or feeling is self-possession. It is the third stage in the therapeutic program. The first two are self-awareness and self-expression. Self-possession is the stage in which the ego functions as the standard-bearer of a self that knows who it is and what it has to do. The self possesses an ego. It is the stage in which the self experiences its being as a fully mature man or woman.

The forward movement in therapy involves analyzing the present-day behavior of the patient in terms of his oedipal and preoedipal conflicts. The transference situation with the therapist is especially important in this regard, since neurotic behavior is most clearly manifested in this relationship. Insights gained in the course of regression are applied to current attitudes and actions. Moving forward also involves grounding a person more fully in his legs and feet so that he can stand for what he believes and have faith that he can stand firmly on his own two feet. It involves increasing the individual's conscious identification with his body through bioenergetic exercises to heighten the sense of self. Thus, the therapeutic process has a dual aspect. The aim is forward toward more sexual excitation and satisfaction, and a greater realization of the self. But this forward movement does not occur unless there is a concomitant backward movement into the past, into the body, and into the unconscious. A tree grows taller to the degree that its roots go deeper and wider. If we wish to jump high, we must first bend close to the ground to get the impetus for the spring. Like a jet engine, we move forward by thrusting backward. In therapy each backward move provides the energy for the leap forward. Regression and progression go on side by side.

Despair, Death, and Rebirth

Patients are willing to talk about the past, but to regress in the sense of reexperiencing the past is strongly avoided. As we have seen, the feelings associated with the past are generally painful. But the past is even more frightening in that for many persons it was a life and death struggle. One survived, but not without some deep feeling of despair—a despair that life would never be more than a struggle for survival. Such despair is a difficult therapeutic problem.

Let me say at the outset of this discussion that there is some feeling of despair in almost every patient.

It may be close to the surface, with the patient himself being aware of it. Or it may be deeply buried and revealed only after the therapy has progressed for some time. In many cases one can see the despair as a hopeless expression in the person's eyes. Often it can be made visible by a light pressure with the fingers on the face alongside the bridge of the nose. This pressure prevents a smile and so unmasks the person. Despair is one of the major reasons a person comes to therapy, because it represents the inner conviction that he cannot help himself. He feels helpless, and that means also hopeless. In some individuals it is a despair "nigh unto death," for the person feels that he might just as well die since there is no use living. When the despair is deep, there generally are suicidal thoughts and feelings associated with it. For that reason despair is a frightening feeling.

Dealing with a patient's despair is very difficult because he sees the despair as relevant to the present. He is in despair about his life and even about the therapy. He will feel or express the idea that therapy is no use or won't help. Since one can't give him any guarantees about therapy, one can't assure him that it will work out all right. Nevertheless, I do offer the patient some encouragement if he will accept the despair. This may seem like a contradiction, but it is true that accepting the *feeling* that it's no use gives the therapy a chance to succeed. Denying one's feelings doesn't make them go away. Nor can one overcome a feeling, which is really an aspect of the self. Painful and frightening as it may seem, the patient has no realistic choice but to accept his feeling of despair.

Accepting despair requires more than a statement to that effect. Admitting one's despair may be coupled with an unexpressed determination not to give in to it. Acceptance means that one makes no effort to fight against the despair. If one accepts it and gives in fully, one *cries*. Crying is the sign of acceptance. Despair may be defined as a seemingly bottomless pit of sadness and sorrow. The person feels that if he let himself down into this pit, he would drown in his sorrow. To prevent this catastrophe he holds himself up and is afraid to let go. But this holding up requires a tremendous effort of will, and when the person gets tired, he falls into the pit and becomes depressed.

Having accepted the despair, the patient is in a position to understand the origin of the feeling. He may be able to relate the despair to his experience as a child that no one responded to his longing with love or to his pain with sympathy. He may have felt terribly alone with a deep sense of hurt, despairing of getting the love and sympathy he so desperately wanted. He might have said to himself, "Give up. It's no use trying to get their love. They don't care." But no child can accept a hopeless situation and survive. He must deny his despair. He must believe that the love is there, that he might have it if he tried harder to be good, to be what they wanted. He must create an illusion that he is really loved but that love is being withheld because he is doing something bad or wrong. He has no choice but to devote his energy to doing what is demanded in the attempt to prove that he is worthy of love.

This attempt inevitably fails. True love is not a reward for doing but is given unconditionally from the fullness of one's heart. Deep within himself the person knew that the attempt would fail. Children are very perceptive, especially with regard to their parents. The child "knows" that he is not loved, but the denial and the illusion are necessary to help him survive until he becomes old enough to be independent. All psychological defenses are means of survival; they become neurotic defenses because they have outlived their usefulness. So the person is back in his despair, now doubly deep because of the failure of his attempt to prove his worth. The patient feels that it is no use to try, even in therapy.

At this point I agree with the patient that it's no use to try. The effort will fail again. If he is trying to gain my love or approval by doing what I expect, it won't work. Trying to overcome the despair won't work either. There is nothing to do. One must give in to one's feelings and, when these are sad ones, cry.

We said in the preceding section that crying is not easy for many people. Severe tensions in the jaw, floor of the mouth, and throat make it very difficult for the person to sob. Tears may come to the eyes, but the voice does not *break* into the deep sobs that convulse the body. Such a sob is a pulse of life traversing the body. But many people maintain a tight upper lip to prevent any breakdown into sobbing.

When a person sobs deeply, the feeling of despair is always lessened. Sometimes, if the crying is deep enough, the person breaks through into feelings of gladness and joy. However, if the crying is shallow or off the surface of the sadness, it may leave the person feeling more despairing than before. He let himself down into the pit, but, since he didn't touch bottom, he became more frightened. Such crying can, indeed, be endless, never arriving to release the sadness or sorrow. It is not a question of how much one cries, but how deeply.

In the body the feeling of sadness is located in the belly. We speak of a belly cry or a belly laugh. To understand the role of the belly in the feeling of despair, we must recognize that an emotion has two components, a mental or perceptual aspect and a physical one, which is the movement or *motion* in the body. Perceiving an internal bodily movement gives rise to a feeling or emotion. When we are frightened or hurt, our guts tighten, our bellies contract and the whole body becomes tense. Crying is the most basic and primitive mechanism for the release of this tension. It is a convulsive reaction that discharges the tension in the guts and in the musculature. At the same time the sound shakes the body loose from its tightness. If we don't cry, the hurt feelings stay locked in the belly and in the tight body. Laughter is also a means of releasing tension. The belly is the pit, but it is only seemingly bottomless. It has a floor, the pelvic floor, and in this floor there are openings. The important one for our purpose is the genital channel. It is the avenue for the discharge of sexual excitation, which also has its primary locus in the belly or lower abdomen. And in the woman the genital channel is also the birth passage for the child, which is conceived in the belly and comes out into the world by passing through the pelvic floor.

I said that each sob is a pulse that flows through the body. When the crying is deep and full, the pulse of the sob goes clear through to the pelvic floor, producing a movement in the pelvis similar to that which occurs in orgasm. The pelvis moves forward spontaneously with each sob as in a sexual discharge, but without the intensity or sexual excitement of the latter. In such deep crying the sadness is discharged and the person feels that he came out of the pit into the sunshine. He no longer has a feeling of despair. He has worked through the grief of the lack or loss of love in his early years.

The pit of the belly is also the locus of the self, as we saw in chapter 3. Persons who suffer from a sensation of emptiness in the belly complain about a lack of sense of self as well as a feeling of despair. Like the flow of feeling in the belly with a strong sexual discharge, deep sobbing leads to a heightened sense of self when the pulse passes through the pelvic floor. The close connection between crying and sexual release is manifest by women who break into deep crying after an orgasm. I interpet this crying as a release of tension similar to the crying of a mother who is reunited with a lost child. In the case of sex, the lost child is the self rediscovered through orgasm.

It is not much easier to give in to such deep crying than it is to surrender oneself to the convulsion of orgasm that it resembles. It takes considerable therapeutic work before the patient is able to do so. For one thing, most of the sexual tensions in and around the pelvis must be released; otherwise, the wave of the sob gets stuck in the belly and doesn't go through. Furthermore, it must be recognized that one breakthrough does not mean that the person is forever free from his despair. The experience may have to be repeated again and again as the patient relives more of the traumas of his childhood. But the bottom was reached and the door opened. It will stay open as he begins to experience in life the joy of full sexual orgasm. If despair is a conviction that one will never feel joyful, the feeling of joy is the best and only antidote.

Despair is often associated with a fear of death. To let down into despair has the connotation for many people of giving up to death. Thinking about these connections, I was struck by the fact that many words in our language that have a negative implication begin with letter *d*. Here are a few: *death, defeat, disillusion, despair, disease, desperation, disaster, derogatory,* and *devil.* I am sure any reader could find other words that have this combination: words that start with the letter *d* and have a negative connotation. *Depression* is another one, and we think of it as representing a down state. This leads to the idea that the word *down* must imply a negative direction in our minds. But the *u* of *up* seems not to have any special significance. Some correlation can be found in the opposition *god-devil.* The letter *g* begins words like *good, generous, graceful, great, gorgeous,* and *gourmet.* These words are associated in our minds with a positive feeling.

There are two other pairs of antithetical words one of which begins with the letter *d.* *Being* and *doing* are one pair; *birth* and *death* are the other. The letter *b* starts the prefix *bio,* which means life. Life can be seen as a rising up, death as a falling down. To be born may signify coming out of the earth; to die is to return into the earth. We are dealing with the upward and downward cycle of life. We humans get up in the morning and lie down at night. Excitement lifts us up; its release lets us down. We charge up and discharge down.

Playing with the sound of the two letters, *b* and *d,* I thought I could detect a difference in their feel. When I pronounce the letter *d,* I sense a downward inflection in my voice and a downward feel in my mouth. The *b* when pronounced seems to have the opposite quality. This may be purely a trick of my imagination, but I am convinced that there is a relationship between the feeling of a word when sounded and the image it represents. All words were originally sounds. We know that the sound of the voice is a direct expression of feeling. The word *sigh* sounds like a sigh and feels like a sigh. I have a feeling that the sound of the letter *d* has a slightly ominous tone.[4] *Damn* invokes the idea of doom.

If a person is to let go of the tensions that hold him up, it is necessary to explore and analyze the association in his mind between letting down and death. This analysis is best done when the patient is fighting against letting go, either in an exercise or in an emotional situation. At that time the association is not an abstract idea but a vivid experience. Here is an illustration. I was working with a woman recently who had suffered from an attack of lupus erythematosis several years before. She had recovered, but minor flare-ups of the disease would occur when she was under sufficient stress. In this session, as we talked about our relationship, a feeling of sadness welled up in her. But she did not cry. I could see her body trying to melt, but it remained frozen. I had her bend forward and touch the floor with her fingertips.[5] When she did so, I asked her what would happen if she let go. She answered, "I would die." "But if you don't let go?" I asked. We were both aware that her illness was related in some way to the tension in her body. She replied, "I will die." She was also aware that the tension involved in holding herself up was destructive to her body and her being.

We talked about her past and her relationship to her parents. She knew that her mother had been hostile to her. She believed, however, that her father had been "there" for her and that he

4. Dr. Michael Conant, one of my associates in bioenergetic analysis, offered an interesting comment after reading this section: "To me *b* is a kiss that reaches out to life, while *d* has a hardening and sneering quality."

5. This is the basic grounding exercise used in bioenergetic analysis. It is described and illustrated in Alexander and Leslie Lowen, *The Way to Vibrant Health* (New York: Harper & Row Publishers, 1977).

cared. Now, she said, she realized that this belief was illusory. It was very painful for her to face the fact that he had used her rather than helped her. It made her feel too lonely and vulnerable. She felt that she would die. All of this was triggered by the discussion of our relationship. She said that she was not sure that I would be "there" for her as her therapist. She sensed her despair.

Here is another case. This particular man was doing a falling exercise, described earlier. In this exercise, when the person feels that he will fall, I ask him to imagine what would happen if he fell. This patient said, "When you told me to say, 'I'm going to fall,' the feeling I had was that I'm going to die. I feel like it's a life and death struggle. If I let go, I'm going to be killed." He pounded both fists against his thighs and added, "I'm going to kill myself if I don't hang in. But if I do hang in, I'm going to die. I'm afraid I'll get cancer of the lungs if I don't stop smoking. But the more I try not to smoke, the more I smoke."

He then related to me how he had almost died as a child. "I had septicemia when I was five years old. I had a high fever, and I was in and out of the hospital for about a year. At times I was comatose. I had to be drained and transfused. I almost died. But I hung in, using all my willpower to live. I know how to exist when it's tough. I don't know how to exist when it's nice."

I have heard similar stories from a number of patients who had been close to death from sickness as children. They recall that at a critical period in the illness they consciously mobilized the will to live. And they believe that it was their will to live that saved them. Since falling or letting down is experienced as a loss or surrender of the will, it can be seen as a danger. On the other hand, living through the will is really dangerous. It requires much energy to use one's will constantly. How long can a person "hang in"? How long can one exist on an emergency basis? Sooner or later the will gives out, and if that is one's only resource, one is finished.

One has to let down to renew oneself. One has to lie down to recover one's strength. Unless one lets go of the day, one can't enjoy the sleep of night. Symbolically, we die each night, but we are reborn the next day. Without death there can be no rebirth. Unless we go down, we cannot rise.

I don't believe that anyone's survival depends on his will to live. The will, as I pointed out earlier, is a psychic mechanism that enables the individual to mobilize extra energy to meet a crisis. The effectiveness of the will depends upon the availability of this extra energy. If a person has used up all his reserves, his will is impotent. In that case we might say, "He has no will to live," but it would be more logical to speak of the person as being depleted energetically. However, it is true that the will as a psychic mechanism is not equally developed in all people. Being a function of the ego, its strength depends upon the strength of the ego. We can say of a person with a strong ego that he has a strong will. But the strongest will is helpless where there is no energy to mobilize. The best general cannot win a war without an army.

Our energy level increases when we are down and decreases when we are up. We are active in the up state and use our energy, while we rest in the down state and restore our energy. This is the normal pattern in a healthy person. Thus, when a person is depressed, he is in a position to restore his energy and come out of the depression spontaneously. It happens often. The inactivity of the depressed state allows the person to rebuild his energy reserves. As he regains energy, he will become active again. But this is not to say that he won't get depressed again. If, emerging from his depression, he goes into a manic, hyperkinetic, or overactive state in pursuit of some illusion, he will use up all his energy and fall back into a depression.

Some people come out of a depression spontaneously; others don't. One difference is the amount of pressure placed on the depressed individual by his family. "Pull yourself together. Snap out of it. Try to do something." They don't leave him alone, and thus they do not allow the natural healing process of the body to operate. Similarly, if the individual labors under a sense of guilt about his depressed condition, he will not recover. This guilt acts like the outside pressure, robbing the person of the peace and rest he so desperately needs to regain his energy. In our culture down is bad and up is good. But since up is tension and down relaxation, this can only mean that all of us have experienced some very painful feelings in the down state.

Here is an example of that connection. One of my patients made a strange observation while doing a breathing exercise. She said, "I just had the crazy thought that if I breathe, I will die." When I questioned her about the thought, she mentioned that she had had an experience as a young child in which she almost died. She related the incident to me. "I was told that my mother and grandmother used to rock me until I fell asleep. One time, when I was about two months old, my mother decided to stop this practice. She would let me cry until I cried myself out. I cried for hours—my grandmother couldn't stand it, but my mother refused to let her go into my room. Finally I stopped crying, and my mother said to my grandmother, 'See?' They opened the door and saw. I was blue. I had vomited and was choking on the vomiting."

Why should breathing evoke this fear? Breathing increases the energetic charge in the body and activates suppressed feelings. If my patient breathed deeply, she would cry. Crying is associated in her mind with hours of torment that ended with throwing up and choking. Not to breathe is equated with not feeling, not crying, not choking, and not dying. Holding the breath is a way of holding oneself up. Letting down and letting go allow one to breathe fully and deeply.

Letting down is a giving in to feeling. But we can't let down if the feelings are so painful that we can't accept them. Here is a case in point. One of my female patients remarked, "If I had to walk around feeling the desire for her, I'd die. The pain is intolerable. The longing is excruciating. I picture her breast so vividly. I see every ridge of her nipple. The feeling is so intense can't stand it." She was talking about a woman she met who was full-bodied, warm, and alive. My patient was thin, contracted, cold, and half dead. She was like a deprived infant who needed a big, warm, and loving mother, a mommy. As an infant she had suffered such a deprivation.

I asked her how she would die. She answered, "I wouldn't sleep. I wouldn't eat. I'd become ill, freeze to death. A body can stand just so much pain. I believe I would die physically. I've seen people go into a state of marasmus. I saw a girl go down to 56 pounds and die. I went through something like that once. I went from 104 pounds to 86 pounds in two weeks. I couldn't metabolize food. I couldn't defecate. I couldn't urinate. My body stopped functioning. A woman nurse in the hospital saved me. She held me in her arms, and my body slowly relaxed and came alive again." With the support she so desperately craved, she was able to let down and live.

People do die when life is too painful. They struggle to keep going for a time, but when their energy is gone, their will to live disappears. In the condition called anorexia nervosa, which afflicts young women mostly, the person stops eating. At this point the body doesn't have the energy to metabolize food. If the condition continues, there is a progressive loss of weight and energy, and the person dies. Suicide is another way out of an intolerably painful situation. Generally, a painful situation becomes intolerable when there is no one to share it with. If we can let down into the pain and cry, we would find that it becomes tolerable. If we can accept the pain, the natural healing process will begin. But we can't let down to nothing. We can let down to the ground if we feel it beneath our feet. We can let down to a friend or therapist who is there for us. But since our mother wasn't there for us when we were young, we have no sense that if we let down, we will find any support. With that feeling, letting down means giving up and dying.

Mark, whose story we heard earlier, felt that his mother was not there for him. At one session, he remarked, "I recoil from the world, but I am afraid I will be left in a deprived state. I feel my chest has been crushed." Mark's chest was so flattened it looked as if it had been crushed. I could sense his feeling of being crushed. Then he asked me, "What can I do? I don't want to be left in the cold."

What can one do? Suppressing the feeling doesn't make it go away. Burying it merely postpones the day of reckoning. I realized that Mark's heart had been crushed by his mother. My answer to him was, "Give in to the pain and agony of your desire and longing."

Mark was silent for a full minute. Then he said, "I just got in touch with something I never told anybody; that if I become substantial and one with my life, I would die. It is my private secret. I've always blamed my mother for my reluctance to be in my own life. But I realize now that if I reach out to life and get it, I would have to face a brutal fact—that I am mortal. It would be the destruction of my grandiosity, of my fantasy of immortality, invulnerability, and independence. I don't need. I can't stand needing and the pain of not getting. It's too much. I would rather die and give up the world. And I did it. I withdrew into myself as into a living tomb. Then I was invulnerable. That was my secret."

The revelation of his secret had a profound effect on Mark. He felt a sense of joyful liberation, as if he had been released from doom and had rediscovered life. He had closed the door of his escape into death. The decision to reach out to life was not a conscious one. It happened, I believe, because his body felt big enough and strong enough to stand the pain. He had experienced pain in bioenergetic therapy and it had not destroyed him. It had actually made him stronger.

It is logical that to the degree that one is afraid to live, one is close to death. The closer one is to death, the more frightened one is of it. Seen in this light, the fear of death reflects the fear of life. People who are not afraid to live are not afraid to die. They do not want to die, but they are not frightened people, and so the idea of death carries no emotional or energetic charge. Frightened people are frightened of dying. However, at the same time, they have a wish for death. For them, it is the dying that terrifies them, not death itself. Dying is a shrinking or contraction of the life energy in the body, which leaves it cold and lifeless. Terror is the same shrinking of the life energy, which stops short of dying. In terror one feels death as in dying one feels terrified. However, dying is experienced as terrifying only when it occurs against the conscious will of the organism. It is a peaceful process when every part of the personality or body surrenders to its fate.

Winnicott, to whom we referred earlier, believes that the fear of death, like the fear of insanity, stems from a "death that happened but was not experienced."[6] He describes such a death as a "phenomenal death," meaning that it happened to the psyche but not to the body. We can understand it by relating it to such expressions as "the life went out of the person," or "his spirit was broken and something died in him." In current language we would say the person was wiped out. Winnicott says, "Death, looked at in this way as something that happened to the patient but which the patient was not mature enough to experience, has the meaning of annihilation. It is like this, that a pattern developed in which the continuity of being was interrupted by the patient's infantile reactions to impingement."[7] Winnicott, then, sees the wish to die (Keats's "half in love with easeful death") as a need to "remember having died; but to remember he must experience death now."

What does Winnicott mean by the remark, "he must experience death now"? He does not explain in the article how this happens in therapy. In my view it means that the patient must experience the original trauma (phenomenal death) as if it were happening in the present. He didn't die then, and, of course, he won't die

6. W. D. Winnicott, "Fear of Breakdown," *International Review of Psychoanalysis* 1 (1974): 103.

7. Ibid., p. 106.

now. But he faced death then; he experienced the feeling that he might die (the shrinking and contracting of his life energy), and he became terrified. To overcome his terror—to live—he mobilized his will, the will to live. From that time on he lived largely through his will, forcing himself to go on, to *do* out of fear that if he let go, he would die. It is like living under the sword of Damocles, constantly threatened by death. Such a life is not only exhausting but hardly worthwhile. One wishes the sword would fall, that death would come to release one from the struggle and the torment. That is the basis of the wish to die.

The therapeutic task is to help the patient let go now before it is too late, that is, before he has a heart attack or develops cancer. He does not risk death but only the momentary feeling of dying. I shall describe how this happened to one of my patients. He was a man in his forties who had a short, thick neck. His holding against letting go was largely concentrated in his neck muscles. He was afraid to lose his head (go crazy). We had worked together for two years, and he had made considerable progress but was still frightened. As he sat facing me, I asked him to put his head in my lap. Then I applied a steady pressure with my fists against his neck at the base of the skull. He was to breathe and let go to me. After about thirty seconds my patient said, "I feel I am going to die. It is getting dark." I realized that he had tightened his neck muscles against my pressure and cut off the blood supply to his brain. I released the pressure, and, as he lay with his head in my lap, I asked him what thoughts he had as he felt he was going to die.

He said, "I thought it could be the end. I couldn't fight you anymore. At that point you let up."

We discussed this when he sat up. I asked him why he was fighting me when he was supposed to let go. He answered, "I'm always fighting. If I don't fight, I'll be killed."

But he wasn't fighting me, he made no aggressive move against me. He was resisting me, and it was the resistance (tightening of the neck muscles) that brought him to the feeling of dying.

Why was he afraid of being killed? Why was he unable to fight? He had made no effort to get away. Because it had happened once earlier in his life when he was a child and unable to fight against the superior force of his father. All he could do, then, was to tense his neck and hope he would survive. He was afraid to lose his head (castration). He defended himself against this danger by overdeveloping his neck muscles. But his very defense endangered his life by constricting the blood supply to his brain. This experience enabled the patient to explore the guilt over his sexual feelings for his mother and to regain the ability to fight. And he found that he could let go to me without fear that I would take his head off.

It is important to realize that a patient's fear of dying has a basis in his fear of life. If a person is afraid to live, he will die. Here is an example of this relationship. A patient, a young woman, had been hospitalized for a nervous breakdown some time earlier. Since her release she had been on medication. She used the medication to cut off her feelings. At the same time she was distraught that she was unable to make any progress toward health. I saw her in consultation and then undertook to help her with bioenergetic therapy. The following incident occurred in our fourth session. I had her do an expressive exercise to help her confront her fear of feeling. The exercise was done with the patient lying on the bed. It involved her kicking the bed with her legs and saying, "Why?" She had a need to express a protest about her life situation. She began the exercise, kicking and yelling "why?" and then she suddenly stopped. She turned to me and said, "I am afraid. I feel I'm going to faint. It started getting black." Then she added, "I'm afraid of the feeling. I feel I'm being carried away by it. It makes me feel I'm going to die."

To understand what happened we must place the events in their proper sequence. As the patient started to let go to the feeling of protest and anger, she sensed correctly that it could carry her away. The feeling that she might lose control terrified her. To cut off the feeling she stopped breathing by contracting her neck muscles. This maneuver cut off the supply of blood and oxygen to her brain, which produced the sensation of faintness and blackness. Then she felt she would die.

I explained this mechanism to the patient, pointing out that she had a suppressed rage that could carry her away if she gave in to it. It is natural for a strong emotion to "carry one away." If we are not frightened of the emotion, we go with it. If we are frightened, we contract against the feeling, which then gives rise to a sensation of dying.

Since the patient understood my explanations, I suggested that she repeat the exercise. She did, letting herself go to it, and it went off well. When she finished, she looked at me and said, "I didn't stop it this time. I didn't feel like fainting." The experience had a dramatic effect upon her. She looked visibly brighter and more alive. It was as if a sentence of doom had been lifted from her. She had made a breakthrough into life. She remarked, "I was never allowed to show any feeling."

After this exercise she described her early life situation as follows: It was nightmarish. She said that she loved her father very much but felt that she was not good enough for him. "My mother," she said, "yelled and screamed at me whatever I did. I felt attacked all the time and terribly alone. There was no one I could turn to. I thought she was going to kill me. I thought that when I went to bed she would take a knife and come after me. I was afraid to die when I was little, but in a way I did feel like dying."

Not all of us have gone through experiences as children in which we were so sick that it was a matter of life and death. But most of us have been hurt to a point where death cast a shadow over our lives. We suffered rejections that broke our heart. If we didn't die, it was because the heart has more than one life, perhaps three. I suggested in chapter 2 that, like baseball players, we are allowed three strikes before we are called out. We experience our first rejection on the oral level, when our mother's love and support are withdrawn because she may have no more to give. It could be when we are weaned after a too short period

f nursing. It could be caused by the birth of another child. We
re terribly hurt, we cry, but we go on. Strike number one. The
econd strike occurs during the oedipal period, on the genital level.
We are rejected because of our sexuality, and our heart is again
roken. We have only one more chance left, but we dare not
ake it. We have to protect ourself and our heart by locking them
way in a closed box or cage (the thorax). We will no longer
pen our heart to the world, and we believe this will ensure our
urvival. But by our very defense, we invite the rejection that will
nally break our heart for strike number three.

If we can accept the fact that what we are afraid of has
appened in the past, we need not repeat the past. We were
children then, fully dependent on our parents for love, intimacy,
and human contact. Our very lives depended on them. We are
adults now, independent in the sense that we can move about and
choose those with whom to share love, intimacy, and pleasure.
If we open our heart, we can be hurt again, but our heart will
not break. A broken heart is caused by a sense of betrayal. As
adults, we cannot be betrayed unless we are naïve. If we are
naïve, we have betrayed ourselves by denying our past.

The repression of the past means that a part of one's life is lost.
One can regain that life only by reexperiencing the past. In
therapy that involves regressing emotionally to an infantile or
childhood state. Every regressive move brings the patient into
contact with some traumatic experience of the past that threatened
his sanity or his life and forced him to armor against the world
and against his own impulses. Like the armor of a medieval knight,
this physiological armoring is a protective shield or shell around
the individual. It is identical with the totality of the muscular
tensions. In its entirety it constitutes the character structure. To
step out of character is like being born. For a conscious individual
it is a very frightening and seemingly dangerous move to make.
The cracking of the shell is equivalent to a confrontation with
death. Living in the shell seems to guarantee survival, even if it
represents a severe limitation of one's being. To stay in the shell

and suffer seems safer than to risk a confrontation with death fo
freedom and joy. This is not a consciously thought-out position. I
is an attitude stemming from a lesson that was once bitterl
learned and is not easily forgotten.

The shell is also a prison. It is a form of protective custod
that the individual fantasizes as the womb. In the shell the eg
hides that part of the self that represents the helpless infant h
is to safeguard from the cruel world. The part of the self tha
represents the infant is the heart. This is clear from our therapeuti
work. If we reach the heart of a person we bring to light th
infant in him. On the other hand, if we make contact with th
infant in him, we reach and touch his heart. But there is anothe
side to this metaphor. The shell that can be conceived as a womb
(retreat into the shell = return to the womb) eventually become
a tomb. The situation is truly tragic. To break out of the shell is t
risk death, but to stay in the shell is a living death that inevitabl
becomes an actual death.

Death is the fate no one can escape. The question, then, is
How does one die? A person can die like a hero or like a coward
The difference is that the hero can face death without fear
whereas the coward can't. But it may be asked, What makes one
person a hero and another a coward? To answer that question
we have to recognize that the hero is characterized more by how
he lives than by how he dies. I would describe a hero as a person
who has no fear of life, who can face life squarely. And, because
he has no fear of life, he has no fear of death. We have seen in the
course of this study how the fear of life develops in people. There
is a saying that a hero dies once but a coward dies a thousand
deaths. When a person has died many times in fear, he ends up
being a coward. His spirit has been broken. Too many of my
patients have been terrified as little children. Each time a mother
looks at a child with hatred in her eyes, it is like a dagger into
the child's heart. If looks could kill, many of us would be long
dead. But while hateful looks do not kill us physically, they break
us psychologically when they are directed at us by our parents.

They force us to build the shells that imprison our spirits. The thicker the shell, the more frightened we are. We become cowards, afraid to break out, afraid to risk death for freedom. And each time we think to break out but fail, we die again in fear.

By confronting each psychological death through therapy, we regain our courage. Facing death, we lose our fear of death. Challenging the terrors of our unconscious, we are like Greek heroes. Should it not be said that the ultimate goal of therapy is to help a person develop a heroic attitude to life?

7/ The Oedipal Conflict Becomes a Fact of Modern Life

The Rise of the Ego to Dominance

The oedipal conflict occurs at a crucial stage in the development of personality, namely, between the ages of three and six. Up to six years the person can be considered a child in the sense that he is still largely governed by the pleasure principle and his ego is very much identified with his body. Physiologically, he is still functioning with his baby teeth. That state changes after six. The child then becomes a youth who is ready for the process of acculturation. In most societies schooling begins at this time, either in a formal setting or in the home. American Indians, for example, make no effort to teach a child the proper ways of acting as a member of society until the age of six. In Japanese culture, too, that age marks the termination of a period of indulgence and the beginning of serious training. Formal education in the United States traditionally starts at six years. We can assume that the ego has now developed to a point where it can begin to assert its dominance over the body and its actions in the name of the reality principle.

To understand why this development is associated with an oedipal conflict in our culture, we need to look at the historical process that led to the rise of ego consciousness. Just as ontogeny recapitulates philogeny on the physical level, so personality development recapitulates the cultural history of mankind. The Oedipus legend lies at a cultural crossroads. It marks the emergence of modern man, who has a developed ego consciousness. Modern man sees himself as a conscious actor in the drama of life, whereas his predecessor felt himself to be part of an unchanging order in which his place was set. This change in consciousness is symbolized in the Oedipus legend.

The historical significance of the Oedipus story was explored by Erich Fromm. Basing his remarks upon the famous plays of Sophocles about the myth, *Oedipus Rex, Antigone,* and *Oedipus at Colonus,* Fromm says, "The myth can be understood as a symbol, not of the incestuous love between mother and son, but of the rebellion of the son against the authoritarian father in the patriarchal family; that the marriage of Oedipus and Jocasta is only a secondary element, only one of the symbols of the victory of the son who takes his father's place and with it all his privileges."[1]

Fromm bases part of his argument on the fact that the myth contains no mention of sexual feelings or wishes on the part of Oedipus toward his mother. His marriage to Jocasta did not

1. Erich Fromm, *The Forgotten Language* (New York: Rinehart & Co., 1951), p. 202.

happen because of any special love for her; she was one of the prizes he received for solving the riddle of the Sphinx and saving the city from her depredations. The other part of his argument rests on the existence of a conflict between a father and a son in each of the three plays. In *Oedipus Rex,* as we have seen, the newborn son is regarded as a threat by his father. Years later, without knowing each other's identity, they fight and the father is killed. In *Oedipus at Colonus,* which is about the final years of Oedipus, there is a violent argument between Oedipus and his son, Polyneices. The latter appeals to Oedipus for help in overthrowing his brother, Eteocles, who has become ruler of Thebes. Oedipus is furious with Polyneices and curses both his sons in the play. Subsequently, the two brothers kill each other.

In *Antigone,* Creon, who is now ruler of the city of Thebes, is opposed by his son, Haemon, for his ruthlessness in condemning Antigone to death. Fromm finds a clue to the myth of Oedipus in this play. He says, "Creon represents the strictly authoritarian principle both in the family and in the state, and it is against this type of authority that Haemon rebels. An analysis of the whole Oedipus trilogy will show that the struggle against paternal authority is its main theme and that the roots of the struggle go far back into the ancient fight between the patriarchal and the matriarchal systems of society."[2]

I agree with Fromm in his insistence that the myth has a deep cultural significance. In speaking of a struggle between patriarchal and matriarchal systems of society, Fromm is not suggesting that the conflict is between men and women for dominance of society. It is a struggle between opposing philosophies, opposing principles, and opposing religious systems. Creon, in the play *Antigone,* represents the patriarchal principle, Antigone the matriarchal principle. Fromm defines the two opposing principles as follows: "The matriarchal principle is that of blood relationship as the fundamental and indestructible tie, of the equality of all men, and of the respect for human life and of love. The patriarchal

2. Ibid., p. 234.

principle is that the ties between man and wife, between ruler and ruled, take precedence over the ties of blood. It is the principle of order and authority, of obedience and hierarchy."

The so-called fight between these two systems took place at the beginning of civilization and represented the clash between barbaric and civilized ways. The matriarchal principle governed society in its precivilized state. However, Fromm's description of that state is too idealistic. There was respect for life but not for an individual life, which could be sacrificed for the common good. Animal and even human sacrifice was practiced in many precivilized societies; blood was spilled on the earth to encourage the renewal of life. Kinship was determined through the mother, which was the bloodline, since the father's role in conception was generally unknown. He was an outsider in the family and had no rights. The responsible head was the mother's brother. It was believed that conception occurred when the spirit entered the woman's body. Like the earth, she was the bearer of life, and blood was the essence of life. Nevertheless, we must recognize that it was a system in which there was no conflict between culture and nature or between the ego and the body.

Another interpretation of the Oedipus myth is offered by Erich Neumann, a Jungian analyst. He views the legend as the story of the ego's rise to power and its challenge to the unconscious. He says, "The world experienced by the waking ego of humanity is the world of J. J. Bachofen's matriarchate,"[3] whose representative is the Sphinx. He describes the Sphinx as "the age-old foe, the dragon of the abyss, representing the might of the Earth Mother in her uroboric aspect."[4] This expression refers to nature as it was experienced by primitive man, in its combined aspect as nourisher and depriver, protector and destroyer, the giver and taker of life. Nature was the great unknown force before which the ego of early man stood helpless and in awe. And it was

3. Erich Neumann, *The Origin and History of Consciousness* (New York: Pantheon Books, 1954), p. 39.

4. Ibid., p. 167.

also the nature of man himself, the great unconscious, against which consciousness and the ego struggled. This condition characterized humanity in the hunting and food-gathering stage before civilization developed as a result of the domestication of animals and plants.

Throughout the early years of civilization the matriarchal principle was still largely dominant. This period is represented in mythology by a dominant female goddess and a youthful male god who is both her son and lover. Attis, Adonis, Tammuz, and Osiris are examples of the youthful gods who are born of the Great Mother, become her lovers, die, and are reborn through her again. These youthful gods are symbols of vegetation, which rises from the earth each spring (birth), returns to the earth in the fall (death), and is reborn next year. In this stage the ego has a youthful quality, and, while it is more developed than the infantile ego of primitive man, it is still largely a body ego, lacking that sense of the will that would enable it to assert its power over the body and the unconscious. For Neumann, the significance of Oedipus is that "only with him is the fatal bond between Great Mother and son-lover finally broken."[5] He represents the victory of the ego over the unconscious.

Because the unconscious, through its association with the body, is identified with the earth and nature, it has a feminine connotation. Consciousness and the ego, as opposing concepts, assume, therefore, a masculine connotation. This permits Neumann to define the difference between patriarchal and matriarchal in psychological terms. He says, "We use the word 'patriarchate' to signify the predominantly masculine world of spirit, sun, consciousness, and ego. In the matriarchate, on the other hand, the unconscious reigns supreme, and the predominate feature here is a preconscious, prelogical, and preindividual way of thinking and feeling."[6]

5. Ibid., p. 81.
6. Ibid., p. 168.

In his recent book *The Origin of Consciousness in the Breakdown of the Bicameral Mind,* Julian Jaynes addresses himself to the same subject. He places this change in the later part of the second millennium B.C. However, Jaynes is not talking about consciousness in general but self-consciousness or ego consciousness. He points out that there is no reference in the Iliad to an ego or I that is capable of reflecting or making deliberate or conscious decisions. The actions of the main characters in the *Iliad* are directed by the gods and are not the expression of a personal sense of will. This leads Jaynes to say that the Iliadic hero "did not have any ego whatever."[7]

Jaynes offers some interesting ideas about the neurological basis for the development of the ego. He postulates that the gods are mental functions associated with the right side of the brain and that they speak to man (functions of the left side of the brain) in the form of auditory hallucinations. The term *bicameral* is used to indicate the existence of two centers in the brain, the right and left hemispheres, which, though normally connected and integrated, can function independently. Jaynes believes that man in early civilization was governed by these two centers; the right hemisphere (god side) provided the directives to action, which the left hemisphere (man side) carried out.

Modern neurological research has shown that the two hemispheres serve different functions. It has been known for some time that the left hemisphere in right-handed people contains the centers for the vocal expression of language. Persons who suffer a destructive lesion of these speech areas lose the ability to articulate and enunciate the spoken word or to make meaningful statements. However, the recognition of language is bilateral. The new discoveries concern the function of the right hemisphere. A lesion in this hemisphere seriously impairs a person's ability to deal with spatial relationships. The recognition of patterns is

7. Julian Jaynes, *The Origin of Consciousness in the Breakdown of the Bicameral Mind* (Boston: Houghton Mifflin Co., 1976), p. 73.

disturbed. The difference in function between the two hemispheres is described by Jaynes as follows: "The right hemisphere is more involved in synthetic and spatial-constructive tasks while the left hemisphere is more analytic and verbal. The right hemisphere, perhaps like the gods, sees parts as having a meaning only within a context, it looks at wholes. While the left or dominant hemisphere, like the man side of the bicameral mind, looks at parts themselves."[8]

There is no reason to believe that the left hemisphere has always been the dominant one. It is true of civilized people for whom analysis, speech, and the manipulation of objects (left-hemisphere functions) are the dominant aspects of behavior. But even among them the degree of left-hemisphere dominance varies. Some people are more intuitive and more creative (functions of the right hemisphere) than others. For example, artists such as painters and composers are less involved with words and analyzing than with sensing patterns and expressing them nonverbally. Broadly speaking, the difference between the two hemispheres can be compared with the difference between the rational approach of the scientist and the intuitive approach of the artist. I believe that primitive man was closer to the artistic temperament than to the scientific one. His work was more creative than productive. He made things not only for use but to express his personality and his religious beliefs. Every product was a work of art.

The world of the primitive mind was quite different from ours. It was not a world of independent objects but one in which everything was seen as connected and part of a whole. The person himself was not a separate individual, since individuality did not exist as a concept in the primitive mind, as Neumann pointed out. Existence or being was dependent on belonging, which was described by Lévy-Bruhl as "*participation mystique*" in the processes of life and nature. In this system the hunter and his prey were united, both were part of the natural order. Success in the hunt was not considered to be simply the result of individual skill, since such skill was not always successful, but equally of some divine or suprahuman guidance. Therefore, a religious or magical ceremony always preceded the hunt and also followed it if the hunt was successful. Since the right hemisphere is our means of apprehending the whole, then it must be the abode of the gods, as Jaynes claims, since they represent the whole or aspects of it. When the gods dominated human life, there was some degree of right-hemisphere dominance in man.

The concept of the matriarchate is similar to the world view represented by the right hemisphere. The matriarchate was overthrown and the right hemisphere became subordinate when the functions of the left hemisphere grew in importance. These are the increasing ability to manipulate things, which is a function of the right hand, the growing use of words to describe and comprehend things, and the capacity to analyze relationships. Jaynes believes that the social and physical upheavals that occurred in the later part of the second millennium B.C. were responsible for the breakdown of the bicameral mind, resulting in the development of ego consciousness. These events undoubtedly were a precipitating cause, but the underlying cause of the change was the growth of left-hemisphere functions, which are identified, as we saw, with the patriarchal principle.

The change can also be described as the move from a subjective to an objective position. Man separates himself out from the whole, which permits him to take an objective view of nature both inside and outside of himself. The ego or I starts as an observer of the self and ends controlling and dominating the self. The ego gains its power through the use of reason and the will. Both of these ego functions are brought into the Oedipus story. Laius and Oedipus both used their wills to counter the prophecy of the oracle, that is, to avoid their fate. This action characterizes a person with a fairly well-developed ego. Jaynes's bicameral man or a primitive would obey the voice or the will of the gods. Then there is Oedipus' answer to the riddle of the Sphinx, an answer that can only be described as verbal, analytic, and logical.

From the foregoing we can conclude that the Oedipus legend

is a story about the rise to dominance of the ego and of the patriarchal social order. However, this victory of the ego and of the patriarchate was not absolute. It did not mean the disappearance of the earth deities associated with the matriarchal order. They were downgraded and assigned to a lower position in the hierarchy of power. The result was the creation of an antithesis between culture and nature, the ego and the body, rational thought and intuitive sensing. This antithesis produced a dynamic tension that furthers the growth of culture, but it also contains a destructive potential in the form of conflict. The patriarchal system is characterized by conflict between the individual and the community, between man and woman, and between parents and children. The Oedipus story as told by Sophocles is about the conflict between parents and children, but on a deeper level it is also about the conflict in the personality of Oedipus himself.

We saw in chapter 1 that the reign of Oedipus as king of Thebes was highly prosperous for twenty years. But the Erinyes, as the fates are called in the play, were waiting. They brought a plague upon the city, ultimately leading to the discovery of Oedipus as the murderer of his father and the husband of his mother. Aghast at this discovery, Oedipus blinded himself and left Thebes to become a wanderer. I was puzzled for a long time by this aspect of the story. Why would the Erinyes punish Oedipus for the acts of patricide and incest, which are crimes against the patriarchal order with which the Erinyes have no common interest? I realized that the real transgression they are avenging and for which Oedipus must suffer is the destruction of the Sphinx.

The Sphinx was one of the original mother goddesses, imported from Egypt, where she was worshipped as a beneficent deity. To the developing Greek ego she was a monster because she demanded the sacrifice of human life. But as an earth goddess the Sphinx ate all her children since they all returned to the earth at death. The female goddesses of the matriarchal order were the rulers of life and death (the fates as weavers of life). As long as these processes remained mysteries, man stood in awe of women and mothers. By solving the riddle of the Sphinx, Oedipus eliminated the mystery upon which her power depended. Of all Greek heroes, he alone acted without the aid of an Olympian god. His conquest represented the victory of the rational mind. He opposed knowledge to mystery and courage to fear. By this deed he became the first modern man.

In the eyes of the matriarchal world, the real crime of Oedipus was the arrogance of knowledge and power. Thus, Sophocles has the chorus say of him:

> Behold this is Oedipus
> Who unravelled the great riddle
> And was first in power
> Whose fortune all the townsmen
> praised and envied
> See in what dread adversity he sank.[9]

It is arrogant to think that one can outmaneuver fate. It is arrogant to believe that one knows the answers to all the mysteries. Oedipus thought that he saw the truth about man, that he understood his nature. But he was blind to the fact that man is the son of woman and must return to his mother, the earth, on his marriage bed and in his deathbed. He who thought he saw clearly did not see that every man marries his mother. In remorse at his ignorance and in self-punishment for his arrogance, Oedipus blinded himself. By turning against his ego, dimming the light of consciousness, he found the peace of the unconscious and of the body. He returned to the realm of the mother-earth goddesses. This denotes a giving up of the arrogance of knowledge and power and an acceptance of humility.

9. This translation of the last lines of the play is taken from Freud's "The Interpretation of Dreams." It is superior, in my opinion, to the translation by David Greene in *The Complete Greek Tragedies—Oedipus the King* (Chicago: The University of Chicago Press, 1959).

The rise of the ego to dominance in the personality of early Greek man produced the first oedipal situation. Since then ego consciousness or self-consciousness has grown and spread. Most people in the industrial cultures of today are egotistic, that is, ego values direct their thinking and actions to a great degree. These values are power, possessions, and progress. These are also patriarchal values, and the family that lives in terms of them is a patriarchal family. Every child growing up in such a family is necessarily subject to an oedipal conflict with the consequences we have seen in previous chapters. Why this happens I will try to show in the next sections.

The Hierarchy of Power and Power Struggles

The important element in the oedipal situation is conflict. Since the oedipal situation is a triangle, there are conflicts between all the parties involved. In the preceding section we saw that conflict between father and son was a major theme in the three plays by Sophocles based on the Oedipus story. But a deeper interpretation revealed that the basic conflict in the plays was between the patriarchal and matriarchal systems of society, a conflict that was resolved culturally in favor of the patriarchate. This resolution meant that the masculine principle, represented by the ego, individuality, and culture, became dominant over the feminine principle, represented by the body, the community, and nature.

The basic conflict in the oedipal situation of the child is, therefore, between the parents. Their relationship forms the base of the triangle, and conflicts in that relationship are the cause of all the problems that develop in the children. I made the statement in the first chapter that where husband and wife are sexually fulfilled by their relationship, the children are not caught in an oedipal situation. We must recognize, however, that in our culture, which is based on the patriarchal principle, the man-woman relationship is rarely free from serious discord. Sexual fulfillment is equally rare. While there are some marriages in which love flourishes, most people erect façades to hide the dissatisfactions and disappointments that exist in their marriages. The façade serves to cover up the failure of the marriage from the public as well as from themselves.

My mother used to say that one should not be surprised at the fighting between nations when there is so much fighting in the home. As long as I can remember, my mother and father were in constant conflict. As a child I was appalled at this state of affairs. I was caught in the middle. Both parents confided in me, and I recognized that each had legitimate complaints against the other. Later, I saw that their personalities were opposites of each other. My mother believed in business before pleasure, my father in pleasure before business. As a result, my mother was joyless and my father penniless, to a degree, of course. Being split between them, I had to find some resolution to my internal conflict, which I did by saying that the business of life was pleasure. But I did not arrive at this solution until I had worked through the fears and anxieties of my own oedipal situation.

I have since come to realize that the situation in my family was not as unique as I once thought. Conflict is more common in marriages than harmony. Why is this so?

The patriarchal order is a vertical hierarchy of power and possessions. The individual at the top, a king or party leader, for example, has the most power, those lower in the hierarchy have less, and those at the bottom have the least or none. This hierarchy also existed in the family, with the father at the top, the mother below him, and the children at the bottom. At the high point in Roman civilization the father had absolute legal power of life and death over his wife and children. Legally, women have been second-class citizens until recently. The property of a married woman belonged to her husband. While much has changed, inequality still exists between the sexes.

Inequality mars the harmony of the man-woman relationship, which should be one of equal sharing in a common effort. The person who feels inferior is resentful of the one who has the superior position. This is especially true where ego consciousness is highly developed, as in our culture. Most people find it humiliating to have to submit to a power they did not grant. One doesn't feel love in this situation, but hate.

In the patriarchal family the inequality extended to sex. Women were subject to a double standard of morality that denied them the right to a full sexual life while it left men free to indulge their desires. The double standard was most strictly enforced in bourgeois society, where the striving for ego enhancement, power, and possessions was greatest. It was less enforced among the nobility, because their ego and power rested on the seemingly solid foundation of birth. It was least enforced in the lower classes, where the striving for power was weak. In bourgeois society a woman's chastity had value in the marriage market. Inevitably, a power struggle developed in every bourgeois home. The man had power through his control of the property, but the woman often countered by withholding her sexuality on the grounds of illness or indisposition. Used consciously or unconsciously, this tactic could be an effective weapon. The woman could also threaten a man with unfaithfulness, which was a real blow to his ego. But this game was played by both parties. The man often stepped outside the marriage for his sexual pleasure.

Fighting between husband and wife is not new. In the past women generally complained that there wasn't enough money, men that there wasn't enough sex. That situation seems to have changed with the demise of the double standard in the sexual revolution of the fifties and sixties. But this change doesn't seem to have reduced the fighting that goes on between the spouses. As long as the issue of power enters into personal relationships, there will be conflict. The unfortunate thing is that parents use their children in their power struggles with one another.

Despite the fact that the man is favored in the patriarchal system, he is not always the winner in the power struggle between husband and wife. And though he may be the financial support of the family, he is not always the boss in the home. He has titular power, but effective power often resides with the woman. Most patients, when asked who was the dominant figure in their homes, said it was the mother. This may have been due to the fact that the home is her domain, a position that society strongly supports because of her responsibility for the children. Actually, family fights are often decided in favor of the person who has the stronger ego and the best developed sense of self. But regardless of who is dominant in the family, conflict between the parents is the base upon which the oedipal triangle rests.

Not only do parents use their children in their fighting with one another, but children take advantage of their parents' power struggle to gain power for themseves. They form alliances with one parent or the other for their own ends. This statement may seem to contradict my previous assertion that children are innocent. They are, but only until they are hurt by the use of power against them. Being lowest in the hierarchy, they are most vulnerable. Parents often unload on their children the hostilities and anger they had toward their own parents but dared not express. Many take out their frustrations on their children. A parent generally feels superior to his child. The simplest way to demonstrate that superiority is to issue an order that the child is to obey without question.

The underlying conflict between parents and children stems from the parents' need to maintain an ego position against the child. This leads to a clash of wills between them. For example, a child makes a request for something (a candy or a toy), which the parent cannot or will not grant. The parent says no. But the child refuses to accept this rejection and asks, "Why?" To that question many parents respond by saying, "Because I said no." The parent's ego quickly becomes involved, changing the situation into a clash of wills. When this happens, the child must submit because the parent cannot allow his authority or power to be challenged. In all fairness, I must say that children can make more demands than parents can fulfill. This is particularly true in our culture, where so many things tempt a child's desire. Parents are often forced to say no. While this answer may distress a child, it will never cause a serious problem unless the child senses that the real issue is one of power and authority.

Another factor that produces a state of tension between parents and children is the pressure of modern living to which parents are subject. They have so many things to do that they don't have the energy or patience to deal with a child's lively nature. It's always "Be still. Keep quiet. Don't move." No child can obey these injunctions, and so a clash develops. I have seen the following scene repeated in different places. This one took place in an airport. A mother with a baby and a two-year-old was waiting to board a plane. The child wandered off, and the mother brought it back. It happened again, and the mother brought the child back angrily. The third time she was furious. She grabbed the child's arm and jerked him back to her seat so violently that he began to cry. In a harsh voice she said, "I told you to stay here." Although we can sympathize with the mother in this situation, we must recognize that the child felt abused and powerless. He could not understand the reason for his mother's anxiety and irritability.

In our culture parents use their superior strength and power to force children to obey their orders. The child feels helpless and powerless. Children, being naturally dependent on their parents, are powerless against them; but only when the parent imposes his will upon the child does the latter become aware of his vulnerability. Normally a child sees his parent as a supporter and protector, not as an antagonist. But when the latter is true, yielding amounts to a submission, for which the child compensates by an inner resolve to gain the power that would enable him to win over the parent. Thus, every submission has a twofold effect upon the child's personality. It diminishes the sense of self, thereby undermining the child's developing ego, and, at the same time, it increases his commitment to the ego as the representative of power. The child becomes ego conscious and ego centered, that is, power oriented. He enters the oedipal situation with mixed feelings: sexual desire for the parent of the opposite sex, fear and hostility toward both parents, and an awareness that sex can be used in the power struggle. It is a highly charged situation that can have only one outcome for the child: the loss of sexual feeling or psychological castration. This result is a direct consequence of the fears and hostilities engendered by the triangle.

The heightening of ego consciousness is not a positive development. It results in an increased self-consciousness, which has an inhibitory effect upon the expression of feeling and upon the surrender to the orgastic release. An exaggerated self-consciousness underlies the schizophrenic state and often ushers in a psychotic break. It is an extremely painful condition. In its less severe form it leads to pathological narcissism.

Conflict becomes an internal state as well as an external condition. Just as man turns against nature in the effort to subdue her, so the ego turns against the body. Through its ability to control and direct volitional activity, the ego can command the body. The will arises through this mechanism. Human beings are the only animals capable of willful actions. Through his will man transcends his animal nature and creates culture, but in the process, he separates himself from nature and becomes vulnerable to illness. That danger can be made clear if we compare the personality to a horse and rider. In this analogy, the horse represents the body while the ego is the horseman. When rider and horse are attuned to each other, like a cowboy and his mount, they can accomplish much and experience pleasure. But a rider who is insensitive to his horse can drive it into the ground. In this manner an ego that is out of touch with the body and under the pressure of a compulsive drive to succeed can push the body to a point where it will break down physically. If a rider is dissociated from his horse, he will get thrown. An ego that is dissociated from the body cracks up.

Let us return to the broad question of the power struggles that go on in the modern family. Most parents will, consciously or unconsciously, raise their children exactly as they were raised. A parent who has had a strict upbringing will tend to be quite strict with his own children. Men who have been beaten by their fathers when they were young often beat their own sons. It is rarely a simple matter of teaching the child to obey, or of applying the rule "Spare the rod and spoil the child." Such behavior on the part of the parent is often personally motivated. The parent resents the idea that his child will be better off than he was. "Why should you have it any better than I did?" is an unacknowledged feeling many parents have about their children. A parent who is egocentric will compete with his own child. He may be jealous of the relative freedom of the child and will try to break the child's spirit as he, himself, was broken. This is illustrated in the following case.

A woman came to therapy complaining of depression, anxiety and feelings of inferiority and inadequacy. Her marriage had broken up recently, and she was left with two teenage children. She had been very dependent upon her husband and had very little ability to stand upon her own two feet. But it was more than a psychological problem. She had very little feeling in her legs and while she knew they were there, she lacked the sense of security that feeling one's legs solidly on the ground provides. The reason for the lack of feeling in her legs was a severe contraction about her waist that appeared to divide her body into two halves. This apparent division was also functional. Her respiratory movements did not pass through the constriction into her abdomen. Since there is no feeling where there is no spontaneous movement, she was in effect cut off from the lower half of her body. Not only did she lack feeling in her legs, but her sexual feeling was also greatly reduced. She had been psychologically castrated as well as made helpless.

One day she was telling me about the difficulties she was having with one of her sons. The boy was rebellious and not obeying her. I could sympathize with her problem because young people growing up in this chaotic culture without discipline can get into serious trouble. However, I was quite shocked to hear her say, "I'll break his spirit. I'll break him in half." This is exactly what had been done to her, and now she proposed to do it to her child. When I pointed this out to her, I was further shocked when she replied, "Well, that's the way it has to be."

I was so angry I couldn't continue the session with this patient. I had been trying hard to help her overcome the crippling that she had suffered as a child, and now she was insisting upon subjecting her child to the same treatment. We had gone into her childhood experiences in previous sessions, and she had told me how her mother had beaten her when she dared to disobey. I realized that she had been "broken" more fully than I had thought. Despite our work, she had not accepted the fact of her own crippling. By denying her hurt and her pain, she was able to inflict it upon another.

Of course, not all parents subject their children to the same treatment they received. Those who are aware of the hurts they experienced from insensitive parents make every effort to spare their children a similar experience. This is generally true of parents who have had therapy. But even in these cases the parent is often aware that his child is reacting to him exactly as he reacted to his parent. For example, a man who was a patient of mine remarked, "I notice that my son is afraid of me just as I was afraid of my father. I wanted to spare him that." He didn't know how it had happened, because he never struck the boy. I pointed out to him that at times when he was upset, his brows descended and a dark look came into his eyes. It was a mixed look of resentment, hatred, and fear. I could easily imagine that a young child seeing that look in a parent's eyes would become frightened.

The look in my patient's eyes was his reaction to his father, of whom he had been afraid. It represented feelings that he had never been able to express. By suppressing them he had structured them into his body and into his character. It became his fate to be resentful, hateful, and frightened, although he had no understanding of the origin of these feelings. And unless his character structure changes, it will become the fate of his son.

In many cases, however, parents act out upon their children the hostility they have for their own parents in more direct ways. I treated a woman some years ago who consulted me because of an uncontrollable rage against a daughter. She recognized that she was destroying the girl, but she couldn't stop herself from berating and screaming at the child. She sensed that she was acting neurotically because the child was neither provocative nor ill behaved. I pointed out to her that while her anger had some validity in other areas of her life, expressing it toward her daughter was unjustified. From what she told me I could see that there was much in this patient's life to make her angry, but she refused to face it. She was sexually frustrated in her relationship with her husband, but she could not talk to him about it. It became obvious to both of us that she was using the child as a scapegoat. But since we could not get at the origin of the anger, the logical move was to discharge it by venting it therapeutically. Simply as an exercise, I had her kick the bed while screaming out her frustration. She also hit the bed with a tennis racquet to discharge her rage. My patient was agreeably surprised to find that her relationship with her daughter immediately improved. She reported that the child was also doing better in school.

Venting the anger in the therapeutic session allows the patient to function more realistically at home. It is like defusing an explosive charge one is carrying about. But this technique doesn't resolve the problem. The patient has to find out why she is so angry. What happened in her past to create such rage? What is happening in the present to maintain it? Also, she needs to restructure her character so that her life is more fulfilling.

When originally questioned about her childhood, the patient, June, said that it was a happy time. Only after the therapy had progressed for some time did it become clear that June and her mother had never got along. She recalled her mother's nagging and critical attitude to her and the lack of any affectionate contact between them. On the other hand, June and her father were close, and she had very warm feelings for him. Sex was a taboo subject in her childhood. No one ever spoke to her about it, but she said that she was spanked more than once as a young child for masturbating, although she didn't know at the time that she was doing anything wrong.

June had a recurrent dream about not being able to open her eyes. In the dream they were closed but not glued, but trying to open them by using her hands and shaking her head didn't help. She couldn't open them, and she felt frightened and frustrated. She said it was like driving a car blindfolded.

The interpretation of such a dream is easy. June can't open her eyes because she is afraid to see something—some image that is threatening and frightening.

Her eyes were ordinarily narrowed and half closed. She needed to open them to see what was frightening her. To accomplish this I used the following maneuver. I asked her to lie on the bed, open her eyes wide, and look at the ceiling. While she was doing this I applied some pressure with my fingers to the occipital region at the back of her head.° June said that she saw the face of her mother. I asked her to focus upon the expression in her mother's eyes and face. To her surprise June saw her mother looking at her with intense hostility. Previously, all she remembered about her mother was her worried and anxious look. Shocked at what she saw, June said, "Why is she looking at me with such hatred? What did I do?"

It took considerable analytic work before June realized that her mother saw her as a rival and threat. Her mother had lost her father when she was eleven years old and had married a man eleven years her senior, who both loved and fathered her. The

---

° The bioenergetic rationale for this procedure is described in my book *Bioenergetics*.

mother had reacted to June as if she was an intruder into the idyllic relationship between the parents. June related that "they held hands, hugged, snuggled, and shared marvelous stories about their courtship with us." June had closed her eyes so as not to see her mother's hostility to her. And she closed her mind's eye so as not to feel her own rage against her mother. But it came out against her daughter.

Feelings cannot be suppressed indefinitely. To suppress feelings is death. They come out often against the most innocent because they are the most vulnerable. Why do parents scream so at children? They take out on children the frustration of their own lives because children are helpless to fight back. Dominating a child gives a parent a sense of power to compensate for the feeling of being powerless that he experienced as a child. This is the essence of the power struggle. If a parent needs someone to dominate, a child is a convenient subject. In addition, parents project onto their children their own sexual guilt and punish them for the same innocent acts (masturbation) for which they were punished as children. In a patriarchal culture the misery is passed on from generation to generation.

Such behavior toward children is inconceivable in most primitive cultures and rarely encountered in Oriental ones. It is not because the lives of these people are without difficulties. They have their share of pain and frustration, which they accept as fate. They lack the egoism that sees everything in personal terms. In our culture, when a child doesn't do well in school, the parent often regards the child's failure as a sign of his own failure. By the same token, the child's success inflates the parent's ego. The ego of modern man is more involved in his relationships than is his heart. Thus, when a child disobeys, it is not a question of right or wrong but a challenge to the parent's ego. Having said no to the child, it becomes a matter of egotistic pride to uphold the no against the pleading or arguments of the child. In many families the child's assertion immediately leads to a power struggle, a conflict of wills, in which both parties are losers because what should be a loving relationship deteriorates to one of antagonism.

It can be argued that all societies, matriarchal as well as patriarchal, have rules of conduct that are enforced by some authority, the chief or the tribal council. The difference between the two systems lies in whether the rule is the accepted practice of the community or is the willful edict of an authority. The latter must create conflict, since it sets the ego of one person against that of another. In the play *Antigone*, for example, Creon, the ruler of Thebes after the departure of Oedipus, says to his son, Haemon:

> Yes, this, my son, should be thy heart's fixed
> law—in all things to obey thy father's will.[10]

Human beings are not born to be subject to another's will. They have not yet been fully domesticated like our beasts of burden. Yet civilization demands that they be harnessed to an economic and political system that limits their freedom and makes them subject to a hierarchy of power. How is this harnessing achieved?

Freud says that "the price of progress in civilization is paid by forfeiting happiness through heightening the sense of guilt."[11] He believes that culture would be impossible without instinctual renunciation, that is, "the nongratification (suppression, repression, or something else?) of powerful instinctual urgencies."[12] This nongratification produces a destructive aggressiveness in the individual, which then must be curbed. Originally this aggression is curbed in the child by punishment or the threatened withdrawal of love. As we saw earlier, the child submits and develops a superego, which is the introjection of parental authority. The superego

10. Quoted in Fromm, *The Forgotten Language*, p. 224.

11. Sigmund Freud, *Civilization and Its Discontents* (London: The Hogarth Press, 1953), p. 123.

12. Ibid., p. 63.

is maintained by the energies of the suppressed aggressive impulses, which are turned against the self, creating the sense of guilt. Thus, the sense of guilt is directly proportional to the degree of suppression. The more one suppresses hostility, the more guilty one feels. One feels guilty for the desire to smash the civilization that denies one fulfillment and to kill the father who is its representative.

Freud claims that "man's sense of guilt has its origin in the Oedipus complex and was acquired when the father was killed by the association of brothers."[13] Whether this is historically true, as Freud believed, is unimportant for our discussion. We have seen that conflict with the father is inherent in the patriarchal system, which, being based on power, invites the struggle for power. Thus, all civilized men who are egotistically oriented and strive for power are guilty of the desire to remove the father or kill him. This sense of guilt develops in the individual as a result of the oedipal conflict. At this time, too, the superego takes a controlling position in the personality, and the character structure of the individual becomes definitively set.

We must remember that the initial move in the Oedipus drama was made by the parent. In the legend it was the staking out of the infant to die that started the chain of events that fulfilled the prophecy of the oracle. It was a hostile act against the child done to protect the father's position and power. Similarly, in the modern family, the oedipal conflict is created by the hostile actions of a parent who sees the child as a threat to his power and as a rival for the affections of his spouse. In my view, the child as he enters the oedipal period is innocent, like any animal. He loses his innocence as he becomes aware of the intrigues and manipulations by his parents to control him, to make him adapt to the culture, and to use him for their own ego needs. In self-defense, he learns to use their tactics against them, but in the process he becomes an egotist like his parents, perhaps even going

13. Ibid., p. 118.

them one step better. There is a saying: "If one fights the devil with the devil's weapons, one becomes a devil."

But why is the process of cultural adaptation invariably associated with sexual repression? I don't agree with Freud that creative achievement depends on the sublimation of the sexual drive. On the contrary, individuals with more sexual aliveness are, often, the more creative persons. But productivity is another matter. If we wish to harness the human animal to the economic machine, we must "break" him as we do other animals that we put to work for us. This can be done only if we tame the free and wild animal *sexuality* of the person. Man learned long ago that he could change the wild animal into a beast of burden by castrating it. This was how he obtained oxen for his plows. Without planning it consciously, he uses the same technique on his own offspring, except that the effective agent is the threat of castration. That threat reduces the intensity of the sexual drive and functions as a psychological castration, making the child amenable to being schooled for his social role as a productive worker. It has the additional advantage of not interfering with the individual's reproductive function. Erich Fromm came to the same conclusion. In a recent study, he says, "The effort made to suppress sex would be beyond our understanding if it were for the sake of sex as such. Not sex, but the breaking of the human will is the reason for vilifying sex."[14]

In describing the social conditions that produce the neurotic character, I may give the impression that in the modern family there is nothing but hostility toward children and a desire to break their spirit. Of course, that's not true. There is love as well as hate, a respect for the child's integrity as well as the need to make him conform. Where the acculturation process is handled with love and respect for the child, he is not severely traumatized. However, I do not believe that even with the best intentions it is

---

14. Erich Fromm, *To Have or To Be* (New York: Harper & Row, Publishers, 1976), p. 79.

possible to raise a child in the modern world without his developing some degree of neurosis. No parent living in this culture can fully dissociate himself from its values. The attempt to do so creates other problems.

We must also remember that in our culture infantile sexuality is not accepted as normal and natural by most parents. As long as we have a hierarchy of values, everything associated with the lower half of the body is viewed as common, vulgar, and dirty. Par contra, we view the functions of the upper half of the body as superior, special, and clean. Knowledge and power are honored, whereas sex and pleasure are devalued. The latter belong to the matriarchal order. Most people are embarrassed when a child touches his genitals in public. Children quickly pick up their parents' attitudes toward sex, namely, that it is bad. These attitudes are so pervasive in our society that I have not found any patient who did not suffer from sexual guilt and castration anxiety. This is true of both men and women.

However, the degree of guilt and anxiety varies among different people. Since they are a function of the struggle for power, one finds less guilt and anxiety in the working classes than in the upper ones. For example, Reich reported that among German working people in the 1920s he found a sexual and emotional health, which were absent in the more affluent classes. If one gauges sexual health by the lack of tension in the body, especially in the pelvic area, one finds more health in the poor people of Latin America than in their richer neighbors to the north. On the other hand, the middle classes everywhere are generally pretty neurotic. Their upward striving for social position and prestige results in great pressure on their children to adjust to the social pattern. In modern industrialized societies, class distinctions tend to break down. In these highly mobile societies, where money and power determine social position, most people belong to the middle class. This is the class in which progress and power are most highly valued.

Progress Produces Conflict

Civilization or the patriarchal system is characterized by its emphasis upon conscious change and upon upward movement. The two are related. Conscious change is called progress, which is conceived as having an upward direction. We speak of the ascent of man, the rise of culture, the climb to success and power. Progress also has a temporal dimension. It implies that the new is always superior to the old, that what is later in time is better than what was earlier. While this may be true in some technological fields, it is a dangerous belief if applied too broadly. It can be extended to imply that the son is superior to the father or that tradition is merely the dead weight of the past. In a culture in which progress is an important value, conflict between the generations will inevitably develop.

There have been and still are cultures in which respect for the past and tradition are more important than the desire for change. In these cultures, conflict between the generations is rare and neurosis is minimal. For thousands of years, even through the greater part of civilization, the pattern of life was for a son to follow in the footsteps of his father as a daughter followed those of her mother. The child wanted no more than to be as big a person as the parent and to do as good a job. This is not to say that the relationship to the parent was always amicable—that is not human nature. It does not mean that every son adopted his father's vocation or occupation. Until recently the choices of ways to earn a living were very limited for the average person. A boy found his place in the world by identifying with and learning from his father, a girl by identifying and learning from her mother. Or, if the family was large, the son might be apprenticed to another man, who became a father surrogate for the same purpose.

Jacob Bronowski, in his book *The Ascent of Man*, describes a nomadic people, the Bakhtiari of Persia, who have followed the same pattern of life for countless generations. Each year they move their flock of sheep and goats over mountains and across rivers in search of pasture; in the second half of the year the journey is repeated in reverse. They cross six ranges of mountains during each passage, marching through snow and spring flood-water, a pattern that has not changed substantially for many thousand years, except that the Bakhtiari now have pack animals.

Bronowski visited these people and filmed them for his television series. What he saw and showed us were boys with wide-open, innocent eyes, who looked at their fathers with admiration and respect. Bronowski's comment expresses his contempt: "The only ambition of the son is to be like the father."[15]

Admittedly, it is a static culture. Here is how he describes their life: "It is a life without features. Every night is the end of a day like the last, and every journey will be the beginning of a journey like the day before. When the day breaks, there is one question in everyone's mind: can the flock be got over the next high pass? One day on the journey, the highest pass of all must be crossed. This is the pass Zadercu, twelve thousand feet high in the Zagros, which the flock must somehow struggle through or skirt in its upper reaches. For the flock must move on, the herds-man must find new pastures every day, because at these heights, grazing is exhausted in a single day."[16]

How Bronowski can describe such a life as being without features, I cannot understand. It is a simple life, but it is also a life of adventure. If survival is the only reward, it is still the greatest of prizes. Traversing mountain passes on foot and horse is a challenge to the courage and strength of any individual. Be-sides the normal concerns of communal living, birth, growth, marriage, and death, which we all share, the Bakhtiari live in the splendor of a nature that is vast, unpredictable, and ever changing.

15. Jacob Bronowski, *The Ascent of Man* (Boston: Little, Brown & Co., 1973), p. 62.

16. Ibid.

Theirs is the wonder of the natural world, ours is the magic (theater, radio, television) and enchantment of a man-made world. The two worlds are different, but to regard the civilized world as superior is typical of the arrogance of civilized man.

Nomadic life is one of physical hardship, with survival always an issue. With its power to ensure our survival, civilization allows us a life of comparative physical ease. The nomad's world is circumscribed and isolated; the civilized world is seemingly open and limitless. But such descriptions do not qualify individual existences. Too many people in our culture live lives that are circumscribed, isolated, and out of touch with the enriching currents of civilization. But I am not arguing for or against civilization. If the nomadic life is not romantic, ours is certainly not ideal. But we cannot go back, even if we wanted to. Civilization is our fate.

What is the fate of the nomad? Bronowski says that the odds for the herdsman that his flock will increase or decrease are always the same, year in and year out. "And beyond that, at the end of the journey, there will be nothing except an immense, traditional resignation."[17] But resignation is not the correct term for the attitude of a people who have the courage to live such an arduous life. Resignation implies that one had a hope for something better. They have no hope or desire for change because they are content with their life. They accept it with an inner peace and calm that we lack. We are the ones who struggle with life to make it better, who cannot accept it, because it ends in death, and in the end it is the civilized person who resigns and dies painfully. For the Bakhtiari who has come to the end of his journey, there is no struggle. He accepts death as he has accepted life, unflinchingly and uncompromisingly.

The Bakhtiari lack the cultural refinements that we associate with civilized ways. Yet, just because of this lack, they have something we have lost, and that is a feeling of harmony, of

17. Ibid., p. 64.

integrity, and of peace of mind. We civilized people are all in a state of conflict, constantly struggling to harmonize the opposing demands of culture and nature, of ego and body, of duty and pleasure. For all of us the struggle is painful, and for some of us it is hell. The Bakhtiari have no such inner struggles. Their eyes are clear; they can sense the wonder and be filled with awe at the grandeur and magnificence of the universe. In my opinion there is no grandeur in our world of subways and skyscrapers, no wonder and no awe. Compared to the Bakhtiari, we live like moles. All we see are dollar signs. Perhaps I am biased. But I see in my native city of New York that as the buildings rise higher, the quality of city life falls lower.

I was particularly struck in reading the account of these people by Bronowski's remark about the relationship of son to father, because it belies Freud's view that the Oedipus complex is inherent in human nature. I believe that this complex arises only when parents have power. Parents have always had authority, but power is a different thing. Authority directs, but power controls. Power represents the ability to impose one's will. The person with authority is respected; the person with power is feared and obeyed. Power creates the kind of inequality between people that is the root cause of all conflict, because no person wants to be subject to another's power. It robs an individual of his freedom, his dignity, and his humanity. Children especially are very sensitive to power manipulations until they learn how to manipulate in turn.

In the long history of human civilization, power has been a limited commodity. Only a few possessed it: rulers, their followers, the rich. And it is in the families of parents with power that the oedipal problem arises. This fact was clearly pointed out by Reich in his analysis of the origin of sexual repression. Basing his remarks upon the study of sexuality among the Trobriand Islanders by the anthropologist Malinowski, Reich remarks, "Children in the Trobriand Islands know no sex repression and no sexual secrecy. Their sex life is allowed to develop naturally, freely and unhampered *through every stage of life with full satisfaction*. The children engage freely in the sexual activities which correspond to their age."[18] Their society showed "no sexual perversions, no functional psychoses, no psychoneurosis, no sex murder." Reich then pointed out, "There is only *one group* of children that is excluded from this natural course of events. These are the children who are predestined for a certain type of economically advantageous marriage. This kind of marriage brings economic advantages to the chief, and is the nucleus from which a patriarchal social order develops. This cross cousin marriage is found wherever ethnological research has revealed actual or historical matriarchy (cf., e.g., Morgan, Bachofen, Engels). The children destined for this kind of marriage are, just like ours, brought up in sexual abstinence; they show neuroses and those character traits with which we are familiar in our character-neurotics."[19]

If Reich's analysis of Trobriand culture is correct, there is a direct connection between the possession of power, sexual repression, and the oedipal conflict. We can see the same relationship in Western civilization. Illegitimacy, for example, was not a problem for peasant families in preceding centuries. Children were generally welcomed on a farm as helpers regardless of their origin. For the same reason, mothers of children born out of wedlock were not looked down on. Farm children did not suffer the same degree of sex repression as did the children of the bourgeoisie who lived in cities. The double standard of sexual morality was most enforced in the families of the bourgeoisie, whose daughters were programmed for advantageous marriages that would further the family's fortunes. This code could be imposed only if children were subject to a sex-repressive upbringing from their earliest years. It was the children of these families that Freud saw in his

18. Wilhelm Reich, *The Function of the Orgasm* (New York: The Orgone Institute Press, 1942), p. 201.

19. Ibid., pp. 202–203.

consulting room at the turn of the century. As long as a major proportion of a nation's population lived on farms in close association with the earth, that nation had a reservoir of people whose emotional health had not been undermined.

The agricultural life, though significantly different from the nomadic existence, had many elements in common with the latter. It was still a natural world in which survival was not guaranteed. Before the introduction of power machinery into farming, the farmer was only slightly less subject to the natural forces than the nomadic herder. He, too, fully accepted the eternal cycle of life, death, and rebirth with no thought that he could or should change it. He was content if his children followed in his footsteps, for survival was still the main issue of life.

The importance of agriculture for the development of civilization is that it not only permitted man to settle down and begin to accumulate possessions but it produced a surplus of food. The existence of surplus food allowed a greater degree of labor specialization, since not everyone had to be engaged full time in the production of food. In addition, surplus food constituted power in the hands of whoever controlled it, for with it one could hire workers or soldiers.

Once people rise above the survival level, that is, when they take the first step upward on the social ladder, they become conscious of their social position. They feel superior to those still on the survival level but inferior to those above. They become self-conscious or ego conscious. People who live on a survival level are not self-conscious because all their energies are engaged in the task of survival. Those of us who live above that level would describe their situation as a struggle for survival. But the word struggle is inaccurate. There is no struggle when one accepts his fate and position. It is the ego-conscious individual who struggles to rise higher in the social hierarchy. The higher he rises, the more ego conscious he becomes, which intensifies the ego drive for dominance and the struggle that it entails. This person calls every step upward progress.

Another aspect of this situation is that this ego drive knows no limits. We rationalize the drive for power by speaking of the security, the comforts, and the conveniences it provides, but when all these needs are fulfilled, the drive for more money and more power continues. Even those at the top keep striving for more power. It seems that once this drive takes hold in the personality, there is no stopping it. I know there are many exceptions to this statement, but I believe it has a general validity. In fact, the drive is not limited to individuals or families. Nations constantly seek more power to dominate other nations. On the deepest level this ego drive for power represents civilized man's desire to control life (nature and fate) because he is afraid of life.

Let us see now how this drive affects relationships in the family. Its very existence presupposes a dissatisfaction in the person with his state of being. The self-conscious individual is not a happy person. He suffers from a deep-seated sense of inferiority for which the drive for power aims to compensate. That sense of inferiority stems largely from the psychological castration the person suffered in the oedipal phase of his development. The result, as we saw, is a power struggle with his spouse that produces resentments and hostilities on both sides, eroding the love that existed between them. Their sexual pleasure is decreased, intensifying the feelings of resentment and hostility. The children are drawn into this struggle. Normally they side with the parent of the opposite sex, to whom they are attracted by their sexual feelings. However, the child is aware that each parent has some validity to his complaints.

When this happens, jealousy is aroused, and all the latent hostility is now focused upon the child, who is caught in the middle. The seductive parent is no help to the child, for in self-defense that parent will deny his manipulation and even accuse the child of being the sexual provocateur. This is easy to do, since the child's sexual feelings are open, while the parent's are hidden. The child is in an impossible situation and must beat a retreat. The child's solution to his dilemma is the surrender of sexual feeling.

With this surrender the child accepts the guilt for his sexual responsiveness and becomes psychologically castrated.

The idea of progress adds further fuel to the oedipal fire. Progress demands that each generation excel the preceding one. The son is to do better and have more power and prestige than his father. The daughter is to have a finer house, a better life, a higher social position than her mother. This demand is imposed by the parents in the name of progress, but in reality to satisfy the parents' need to rise higher in the social world. For the mother, her son's success vindicates the sacrifice of her sexual fulfillment and happiness. For the father, the boy's success is a substitute for his own failure. The interest of the parents in the daughter's success has a similar motivation.

When such expectations are placed upon a child, whether openly expressed or not, they intensify the oedipal conflict. The boy is forced to compete with his father, and so he measures himself against him. Seeing the discrepancy in the size of their sexual organs, the boy becomes very conscious of his inferiority, a consciousness that may stay with him throughout his life. This feeling of inferiority is responsible for the tendency men have to compare their genital organs with those of other men. It also increases the drive for power to compensate for this feeling. Being set up to compete with his father produces in the boy a fear of his father, which is experienced as castration anxiety.

There is, however, another side to this picture, which is that the boy also believes that he is superior to his father. He is expected to outperform his father. And his mother may look upon him as in some way better than his father. Then, as he grows older, he picks up from his culture the idea that older people, including his parents' generation, are passé, behind the times. Very many young people believe that they are smarter and more sophisticated than their elders. In some cases this may be true, given the early exposure of children to sex and violence on television. Thinking they are superior, these young people are quite resistant to learning from those who are older or in authority.

Too often they are contemptuous of old, established ways. This contempt covers both their fear and an underlying sense of inferiority.

The boy also feels that to surpass his father is to displace him in his position as husband and head of the family. The parents are not thinking sexually, but the child is. Success means to win over the father and, therefore, to have the mother. This is what Oedipus did. Seemingly, this is what the father is encouraging, but, also unexpressed, is the threat of castration for the child's daring to compete. However, if the boy doesn't succeed, he is also blamed In some cases the danger of success is so great that the person would rather fail in all endeavors than risk the challenge. In others success in the world is achieved only after the child has accepted his castration. He is allowed to succeed because he is doing it for his father. This was true of Robert, whose case I described in the first chapter. The dynamics for the female child are pretty much the same.

Children growing up in this modern culture cannot avoid the oedipal situation or the conflicts that surround it. There seems no other solution than the one Freud saw, namely, the suppression of sexual feeling under the implied threat of castration and the submission to the demand for progress. Having accepted defeat, the child slowly sets about to reverse it. He commits himself to the goals of power and progress. With power he need not be so frightened. With more power he might even overcome his fear of castration. With further progress he could deny the existence of the oedipal problem and convince himself that he is the liberated generation. But the fates are not deceived, they are waiting. Despite our power, or because of it, as in Oedipus' case, we are visited with a plague of mental illness. More progress is not the answer. Our way out of the trap is the one Oedipus took, namely, the attainment of wisdom and humility through the surrender of the arrogance associated with ego consciousness. There is an underlying theme in Greek mythology pertinent to this issue. If the hero "acts in the arrogance of egomania, which the

Greeks call hybris, and does not reverence the *numinosum* against which he strives," it must end in disaster, death, or madness.[20] Oedipus, however, did find the peace of mind for which we are all searching.

20. Neumann, *The Origin and History of Consciousness*, p. 188.

8 / The Wisdom of Failure

The Riddle of the Sphinx

When the plagues hit Thebes, Oedipus consulted Tiresias, a blind seer, just as today a person suffering from the modern plague of emotional illness would consult a therapist. A seer can predict the future because he can *see* into the nature of things. But Tiresias was blind: the vision of the seer is not a function of ego consciousness like ordinary sight but of the unconscious or god-like function of the right hemisphere, as Jaynes believes. The conscious eye can be deceived by the appearance of things, which often contradicts their true nature. With people, it is a general rule that the more elaborate the façade, the greater is the inner emptiness. A seer must understand human nature if he is to predict the fate of man.

An ideal therapist should be a seer like Tiresias, able to read character and predict fate. We turn to him for counsel because we expect him to be wise and to have an understanding of human nature. Without that understanding he is not able to help his patients heal the splits in their personalities that destroy their inner unity and harmony. In this chapter let us look at the nature of man and try to arrive at an understanding of wisdom. We shall see that the riddle of the Sphinx contains some important keys to an understanding of human nature if our analysis goes deeper than the accepted answer.

Oedipus said that *man* was the animal who walks on four legs in the morning (infancy), two legs at midday (maturity), and three legs in the evening (old age). While this is the correct answer to the riddle, it leaves unanswered the more important question: What is the nature of this creature who has three different ways of standing or being in the world? I stated earlier that Oedipus was guilty of the arrogance of knowledge; he thought he knew. None are so blind as those who think they know.

Let us examine the three stages in the life of a human being to see what they mean. As an infant crawling on all fours, man is like all other animals. The animal is characterized by the way it lives fully the life of the body, freely following its impulses and knowing only the need to satisfy its wants and desires. The human infant is exactly like that. It is born a mammal, more helpless and more dependent than other mammalian young, but with the same instincts for survival. A basic instinctual action, common to all mammals, is sucking the breast for nourishment. No one has to teach the newborn infant how to perform this action; it is part of its nature. In primitive and nonindustrial cultures children are nursed up to five years, long past the time when the child is able to stand on its own feet, speak, and eat solid food. This long period of nursing not only fulfills the child's oral needs, it strengthens its animal nature, which is the base of its being. Neurosis is marked both by some degree of sexual disturbance (orgastic impotence) and also by a disturbance of the sucking impulse. The latter is manifested by an inability to suck air fully and deeply while breathing.

The second stage begins before the first has ended. It represents the phase of man's existence when he is most human, that is, when he is able to speak. The use of language is the most human attribute. It is closely related in time to the ability to stand on two legs. A child says his first words around the time he takes his first steps, at about one year of age. Speaking and standing on two legs separates man from the other animals. He now has a different relationship to the world about him. With his focused vision he looks out upon the world, and it is his nature to seek to dominate and control it. He is no longer a passive participant in the events of nature. By his manipulation of the environment, he imposes his will upon nature. He becomes a creator. As a creator man identifies with God, whom he sees as the creator of the universe. In this stage of his life man aspires to be godlike; that is, he strives for omniscience, omnipotence, and immortality, the attributes of the godhead. He looks to the heavens for his inspiration and his knowledge.

The idea that man has a dual nature is a common one. Erich Fromm speaks of man's "paradoxical nature, half animal, half symbolic."[1] Our predicament has also been described as one in which we are simultaneously worms and gods. This duality can also be expressed in terms of the ego and the body, self-consciousness and unconsciousness, the left and right hemispheres. Although this duality is inherent in the nature of man, it developed through a historical process in which ego consciousness came into being and the matriarchal order was replaced by a patriarchal one. We have also seen that the tension between the dual and antithetical aspects of man's nature renders him vulnerable to mental illness.

The riddle of the Sphinx adds a third stage to the life of man. Without this third term it would seem that we are doomed to lead

1. Erich Fromm, *The Heart of Man, Its Genius for Good and Evil* (New York: Harper & Row, 1964), p. 116.

a divided existence. What is the meaning of the third stage when man walks on three legs? This is indeed a strange creature, neither man nor beast; or, perhaps, at this point he is fully man and beast like the Sphinx. A third term is always necessary to understand dualities or contradictions. In dialectical thinking this third term is called the synthesis and represents the reconciliation on a higher level of the opposition existing between thesis and antithesis. Birth and death can be viewed, for example, as a dialectical relationship arising out of life. Birth is the beginning and death the ending of life and, thus, they are opposite concepts. The synthesis is rebirth or new life, which emerges from their interaction. Without birth and death there would be no rebirth or new life.

An old man can no longer support himself on two legs, hence the cane. He no longer aspires to be godlike. Nearing the end of his life's journey, he is weary. He accepts his mortality, and so death loses its terror. Death is often seen by older people as an earned rest, a welcome surcease from life's toil, a return to one's forefathers. In many primitive cultures old people go away voluntarily to die so as not to burden the younger generation. They do it without fear.

Rebirth is not necessarily reincarnation. It is first a return to the source of life. The body goes back to the earth from which it came, and the spirit becomes part of the cosmic energy ocean. The two will come together again in the creation of another living body. The individual returns to the universal and ceases to retain any individual character. Like drops of water that fall into the ocean, we lose our separateness. The analogy with the ocean is apt, for life as we know it began in the ocean. Each life crystallizes out of the universal matrix. That is why an infant feels so much part of the whole, why a child feels such a close relationship to all living creatures. His boundaries have not yet been fully established, and he is still open to all kinds of influences.

The second stage is marked by a heightened sense of individuality. This is certainly due to the development and growth of the ego, which endows the human being with a conscious sense of self. But individuality means separateness. We no longer see ourselves as part of the broad process of life on earth but as unique beings whose separateness is more important than our commonality. We are not just self-conscious; we are ego conscious, in fact, egoistic. And since our egos will not survive the death of the body, we live in fear of death. Persons who are not involved with their egos, who retain a strong identification with their animal nature, are not frightened of death.

As one grows older, the sense of separateness is slowly reduced. Old people do not live on an ego level. Their concerns are not about their individuality but about the river of life, the family, the community, the nation, people, animals, nature, life. They can die easily if they are assured that life will continue positively, for they feel part of the river again, and soon they will be part of the ocean. When they are very old, they no longer belong to our time and space but to all time and all space. Laurens Van der Post reaches a similar conclusion after observing two old Bushmen facing death because they can no longer keep up with the community. "We will have the courage to meet it and give meaning to the manner of our dying provided we, like these humble, wrinkled old Bushmen, have not set a part of ourselves above the wholeness of life."[2]

Now, let us examine each of these stages in more detail. Notice that the three stages of man are also related to three different time perspectives. The infant, like all animals, lives fully in the present. An adult, on the other hand, lives partly in the future. He conceives and plans for future needs. Human beings can project part or all of their consciousness into the future, an ability that can produce a momentary disruption of their perceptions of reality. A person can slip into so vivid a daydream that he loses his awareness of what is happening to him. Man's creative ability is directly

2. Laurens Van der Post, *The Lost World of the Kchahais* (London: The Hogarth Press, 1969), p. 253.

dependent on his ability to project his consciousness into the future.

The different time perspectives of a child and an adult are related to the basic principles underlying human behavior, the pleasure principle and the reality principle. The former states that organisms strive for pleasure and to avoid pain or stress. All living creatures, including man, obey this principle. It completely governs the behavior of a child. But in the case of an adult, there is a secondary principle that modifies the action of the first one. The reality principle states that pleasure can be postponed or a pain tolerated for the sake of a greater pleasure or to avoid a greater pain in the future. The operation of the reality principle depends on the ability to anticipate a future situation. All animals have this ability to some degree, since it is the basis for learning. In the adult human being, however, this ability is so much more highly developed and conscious that the difference in the degree becomes a difference in kind.

Trouble arises when we are unable to keep a balance between these two perspectives. With increasing industrialization, the tendency in any culture is to focus more and more upon the future. Almost everyone, from the child starting school to the largest nation, is involved with plans, projects, and pursuits. It is not simply a question of reaching a particular goal. As soon as one is reached, a new one is set. This is called progress. It engages people in unending activity, doing, the antithesis of being. We are so trained to look ahead that no sooner do we begin our careers than we are thinking and planning for our retirement. As soon as a child enters school or even before, he and his family are planning for college. People work to build an estate for the time they retire or die. Too often the latter happens first.

This exaggerated focus upon the future robs the present of its meaning and pleasure. And, since the future grows out of the present, the loss of the present turns the future into a dream or an illusion. It is like trying to build a house without a foundation. All that one can produce is a castle in Spain. It is not surprising that so many people end up in depression or have so little sense of being. When the future supersedes the present, when doing negates being, we are in trouble. A proper balance can be obtained when a person or a society is grounded in the body, the present, and being. Then the ego, the future, and doing rest upon a firm foundation. On a deeper level, the foundation itself rests upon one's being part of the earth and of nature.

What is the time perspective of the third stage of life? If the infant lives in the present and the adult in the present and future, what about an older person? As one grows older and the eyes dim with age, the future fades, the present is clouded, but the past becomes vivid and real. It is typical of old people to look backward in time. This is truly an amazing phenomenon. It means that old people are our links with the past and thus serve a very important function in society. The past can be read in books, but when it is recounted by an older person who has lived it, it has a different reality.

The concept of three stages in the life of man or three terms in any analysis of life functions is dialectical. There is an original unity that through the action of consciousness splits into opposite or antithetical aspects to seek a synthesis on a higher level. The dialectical principle can also be applied to the way information is processed. The two antithetical ways of processing information are understanding and knowing. Day-old chicks from a hatchery "know" what food to eat. But knowing is not the right word here. They receive information from their organs of sight, smell, and taste that is unconsciously processed to guide their actions. I call this understanding. Knowing denotes that the information is processed consciously. Let us examine each way in more detail so we can arrive at the synthesis.

The second edition of *Webster's New International Dictionary* quotes Coleridge as saying that understanding is "the power of dealing with the impressions of sense and composing them into wholes." This is what chicks do when they pick up and eat some things while leaving others. They understand what is good for them and what isn't. Infants have the same ability. Of course, this understanding is limited to those sense impressions the meaning of which their minds have learned through the evolutionary history of the species. Understanding means "what stands under." Under a child—or even a chick, for that matter—are millions of years of evolutionary history that have informed the body-mind what it means to be a child or a chick. Understanding is diffused in the tissues of the body, which sense and respond intelligently to the natural environment. Seifritz, who spent many years studying the slime mold, comments about protoplasm, "I cannot say that protoplasm is intelligent, but it does the intelligent thing."

Interestingly, Jaynes also derives understanding from what stands under. In the hierarchy of power in the bicameral kingdoms, man stands under his god. Interpreting a carving on a stele dating about 1750 B.C., Jaynes says, "Hammurabi listens intently as he stands just below him ("under-stands")."[3] Since the gods, according to Jaynes, are a function of the right hemisphere, which is concerned with wholes, we can relate understanding to that hemisphere, in contrast to knowledge, which would be a function of the analytic power of the left hemisphere.

Knowledge belongs to the second stage of life, the uniquely human stage. The dictionary defines it as the acquaintance with facts, truths, and principles derived from study and investigation. It concerns the conscious acquisition of information. It involves the use of language and other symbols. If understanding is related to the feeling processes of the body, knowledge is related to the thinking processes of the mind. Broadly speaking, understanding is a sensing from below, from the body, whereas knowing is seeing from above, from the mind or head. The distinction between understanding and knowledge is clear when we consider sex. I believe that an infant understands what sex is. This should not surprise us. He is not long removed in time from his conception

3. Julian Jaynes, *The Origin of Consciousness in the Breakdown of the Bicameral Mind* (Boston: Houghton Mifflin Co., 1976), p. 199.

in an act of sex and closer even to his birth, the end product of that act. Sex is part of his nature, but at this stage he has no knowledge of these things.

Knowing is a function of the ego, which, as it develops, will eventually take an objective and superior position with regard to the body. It would be very nice if our knowledge grew as our understanding deepened, but unfortunately this rarely happens. Very often what we think we know contradicts our understanding, and in the conflict between the two we tend to rely heavily upon knowledge and deny our understanding. Let me give an example. We know that power is an important force in this world and that without it we are vulnerable. We are willing, therefore, to make enormous sacrifices for it. We sacrifice our pleasure, our integrity, and our peace of mind for power in the form of money and success. We *understand* that pleasure, integrity, and peace of mind are essential to our well-being but we don't *know* this is so. It is not a provable fact like the effect of power. So we tend to ignore that understanding.

Here is another example. Pediatricians have studied the dietary needs of infants for a long time and have acquired some knowledge of this subject. Primitive people lacked this knowledge, but they had an understanding of how to nurse their children, and it worked. However, as our knowledge increased, breast feeding diminished. People seem to put more faith in knowledge than in understanding. Yet another example: We all understand that man is a part of nature and that his existence is dependent on the ecological balance in nature. But as we have gained knowledge of nature's laws and learned how to control it to provide for our needs, we have tended to ignore the understanding inherent in our animal nature.

Why? Well, knowledge is power, the power to control the results by manipulating the causes. This gives man the impression of being godlike, allaying his anxieties and assuaging his insecurity. Understanding offers no such illusory rewards. But these are illusory rewards because as our power increases we seem to suffer from more anxiety and insecurity than before. And more and more people need therapy to cope with these dis-eases.

The weakness in our reliance upon knowledge and power is that the former is imperfect and incomplete and the latter too limited. Only God is omniscient and omnipotent, and it is an illusion to believe that we can become gods. Our knowledge must always remain partial, because we are only part of the whole order of nature. We can only see one aspect at a time. In physics this is known as the principle of uncertainty. This states that with respect to very small particles such as electrons, if we know their position, we cannot determine their direction of movement or speed. If we ascertain the latter two, we cannot know the position. Unfortunately, the average person in our culture is schooled to believe that knowledge is certain.

When the facts are known through one's personal study and investigation, one's knowledge is fairly certain. However, too much of the knowledge that we take for granted represents the dicta of "authorities," who, too often, speak as if they had the omniscience of God. And when knowledge is presented in book form, people respect it as if it were holy. This is dangerous because it subverts the role of understanding. Instead of basing knowledge upon understanding, we try to derive our understanding from knowledge. This is like turning a house upside down and resting it upon the roof. No parent can understand a child by reading books on child psychology, and no therapist can understand a patient by studying books on clinical psychology. Understanding is an empathic process that depends on the harmonic response of one body to another.

This is not to negate the value of knowledge. It is merely a question of priorities. When I work with a patient, I rely heavily upon my empathic response to the person. Through my body I can sense how he holds himself and how he stands in the world. Until I get a feeling of the person, I can't make a move, for I would have nothing to go on but knowledge, and my knowledge may have no relevance to where this patient is at. The empathic response comes up spontaneously from my unconscious, and once that happens I can use my knowledge to interpret my response to the patient. To operate in this fashion I must trust my sensing. Not to do so is to lack sense.

Now let us turn to the third stage of man, in which we may find a synthesis of the conflict between knowledge and understanding. That synthesis is called wisdom, which we associate with an older person. Wisdom is the realization that knowledge not based on understanding is meaningless because it has no reference to the whole. On the other hand, understanding without knowledge is impotent because it lacks the factual information needed to control a situation or effect a change. An older person has lived in the present as a child, looked to the future as an adult; now, looking backward, he can see what it is all about. Wisdom is the realization that life is a journey, the meaning of which is found in the voyage and not in the destination. A wise person is like the Sphinx in that he has reconciled within himself the opposing forces in human nature, the animal body and the godlike mind.

Basically, therapy involves the acquisition of wisdom. One looks back to the past in an effort to reach an understanding of one's self, which, when added to one's knowledge of life, produces wisdom. Since the past is buried within the self, in the unconscious, looking backward also means looking inward. Understanding that is gained in this search is called insight. In bioenergetics this search is made along two parallel paths: through the analysis of memories, dreams, associations, and the transference situation; and through the body, the repository of all experience. I have else-where described the bioenergetic approach, and I would refer my readers to that study.[4]

One doesn't have to be old to acquire some wisdom. It would develop naturally if the knowledge we learned was integrated with the understanding we had, if our heads were truly one with

4. Alexander Lowen, *Bioenergetics* (New York: Coward, McCann & Geohegan, Inc., 1975).

our bodies. But this is not the way of our culture, which splits these aspects of man. To gain wisdom today one has to have lived long enough to be able to look back into the past with some objectivity. This explains why Jung believed that analysis works best with people over forty. It also explains why it is difficult to do conventional analytic therapy with children and adolescents. Children live too fully in the present, while the eyes of adolescents are turned to the future. This is as it should be, for young people need their dreams and children need their innocence. But often they also need help. There are many ways they can be helped. Working with the body, in my opinion, is one of the better ways. Family therapy is another effective approach, which by focusing on the interaction between parents and children opens the doors to communication between them.

Gaining wisdom is a process of seeing and accepting the contradictions in human nature, including that of our parents. At first we are angry, even furious, at their lack of love, their manipulation, and their insensivity. We feel the sadness of their unresponsiveness and we experience the fear that their disapproval and hostility aroused. We cry, scream, and rage because of the pain that is in our bodies from these early traumas. These feelings are valid, for they are us and we are them. Every feeling is a self-perception (to feel is to perceive the self in motion-emotion). Denying or suppressing a feeling reduces and deadens the self. But in time, as our pain is released, we also begin to understand our parents in terms of their own life situation. Then, as we become free from our bondage to the past, we realize and sense that our parents did love us as much as they were able. For there is no life without love.

Wisdom means seeing into the heart of things, beneath the surface of our contradictions, where there is neither good nor bad, neither right nor wrong. It means seeing the human being as the animal he is, struggling to gain security yet be free, to be productive but also joyful, to seek pleasure but also to know pain, to hope for transcendence and yet be content that one is contained within a finite body. It is to know that love does not exist without possibility of hatred. It is to know that there is a time for living and a time for dying. It is to know the glory of the blooming of life that seems to fade all too quickly but that leaves behind a seed that will bloom in its season. It is to know that the individual exists to celebrate life.

Reconciling the Contradictions

Human nature is full of contradictions. One of them revolves around the much debated question of free will. Is our behavior a matter of choice, or is it conditioned and determined by past experience?

We all believe that within limits we consciously choose how we will react to situations. Do we not deliberately choose the clothes we put on in the morning, the food we eat, the careers we pursue, and the persons we marry? Can we not choose to be honest or deceitful, kind or cruel, generous or selfish? Denying that an individual makes choices in his life clashes with our self-experience. On innumerable occasions throughout the day we consciously and deliberately choose to do some things and not to do others. As long as we are conscious and in full possession of our faculties, it seems to us that we have a choice.

Yet all analytic evidence points to the fact that our behavior is determined by past experience. Those of us who practice any form of analytic therapy study a person's past to understand why he feels and behaves as he does in the present. If we probe deeply and carefully into the person's unconscious, we can generally come up with some answers to explain his behavior. Here is an example.

A person comes for help because he cannot establish significant relationships with other people. He fears rejection, he feels rejected, and he acts in such a way as to provoke rejection. He cannot open up and reach out to people. Though he desperately wants contact with others, he withdraws and closes up when it is offered. Why? In such a case analysis invariably reveals that the person experienced a severe rejection in early childhood, which was so painful that he contracted and closed up in self-defense. As an adult, he feels that he dares not risk another rejection because he may not survive it. He avoids that danger by keeping apart, withdrawn and in a state of being rejected. It does not hurt if one is rejected for not opening up. It hurts only when one opens himself, reaches out, and is then rejected. As long as he stays contracted, there is neither hope nor pain, just aloneness.

Can one speak of choice in a case like this? Does a person have a choice whether to put his hand into a fire or not? If one has been burned touching a hot stove, one will be cautious touching any stove again. But only a fool will take a chance if he has been burned twice. Past experience structures our behavior to ensure survival. We do not close up, armor, or withdraw through choice, but out of necessity. No one deliberately chooses a neurotic style of life, since it is a limitation of being. The armoring process is a means of survival, a way of avoiding intolerable pain. Then, when the closing up or armoring has become structured in the body, that is, has become unconscious, we no longer have a choice in the present whether to open up and reach out or not. A locked door cannot be opened without the key.

Psychology is of relatively little help in this situation. A person can be made aware that in the closed-up state he will always feel rejected; that if he doesn't open up, of necessity others will reject him. But he cannot change his way of being by making a decision. This is because the conscious control of behavior is limited to volitional actions. The conscious mind, acting through the ego, commands the voluntary movements of the body. But this command was surrendered over those movements concerned with suppressed feelings. The suppression of feeling entails a state of chronic contraction in the muscles that would express the feeling. Chronic muscular tension is unconscious; that is, the person doesn't feel the tension or the muscle and, therefore, has no control over its movement. Besides, feeling in general is not subject to volition. A person can will himself to make the action of reaching out, but, without feeling, the movement is mechanical and ineffective. There is no way one can *directly* affect the unconscious bodily processes that have shaped the personality and determined its responses.

Consider the case of a person who struggles with an inordinate need for power and control. Invariably, analysis will show that as a child he suffered from a sense of helplessness and impotence that he felt threatened his survival. His drive for power can be seen, therefore, as a means to ensure his survival. Again, it was not a matter of choice but of necessity. Or we can take the case of a person whose behavior is submissive and passive. Is this the result of choice? Once more, analysis would reveal that it wasn't, that this pattern of behavior was adopted in order to survive. As the child experienced his family situation, it was either submit and survive or rebel and be destroyed. This cannot be regarded as a choice.

These analytic findings (some of which extend back over three quarters of a century) cannot be disputed. There is overwhelming evidence that even our so-called choices of career, mate, place to live, etc., are largely determined by our early experiences. As we get to know ourselves through analysis we realize how much our responses as adults were conditioned by events in our childhood. I cannot eat oatmeal today because as a child I choked on the lumps. My mother nonetheless insisted that I eat it. Innumerable instances of this kind of conditioning can be culled from anyone's life story. It makes one wonder how much choice one really does have in life.

However, acceptance of the concept of determinism poses a big dilemma. If behavior is largely predetermined and little is subject to the will, how responsible is a person for his actions? What position shall we take toward criminal behavior, which in every case where the analysis of the person's background is deep and thorough can be shown to be conditioned by early life experiences? Shall we say that such behavior is to go unpunished because an individual cannot be held responsible in situations in which he had no choice?

Obviously society can only function on the assumption that an adult individual is responsible for his actions. Social living would be impossible on any other basis. But this assumption implies the existence of a free will and the opportunity to choose between right and wrong. According to Genesis, when man ate the fruit of the tree of knowledge, he became like God, knowing good from evil. He gave up the innocence that characterizes the animal and in doing so lost the paradisical bliss of ignorance. With that knowledge man became Homo sapiens. Knowing right from wrong, he can be held responsible for his actions. It is on this principle that we excuse crimes by little children, who are still considered animals, and the insane, who are unable to judge.

The contradiction between determinism and free will cannot be resolved. Looking *backward*, it does seem that our behavior is predetermined. Looking *forward*, it seems that since we know right from wrong and have a will, this knowledge can be used constructively or destructively. If we say that both views of the human condition are valid and that it is a matter of which way we look, we gain some wisdom. We have reconciled the contradiction. Wisdom is the ability to look forward and backward, to see both sides of life with no illusions.

But isn't it an illusion to think that man *knows* right from wrong? He is taught certain rules of conduct by his parents, who got them from their parents. These rules vary from one culture to another, yet each culture believes that its rules are based upon a knowledge of right and wrong. If that belief were valid, man would be like God. But if this belief is an illusion, we may recognize that perhaps the illusion is necessary to endow the rules with a superior authority. A society will adopt certain rules of behavior to facilitate social living, and, if the community prospers, the rules will gradually become established truth for that community. One may then forget that they have become established by custom and not by divine law. The important question about any rule of conduct is whether it promotes the welfare of the community. A wise man can accept and live with this contradiction. He is not troubled by such statements as "it seems." He has no illusions about the certainty of man's knowledge.

The issue of free will versus determinism is not just a philosophic question. It lies at the heart of the therapeutic undertaking. How much choice does a patient have about his neurotic behavior? In working with a patient I always take the position that he is helpless to change his condition. If I didn't believe this, I would have to accuse him of malingering, of choosing to be ill for the secondary gains that illness can provide. Playing sick is one way of getting attention. And self-destructive behavior is one way to get back at someone. A child, for example, will not eat his dinner to spite his mother. But in this case we can surmise that the negative behavior is adopted because a positive attitude would be more painful. A child may forego dinner if eating it requires that he also swallow his humiliation or hurt. We can also understand that the child who has to play sick to get attention may be really sick at heart for the lack of attention.

But if a patient is powerless to overcome his neurosis, what responsibility does he have? He is, of course, responsible for his life just as any other adult is. No one can breathe for him, feel for him, or live for him. If he doesn't live his life it is lost. He owes this responsibility to himself. Part of this responsibility involves self-understanding, which includes a sensing of the fears, anxieties, and guilts that block him from being fully alive. No one can overcome his own fears, for that is equivalent to using the self to surmount the self, an impossibility. A patient doesn't get better by overriding his difficulties, but by accepting and understanding them. He learns that his fears and anxieties stem from early life situations that no longer exist except in his imagination. If he can surrender the defenses of these situations, he can experience a liberation from the fears, anxieties, and guilts that limit his being.

Giving up one's defensive posture and attitude requires no effort of will. It is what we therapists describe as "letting go." If anything, it is a letting go of the will, a surrender to the natural and spontaneous processes of the body and life. While the defensive system developed originally as a means of survival, in the present it constitutes a defense against life and represents a fear of life. It was erected through the use of the will, and its persistence is tied to the continued use of the will, though that use is unconscious. The patient needs to become aware that he is using his will, making an effort, or doing something unconsciously as a defense against life.

I shall illustrate this idea. The basic mechanism for the suppression of feeling is the inhibition of respiration. By reducing the intake of oxygen we dampen the metabolic fires and lower our energy level. This, in turn, decreases the intensity of our feelings and makes them easier to suppress or control. To mobilize suppressed feeling it is necessary, therefore, to get the patient to breathe more deeply. This is the technique that Reich used with me when I was his patient. It is a powerful technique and, at times, strong feelings erupted in me.[5] Many other times, however, I lay on the bed breathing and nothing happened. I was breathing too shallowly. Reich, who was sitting facing me, would then tell me to breathe more deeply. In response I made an effort to do as he directed, but this didn't work either. The effort required the use of my will which had an inhibiting effect upon feeling and emotion because of the conscious control involved. For the same reason, breathing exercises do not arouse feelings. It is a matter of letting the breathing happen rather than doing it.

I was supposed to let go, to give in to the spontaneous breathing of my body, for only in this way could I attain the full potential of my orgastic potency. The full orgasm is the most intense spontaneous activity of the body. One doesn't "do" an orgasm and one doesn't have to "do" breathing. The latter, like the former, is a

5. I have described some aspects of my therapy with Wilhelm Reich in the first chapter of my book, *Bioenergetics*.

natural, involuntary activity of the body. My shallow breathing was due to the fact that unconsciously I was restricting my breathing, partially holding my breath, because I was afraid to give in and let the involuntary processes of the body take over. This realization allowed me to let go, and I began to cry. I became aware of how much I held back from expressing my feelings. "Holding" by tensing muscles is a doing, an action of the will. Letting go is a stopping of the doing that allows life to flow. Life is spontaneous movement that doesn't require the use of the will.

The will is a function of the ego and represents the ego's control over volitional movement. Through this control the ego can mobilize actions that run counter to the immediate body feeling. A person may feel like quitting a race, but his will can drive him on to victory. He may be scared to death facing a danger, but with sufficient willpower he can master his fear and overcome the danger. The will is not a negative force, though it can be used against the best interests of the person. It is an extra force that will drive the body when feeling is inadequate for the task. Normally it is used only in emergencies.[6] When the will takes command, the body is harnessed by the ego as a horse is harnessed by a driver. The will is also the way an individual is harnessed to the patriarchal system and its values: power, productivity, and progress.

The contradiction in modern thinking is that power and productivity make one free. The logic behind this belief is that with enough power a man can do what he wants. There is no question that man's ability to *do* has increased vastly as he has gained knowledge and power. And from one point of view it can be argued that his greater mobility and wider scope of action represent more freedom than his forebears knew. Jaynes describes early civilized man as a slave of the gods. We think of the

6. See Alexander Lowen, *The Betrayal of the Body* (New York: Collier Books, 1969).

animal as being a slave to its instincts. But we are equally bound to our system by a sense of guilt, as Freud pointed out. We are literally bound by chronic muscular tensions that limit our respiration, depress our energy, and inhibit the free expression of feeling. In effect, we are dominated by an ego that can be as tyrannical as any despot.

The human dilemma arises because the effort to overcome nature or fate can lead to a more horrible fate than the one the person is trying to avoid. Thus, it seems that the more external security man builds for himself, the greater is his inner insecurity. Similarly, it seems that the more external freedom he gains, the less internal freedom he has.

One of the contradictions in human nature is that the awareness of freedom is conditioned by its loss. We think of an animal living in the state of nature as being wild and free because it can do what it wants. It can act freely upon its desires. However, the animal itself is not conscious of being free. That consciousness can arise only when the state of freedom can be contrasted with its opposite. Only when one has lost freedom can one become conscious of what freedom is. Consciousness develops through the recognition of opposites.[7] By the same principle, the conception of love can only arise from the experience of its loss. An infant who has not experienced that loss is aware only of the pleasure and fulfillment of his being. Like an animal, the child lives in the bliss of ignorance: innocent and unknowing of fate. An adult who has a developed ego consciousness looks to the future and conceives of fate. But by that very ability he risks losing his freedom in the struggle against fate.

The concept of freedom is associated with the idea of choice in the sense that without the right to choose, there is no freedom. Certainly, denying a person that right when choices are available limits his freedom. On the other hand, the absence of choice does

7. Erich Neumann, *The Origin and History of Human Consciousness* (New York: Pantheon Books, 1954).

not represent a loss of freedom. For example, in homes where everyone eats whatever is prepared for the day, no one feels constrained by the lack of a choice. In fact, the availability of choices is often experienced as a restriction because of the necessity to make a decision. Trying to choose an entrée from a menu where all the entrées have the same appeal can even be slightly painful. One doesn't feel free until the decision is made. Thus, if freedom means choice, which requires a decision, one ends with a burden that is a loss of freedom. How much easier and more pleasurable life can be when one doesn't have to make a decision because one's desire is so clear and strong that it leaves one with no choice in behavior.

Speaking personally, I hate having to make a decision. I feel trapped by the process. I have rarely made the right decision in my life. All the good moves I made, those that had a constructive effect on my life, were not the result of deliberate choice. I acted because my desire was so strong it allowed no choice. I didn't choose my wife; I fell in love with her. I didn't choose to fall in love; it hit me out of the blue. And so there were no regrets and no "what ifs" to mar my commitment to marriage. Nor did I choose my career. I had never seriously considered becoming a doctor until I met Wilhelm Reich and became involved in his kind of therapy. Once I did become involved, I felt I had to become a doctor. Looking backward, it seems a matter of fate. There was no question of choice. If there is no weighing the alternatives, there is no ambivalence and one's commitment is wholehearted.

In situations where action flows directly from feeling, one has the greatest *sense* of being free. Interrupt this flow and the sense of freedom is suspended. We should think of freedom as equivalent to being. We can picture freedom as a stream leaping down a mountainside, as a river flowing to the sea. The river is simply obeying a law of nature, gravity, but in the process of fulfilling its destiny to reach the ocean, it is free. It loses the image of freedom when it is dammed. Stopping the flow denotes a loss of freedom. The river in its flow to the sea is simply being a river. It stops being a river when it is dammed, and becomes a lake. There is also a life current in a person, which flows through time as the river flows through space. Its destiny is to merge at the end of the individual's life in the great ocean. We can go with the current, or we can try to slow it down or to stop it. In the latter case we will lose our freedom and still not overcome our fate.

It is a seeming contradiction to say that we are most free when we have no choice, when we are simply fulfilling our being, because the consciousness of freedom is associated with the idea of choice. This contradiction, like the preceding one, arises from the dual nature of man. As a child or animal, he is free but doesn't know it. As an adult who aspires to be god, he equates freedom with the ability to assert his will. Both positions are equally valid. Freedom in nature is different from freedom in culture. In the latter situation the inability to assert one's will denotes submission to the will of another. It is a loss of freedom since it is a denial of the right to express one's feelings. An individual may not have the right to do what he wants, but we insist that he should have the right to *say* what he wants. In nature or culture, freedom cannot be separated from the right of self-expression.

In most cases it is this right that is denied the individual. He is schooled to accept the values of a culture that places power over pleasure, productivity over creativity, and material progress over spiritual harmony. He is indoctrinated with the idea that thinking is a superior virtue to feeling and that achievement is the goal of life. He doesn't sense the loss of freedom in being harnessed to the industrial system. Now, I am not advocating that we surrender our aspirations, deny our minds, and revert to being pure animals. That is not a pronouncement of wisdom. Wisdom is balance, and a three-legged stance (old man), like a three-legged stool, offers the best balance. When one has become older, one knows that doing is valid only when it enhances being and that thinking makes sense only if it stems from feeling. One knows that computers cannot provide the answers to human problems. These have to be handled by people who feel and think. Our need today is for more feeling.

When feelings are strong, one knows what one wants. Then one has to think only about how to get it. But even here one's feelings can guide one. The result is a type of behavior that is open, direct, and in most cases, effective. Difficulties arise when feelings are ambivalent or when they are suppressed and the person doesn't know what he wants. In this case one is required to think and to make decisions that can never work out for the best, since the conflicts underlying the ambivalence or the suppression of feeling have not been resolved.

If therapy is to help a patient become free (no other goal is meaningful), it must help the patient reestablish his identity with his animal nature. As a result of modern science and technology, we have become alienated from nature, with the result that we are trapped in a man-made world with a corresponding loss of freedom.

It is the loss of freedom, the sense of being trapped, that is responsible for the violence in the world today. Restrict the freedom of any animal and you will have a violent creature on your hands. Man is no exception. We canot blame the violence upon economic factors. People have lived peaceably in their communities under conditions of much greater economic hardship. Injustice can lead to revolt and rebellion, but the violence is purposeful and directed. Much of the violence in the modern world is senseless and destructive. And yet it is not unnatural. Trapped animals will fight each other when they cannot direct their aggression against the cause of their loss of freedom.

There is another contradiction in human nature that is related to all this and is manifested in the conflict between the individual and the community. Man is a social animal; he lives in groups. The group, and later the community, was necessary for his survival. It was within the context of communal living that speech and the function of abstract thinking developed. The settled community provided the matrix for the growth of culture, which then allowed man to expand his ego and gain a sense of will. In effect, the community and culture have functioned to further the person's sense of his own individuality. One is an individual whether one is part of a community or not, but only within the framework of a community is a person conscious of this individuality or of himself.

However, the focus upon the self or the ego acts to separate persons and diminish the cohesive forces that hold a community together. The conflict between individuality and community is particularly evident in our culture, where the thrust to an ego-centered position is causing a breakdown in community functioning. No community can exist if each member is interested only in his personal welfare, yet no one wants to sacrifice any aspect of his unique individuality for the community. Current political thinking sees society or the community as existing for the benefit of the individual. While that is true, this sort of thinking fails to recognize the interdependent relationship of these forces.

When communities disintegrate, individuality deteriorates. People lose the sense of their individual meaning or worth and become units of a mass. They feel alienated, not unique. Or they become egocentric and try to create an image that will distinguish them from the crowd. They may become rich or famous and thus stand out, but they are not unique, for they represent merely a different stratum in the mass structure.[8] No group is more alike than our TV personalities, who must all live according to the same image: the image of success.

To exist, every social organization must place some restrictions upon the freedom of its members. To further the common goal, it must limit the rights of the individual. If the restrictions are too severe or the limits too narrow, the freedom of the individual may be curtailed to a point where the sense of individuality is reduced. But the absence of limits can have an equally harmful effect upon the sense of self. A body of water flowing down a

8. For a full discussion of the nature of individuality see my book, *Pleasure* (New York: Penguin Books, 1975).

mountain is not a river unless it is contained within banks; it is a flood. The lack of structure leads to chaos, not liberty. Without boundaries the self cannot be defined.

These ideas have particular relevance in the upbringing of children. We have seen how an authoritarian family structure can crush the spirit of a child. It would seem psychologically desirable, then, to give the child complete liberty, encourage its self-expression, and support its independence. Unfortunately, the permissive atmosphere doesn't seem to work out either. A family is a small community and depends on the cooperation of each member. But this cooperation cannot be a matter of choice. Each member has an obligation to the family that defines the function of the individual in the community. Without the responsibility (i.e., ability to respond to the needs of the community), the person is like a leaf blown from a tree. We are beginning to see that the child-centered home does not produce individuals who have a strong and sure sense of self. It is a paradox of life that freedom is dependent on boundaries and structure.

The Wisdom of the Sphinx

The Sphinx was originally an Egyptian deity best portrayed by the famous statue discovered near the pyramid of Cheops at Gizeh. It dates back to about 2000 B.C. Known as the Great Sphinx, this statue has the head of a man and the body of a lion. The combination represents the union of important virtues. The lion denotes courage, *vide* our expression "lionhearted." The human head denotes intelligence. The combination of the human and the animal represents a reconciliation of the antithetical aspects of man's nature. Another interpretation is offered by John Ivinny, based upon an inscription that describes the Sphinx as representing three gods in one. He says, "The whole is thus a symbol of the resurrection, or the sunlike cycle of human birth, death, and rebirth."[9]

9. John Ivinny, *The Sphinx and the Megaliths* (New York: Harper & Row, Publishers, 1975), p. 15.

One other feature of the Sphinx is worth analysis. Its eyes and ears are open, but its mouth is closed. This could mean that it sees and hears everything but says nothing. We speak of a person as being Sphinxlike when he keeps his mouth shut to guard a secret. The Sphinx may be regarded as the guardian of an eternal secret, as the Great Sphinx is seen as the guardian of the pyramid of Cheops.

If that is the case, can we guess its secret? What wisdom does the Sphinx have to offer us? I would like to suggest, first, that the Sphinx symbolizes the idea of changelessness within change. The pyramid can be a symbol of static permanence, while the Sphinx would represent dynamic permanence: the rising and setting of the sun, the flood and ebb of the tides, the birth, death, and rebirth of life. No day is exactly like another; no life is identical to its predecessor; everything changes, but the process is always the same, changeless. The French have a saying that expresses this idea beautifully: *Plus ça change, plus c'est la même chose*. This is a remark of wisdom because only by looking backward can one see that below the surface life goes on the same for each generation. Each struggles with the same problems of making a living, raising a family, sickness, old age, and death. When I was young, my mother warned me, saying, "You think it will be different when you have a family. You will see." It was different, but not that different. She probably had the same experience comparing her life with her mother's.

My second suggestion is that the Sphinx symbolizes the idea of change within an eternal order. The fact that the statue represents living creatures denotes change to me. Everything in life changes with time; only the order is immutable. The pyramid allows no such interpretation. It and the mummified pharaoh entombed within represent the eternal order, namely, God. Human creatures and creations are impermanent. To think otherwise is an illusion.

Both suggestions can be seen as principles capable of guiding human behavior. Their aim would be to keep man grounded in the reality of his being and to prevent the egomania that could destroy his humanity. Given the power that the ego can command in the modern world, it is easy for a person to lose his humility and see himself as godlike. This means that he takes the responsibility for his fate. We are indoctrinated by our culture with the idea that our success or failure is in our own hands. The effect of this position is to burden the person with the modern equivalent of guilt—the fear of failure.

Every patient suffers from a fear of failure or a sense of being a failure. He comes to therapy complaining about depression, anxiety, or a general feeling of malaise and dissatisfaction. But beneath the complaint, the person suffers from a sense of failure as a lover, a spouse, a parent, or in his business or vocational life. Sometimes the breakup of a marriage will bring a person to therapy because of a sense of failure, but this is rarely acknowledged. However, in all cases, the patient wants help to overcome his failure and become successful. Success is associated with feeling good and up, failure with feeling bad and down. We all want to ride high on the wings of success. In my opinion, it is a sure prescription for neurosis.

What is success or failure? Let's consider the following case. The man in question had been in treatment with me for a short time. He was having difficulties in his relationship with his wife, and he was confused about his role as a man. One session he came in complaining about his sexual functioning. The previous night he and his wife had been to a sex party, where partners were exchanged. This was some years ago, when such evenings were considered to be a sign of liberation. His wife took off with one man, while he and another woman went into a bedroom to have sexual relations. But try as he might, he had difficulty getting and sustaining an erection. He felt humiliated and a failure. He wanted to know what was wrong with him.

I suggested to my patient that perhaps he wasn't excited enough by his partner to have relations with her. He had said nothing to indicate that she was attractive or desirable. In reply he assured me that he wanted to have sex with her. Maybe he did, but, obviously, no such desire was manifested by his genital organ. He became angry with me for saying this. I pointed out to him that the desire could have been in his mind but not in his body, that his interest in sex with this woman was egotistic and not due to passion. He wanted to prove something to her and, probably, also to himself, and in that sense he failed.

I have rarely heard a man complain about a lack of sexual satisfaction in intercourse. Whatever his difficulty, loss of erective potency or premature ejaculation, it is seen as a lack of manhood, an inability to perform, a failure to measure up to some image. Admittedly, such sexual problems denote a disturbance in the personality that can be judged as masculine weakness. But to regard a personality disturbance as a mark of failure is in itself a clear indication of neurosis.

Let us look at this question of failure in the context of a different body function. One of the most common complaints of patients is tiredness. Often the feeling of tiredness becomes more acute as the therapy progresses. It can develop into a feeling of exhaustion. This feeling of fatigue is almost never accepted by the patient as a normal body condition. It is invariably regarded as a mark of weakness, as denoting a failure of the therapy and of the person's will. He complains that he lacks the drive he formerly had, that he isn't able to do as much as before. The implication is that being tired is "wrong," a sign of failure. The belief is that one should be active, productive, and efficient. This image constitutes an ego ideal that the person has incorporated from the teachings he received at home and in school. Since the person is consciously identified with his ego, he uses his will to drive himself to the realization of the ideal. By definition, ideals are never realized. This means that the person is driven by a continuing force to do, to produce, to achieve (whatever it takes to fulfill the image). The drive is a compulsion and constitutes neurotic behavior. No wonder the person is tired. Feeling tired can be interpreted as a statement by the body that it is "tired" of being harnessed by the ego to fulfill an image that has no relation to the body's needs. There is no purpose in achieving if the achievement does nothing to maintain or enhance the pleasure of being.

Most patients believe that being tired is a neurotic symptom. They see emotional health as the ability to go, to do, and to produce. Where they are going or what they are doing is largely irrelevant. This is the "action" generation, out to set records. Their ideal is superman, almost a god. Unconsciously, they compare themselves to the machines that dominate life in the industrial world. The only possible outcome of this situation is people breaking down. They become tired from the effort to achieve an unattainable goal, the ideal, and depressed by their failure. Both the tiredness and the depression can have a positive value for the person if he recognizes their relation to his life-style. Being tired can make a person conscious of the needs of his body. It can make him realize that the body is not a machine or an instrument of his ego. Being depressed can make one aware that he was pursuing an illusion, the ego ideal. For example, one of my patients who suffered from depression told me how she was supposed to take care of her mother and her sister. Being the older child, she was the responsible one in the family. That role is commonly assigned to the oldest child in the family. After telling me this, she remarked with mixed feelings, "I failed both of them. I should be God Almighty!" She felt both guilty and resentful. She didn't recognize that in attempting to fulfill this impossible role, she lost much of her life and became depressed.

It is significant that the feeling of tiredness becomes stronger after the therapy has made considerable progress. While the neurosis is in full force, the person is like a cliff-hanger who dares not let go because he doesn't know where the ground is. The neurotic, too, as we saw earlier, holds on for dear life or to guard his sanity. Neither can he let himself feel tired, because doing so would threaten his survival. Only after one is safely on the ground can one afford to give in to the feeling of exhaustion. Both the cliff-hanger and the neurotic have every reason to be exhausted. The neurotic is also holding on physically in the form of chronic muscular tensions designed to suppress feeling. Exhaustion effectively stops the compulsive drive to go and to do. Giving in to the tiredness, which is a giving in to the body, would have the same effect—it would allow the person to recover his energy and renew his enthusiasm for living.

Depression and tiredness are endemic in our culture, and this is some indication of how pervasive the drive for success is. Most people are hung up on the image of success because they associate success with happiness, even though they know that successful people are not happier than others and often have more problems. Still, the idea that success means fulfillment has a powerful hold upon our minds, which can be understood only if failure is equated with death. I use "death" in the sense of some terrible thing that will happen to the person. Until recently I was not sure what calamity lurked in the deep recesses of people's unconscious. Many people are afraid that if they let go, they will die. We have seen that the fear of life translates itself into a fear of death. But I didn't believe that the fear of death was as universal as the fear of failure.

The answer became clear through a falling exercise I did with a patient.[10] This exercise was previously described on p. 76. I repeat it here for convenience. In this exercise the person stands with his weight upon one bent leg while the other touches the ground lightly behind him for balance. He is instructed to hold the position as long as possible. It becomes very painful, and sooner or later the person will fall. To prevent any injury a mattress is placed on the floor before him. The value of the exercise lies in the experience of falling anxiety and in understanding what that means to the patient. When the struggle not to fall becomes intense, the person is asked to express all his thoughts about what falling means.

10. See my book *Bioenergetics*, for a full discussion of the significance and use of this exercise in falling anxiety.

When this patient first tried the exercise, he fell too quickly, indicating that he was afraid to confront his anxiety. He repeated the exercise twice more. On the third try he stayed up longer, which greatly increased the pain. Mustering his will he exclaimed, "I won't fall. I won't fall." When I asked him what falling meant, he said, "Falling is failing. I am afraid to fail." I asked, "Why? What danger does failure pose?" He replied, "If I fail, I'll be broken." Falling also entails the risk of breaking. When he fell, he broke into deep sobs. Lying on the mattress, he remarked how relaxed he felt. His fear of breaking proved irrational, but he did break down into crying. It became clear to me, then, that falling or failing evokes the fear of being "broken."

If we ask where this fear comes from, the answer is—from the oedipal situation. But in this context that term includes all the events in the upbringing of the child culminating in the experience of the oedipal situation. By the age of six almost all children in our culture are "broken in" to its ways and values. The final step in this process is the implied threat of castration that the child experiences in the oedipal situation. Some become rebellious and violent later in reaction to being broken. Most, however, submit, accepting the demands of the culture, and become the producers, the achievers, the strivers for success and power. They deny being broken or that any castration took place. These are the people, however, in whom the fear of failure is greatest. For them, success supports their denial.

There is another strong motivation for the drive for success, and that is the need for approval. The person striving for success is trying to prove to his parents that he is worthy of their love. He is correct in assuming that their love is conditional and depends upon his acceptance of their values and his submission to their authority. But when success is attained, it doesn't fulfill the need. He gets the approval but not the love. Or, the person is loved for his success but not for himself. Since the achievement doesn't gain its end, one must try harder, achieve more. When one is seeking to obtain the pot of gold at the end of the rainbow, the striving is endless.

Whatever the motivation of the success drive, it ends in failure as far as the person is concerned. He may have attained a seeming success in the eyes of the world, but he is a failure in his own eyes whether he admits it or not. He failed to prove that he was not castrated or that he was worthy of love. He senses that his behavior is neurotic, but he hopes to prove by his success that he is "okay." How can a person prove that he is not neurotic? The need to prove it betrays a neurotic sense of inferiority and insecurity. A healthy person doesn't go about trying to prove himself. He accepts his being however it is, and he accepts his fate whatever it is. The other animals are not troubled by such problems. A dog is content to be just a dog. Why is the human animal not satisfied just to be? Man is the only animal who was kicked out of paradise by God for eating the fruit of the tree of knowledge. I imagine that he is trying to prove that he could build a better paradise than the one he lost.

It might seem from the above that I am advocating the abandonment of all effort and achievement. That isn't my thesis, nor would it be a wise position. Letting go does not mean regression to an infantile way of being. Doing and achieving are neurotic only when they are used as substitutes for being. There is pleasure in doing even when it requires an effort, provided it is not a compulsive activity. Success has a sweet taste when it comes by itself but a bitter one if the person has sacrificed himself for it. Also when success comes by itself, the person doesn't experience it as success. He mightly simply say, "Something nice happened to me." And since there is no striving, there can be no failure either. Where life is not measured in terms of achievement, there is neither success nor failure, just the pleasure and pain of being and doing.

Man's glory is in his aspiration to be godlike, not in his achievement. The aspiration is reflected in his bearing: he stands on two legs with head held high, he acts with dignity and moves with grace, he looks at the earth with its myriad creatures and sees how beautiful it is. He alone of all animals can appreciate the magnificence and splendor of God's creation. In this appreciation he is truly godlike. But if he has the arrogance to think that he can do it better, he becomes a devil. Lucifer was one of God's trusted angels. His name means "light," the light of consciousness and intelligence. He was a shining light in the kingdom of heaven until he presumed to challenge God as a superior. Similarly, the inflated ego of modern man becomes a devil when it is not subordinated to the primacy of the body.

The attempt to transcend our animal nature must end in failure. We are fundamentally animals, different in degree but not in kind. We are born and die as they do. We all share in the great adventure of living. What we do is not important; it is how we live our lives that counts. It is not the end that matters (we all come to the same end) but the journey itself. Achievement can add spice to living, but it is not living in itself. Living takes place on the bodily or animal level. And on this level the important thing is feeling. Only living organisms can feel. The question is not whether we achieve anything but whether we live our lives fully. To live fully is to have all one's senses and feelings available for the experience of living.

Success and failure are ego concepts. On the body level, success is experienced as rising and failing as falling. Falling is part of life. If there is no falling, there can be no rising. If there is no death, there can be no rebirth. Rising and falling, expanding and contracting, are what life is about. If we are afraid of life, we are afraid to fall. We are afraid to fall asleep and afraid to fall in love. Persons who are blessed with health and have fully lived the day welcome the sweet rest of sleep. By surrendering to its oblivion they awake in the morning renewed and refreshed. The best example of this cycle of life is the function of the phallus. It rises with desire and falls when the desire is spent in satisfaction. Who would want to have a perpetual erection? Who would want to be driven by a desire that can never be fulfilled? How beautiful it is to rise and soar on wings of desire when we know that fulfillment is possible and that we shall return safely to earth.

The coming down is the important part, for this is where the true pleasure and satisfaction are experienced. Going up is exciting and tensing, but coming down is satisfying and releasing. Children know this from their swings; the pleasure and thrill of the descent is what they seek, that lovely sensation in the pit of the belly as one goes through the fall. The higher the swing flies, the greater the pleasure when it comes down. Riding a roller coaster provides a similar experience. There is excitement, tension, and anticipatory pleasure in the ascent. Then, as the cars reach and pass the crest and start their plunge, one knows the thrill of the fall. And after the ride is over, one has a sense of satisfaction as if one had accomplished something meaningful.

Now suppose the swing or the roller coaster was arrested in its elevated position—what would one feel? The real thrill of the descent would be lacking. One could, of course, have the satisfaction of being "above it," superior to those below, looking down on them. But this satisfaction is limited to the ego. As far as the body is concerned, one is "hung up" and unable to discharge the excitation resulting from the ascent. Soon even the ego satisfaction palls and one becomes depressed.

The aspiration to be godlike is expressed in some creative action. It doesn't matter what one creates. It is the act of creation that is godlike, not the product. Thus, the simple act of making wine or bread, using one's imagination to effect a transformation of nature, is the kind of creativity that is associated with the godhead. Gardening and farming are similar activities. In all these activities there is a rise and fall of excitement, a buildup and discharge of tension. In making bread, for example, the excitement mounts until the bread comes out of the oven. At this point we turn to the satisfaction of consumption, which is the pleasure of descent. Think how hung up we would be if we were not allowed to eat the bread our mother baked.

Where production and consumption are closely linked, as they are in simple communities or on a farm, people don't get hung up on their accomplishments or achievements. The reward in terms of pleasure and satisfaction for their creative effort is immediate. In our modern, technological cultures, the focus is upon an indeterminate future, when all problems will be resolved, all difficulties overcome. We live for a utopia, a new Garden of Eden, man-made this time through science. Meanwhile our pleasures are momentary respites, our repose a temporary rest before we resume our upward climb again. We are hung up on the illusion of success, and so we aim constantly higher: more production, more knowledge, more power, more, more, more.

We seem to be terrified of the descent. It represents falling, failure, and fate (death). The original Garden of Eden was man's home before he lost his innocence and fell from grace, that is, while he was still an animal and had not begun his ascent (Jacob Bronowski, *The Ascent of Man*). Innocence can never be recovered. But need we delude ourselves that we will ever arrive at the abode of the gods in our lifetime? Can we not accept the idea that the effort to transcend the animal state is meaningful only if one can descend to enjoy that state? It is exhilarating to let our imaginations fly, but it is necessary to keep our feet on the ground. It is exciting to think, but fulfillment and satisfaction are bodily events. The life of the body is where being is realized.

Wisdom is the recognition that what goes up must come down. I was a modern, ego-conscious young man who aspired to rise up in the world. I wanted success and fame. Despite my graduation from law school summa cum laude and my earning a doctor's degree in law, magna cum laude, success and fame in the practice of law eluded me. It was the time of the Great Depression, and I couldn't even make a living. That failure, however, was fortunate. It forced me to look elsewhere. In pursuance of my interest in the body-mind relationship I met Wilhelm Reich and underwent a training therapy with him. My goals now were to become a doctor, to practice Reichian therapy, and to attain full orgastic potency; but I was still committed to the drive for success and fame.

Now, having founded an institute and written many books, I am seen by people as famous and successful. But measured by the ambitions of my youth I am a failure. My aspirations have not been realized; the dreams of my youth have not materialized. I am still an imperfect creature. I sit on no Olympian heights. I have known the ecstasy of full orgasm on only a few occasions. I am not free from tensions, problems, or daily cares. My books are not best sellers, and my institute is small and struggling. But I have consistent pleasure in my life and my work. However, pain is not absent either. The big change in my life occurred some years ago when I accepted my failure. Since then I have gained peace of mind, inner contentment, and some wisdom. Part of that wisdom is the realization that success and failure are not valid criteria for living.

Failure has always had a positive effect upon me. It has been my best teacher. It made me stop and look at my self-destructive behavior. It enabled me to make a fresh start, with all the excitement and enthusiasm of a new beginning. And by accepting failure I became free from the struggle to overcome an inner sense of failure. I started this study by discussing the problem of people's inability to learn from experience. I believe that a major factor is their unwillingness to accept failure. They are determined to succeed and so will make the same mistakes again. Accepting failure is not resignation but self-acceptance. No real character change occurs in therapy until the person accepts himself as a failure. This acceptance liberates the energy tied up in the struggle to succeed and to prove oneself and makes it available for growth. In the same way, the acceptance of fate changes one's fate. By giving up the effort to overcome fate we let go of our neurotic character structure, and a healthy character can develop, which determines a different fate.